LEGENDARY LOCALS

OF

CHUGIAK-EAGLE RIVER

ALASKA

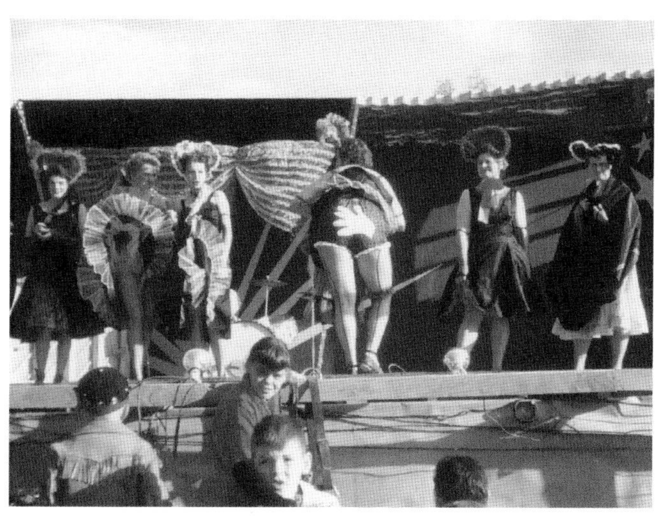

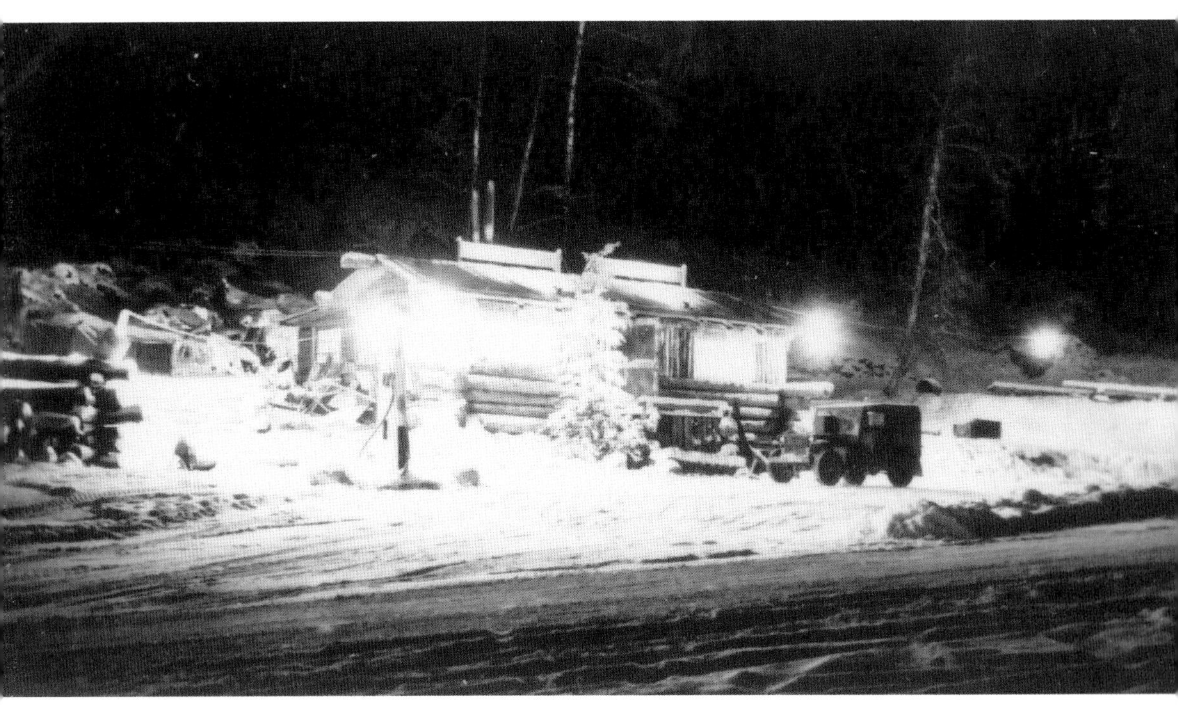

Parksville

The Chugiak Coffee Shop, also nicknamed "Parksville," was a favorite place to stop for coffee, sweets, and good conversation as soon as it opened in 1947. Owners Justine and Cloyce Parks installed a gas pump and a neon sign to beckon customers driving along the Palmer Highway. (Courtesy of the Chugiak-Eagle River Historical Society.)

Page 1: Chugiak Belles

Pictured are the Chugiak Belles dancing at the community's annual spring carnival in 1955. For more information, see page 117. (Courtesy of the Chugiak-Eagle River Historical Society.)

LEGENDARY LOCALS

OF

CHUGIAK-EAGLE RIVER

ALASKA

CHRIS LUNDGREN

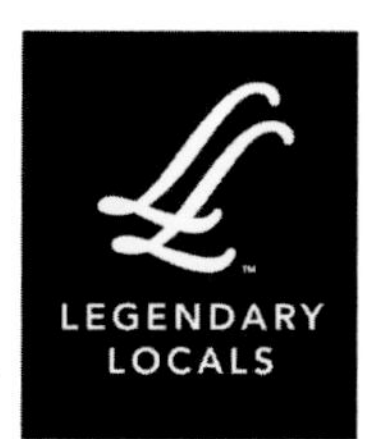

ISBN 978-1-4671-0136-3

Legendary Locals is an imprint of Arcadia Publishing
Charleston, South Carolina

Printed in the United States of America

Library of Congress Control Number: 2013950054

For all general information, please contact Arcadia Publishing:
Telephone 843-853-2070
Fax 843-853-0044
E-mail sales@arcadiapublishing.com
For customer service and orders:
Toll-Free 1-888-313-2665

Visit us on the Internet at www.arcadiapublishing.com

Dedication
To Carl and our shared history, and to Eric and Perry, our contributions to the historical record

On the Front Cover: Clockwise from top left:
Chugiak Belles, dance group (Courtesy of the Chugiak-Eagle River Historical Society; see page 117), Tom Huffer Sr. and Tom Huffer Jr., coaches (Courtesy of Stella Huffer; see page 106), Natalie Haskell Brooks, music teacher and volunteer (Courtesy of the Chugiak-Eagle River Historical Society; see page 67), the Haik family, owners of Spring Creek Lodge (Courtesy of the Chugiak-Eagle River Historical Society; see pages 42, 43), the Stockhausen family, homesteaders and owners of a bar and liquor store (Courtesy of Darlene Stockhausen Halverson; see page 41), Harry McDonald, father of hockey in Chugiak-Eagle River (Courtesy of Carole McDonald; see pages 104, 105), Barbara Erickson Jordan, longtime owner of Frontier Fabric & Craft (Courtesy of Lee Jordan; see page 33), Bill Stephens, co-owner of the Dari Delite and later owner of Peters Creek Fuel (Courtesy of the Chugiak-Eagle River Historical Society; see page 39), and Paul Swanson, one of Chugiak's earliest entrepreneurs (Courtesy of the Chugiak-Eagle River Historical Society; see pages 28, 29).

On the Back Cover: From left to right:
Homesteader Til Wallace (Courtesy of Til Wallace; see page 26), coach Andy Kirk, at the far right, with the Chugiak High School Century Club bicycle riders (Courtesy of Jinny Kirk; see page 80).

CONTENTS

ACKNOWLEDGMENTS

Topping my list of thank-yous is Phyllis Smith, president of the Chugiak-Eagle River Historical Society (CERHS), for putting me in touch with Arcadia Publishing editor Erin Vosgien in the first place. If not for Phyllis, another writer might have had all the fun. Phyllis answered abundant questions as I wrote the book and, even more importantly, edited the manuscript for accuracy. I also thank Jinny Kirk, founder and past president of CERHS, who was my first contact with the group back in 2006. Jinny has always cheerfully answered my questions and pointed me in the right direction. Grateful chuckles go to the CERHS Finish-it Friday Crew for sharing funny stories about the early days; there are times the group should be called the "Hysterical Society." A heartfelt thank you has been reserved for Lee Jordan, author and founder of the *Chugiak-Eagle River Star* newspaper, for being the chronicler of life in Chugiak-Eagle River as well as our first and only mayor. As always, Lee has been generous with his time, energy, considerable knowledge, and photographs. I also thank *Anchorage Daily News* reporter and former *Star* editor Mike Nesper for helping me locate photographs even while he was under deadline. I am grateful to Susie Gorski, executive director of the Chugiak-Eagle River Chamber of Commerce, for her consultation early on in the project. Thanks go to Erin Vosgien, my thoughtful and thorough editor; Legendary Locals manager Kris McDonagh, who helped see the project through; and production editor Laura Saylor for her attention to detail and creative problem solving. "Thin Q's" go to my family: son Eric, indispensable tech consultant and photographer, and son Perry, super-reliable backup photographer, as well as my husband, Carl, a legendary local in his own right who kept our family on track and provided feedback on the manuscript whenever asked. Finally, immeasurable gratitude goes to the men and women inside these pages whose rich and complicated life stories have been condensed into just a few hundred words.

INTRODUCTION

In so many cities and towns across the country, history stands apart from day-to-day life. Museums, street signs, and commemorative plaques are among the few clues to the past. Not so in Chugiak-Eagle River. History lives on in the faces of our neighbors—the homesteaders and their children and grandchildren, the entrepreneurs, and the first schoolteachers. Original buildings still stand. If you drive out Eagle River Road, you will pass large homes that started as prove-up cabins. The road dead ends at the Eagle River Nature Center, once part of a homestead and landmark restaurant and bar. Heading up the Old Glenn Highway, you will pass the Chugiak Post Office from 1947 and Chugiak's lone territorial school from the 1950s.

Less visible but still present are vestiges of an earlier history. The Eugene and Cleo Vick cabin from 1917—acquired by Frank and Fina Siebenthaler in 1929—sits on the property of Birchwood Christian Camp near Beach Lake in Chugiak. Both couples reportedly raised mink and fox.

Older still is St. Nicholas Russian Orthodox Church, which dates back to 1870 (according to the National Register of Historic Places) and is located north of Chugiak in the native village of Eklutna. Eklutna itself is an active village and also a former encampment of the Dena'ina Athabaskans, a nomadic people who fished, hunted, gathered, and trapped in the expanse of land between the Chugach and Talkeetna Mountains for more than a thousand years before any Westerners showed up.

Conversely, a wave of permanent settlers arrived in Chugiak-Eagle River in the 1940s and 1950s with one thing on their minds: homesteading. Many were soldiers or civilians with jobs on Fort Richardson Army Base. Others were adventure-seekers or self-starters. All were willing to sweat.

Homesteaders were experts at pressing ahead despite physical discomfort. They brushed off cuts, sprains, blisters, and backaches like so many mosquitoes. Although each homesteader (or homesteading pair) worked independently, a culture of cooperation and interdependence sprang up among them. Within a short span of time, they had built a small community, and in 1947, it was christened *Chugiak*, or "place of many places," in the Dena'ina language. The Chugiak Territorial School educated first- through eighth-graders and provided a community center when it was built in 1951. Its name was changed to Chugiak Elementary after statehood in 1959.

In the early years, many people had considered Eagle River to be little more than the south end of Greater Chugiak. The community's separate identity was sealed with the establishment of a post office in 1960 and the construction of Eagle River School, for grades one through eight, in 1961.

Many locals had been against statehood, pushing instead for a self-taxing, self-governing commonwealth. Most of those in favor of statehood wanted Alaska to be able to regulate its own mines and fisheries. After both houses of Congress passed the Alaska Statehood Bill in the summer of 1958, residents lit a bonfire of scrap lumber and tires that shot a plume of black smoke into the sky. Statehood was coming, and the people of Chugiak-Eagle River would adapt to the idea and celebrate in their own way.

In 1960, a local, grassroots advocacy group called Operation Chugiak High School began petitioning the state for a secondary school in Chugiak. Their reasons were practical: more than 170 local teens endured a 90-minute bus ride on hazardous roads to and from Anchorage each day. Four arduous years later, Chugiak High School opened its doors, instantly becoming a source of pride and a focal point for the community.

The high school had been constructed with state money but would be operated under a newly formed Greater Anchorage Area Borough, or GAAB. The GAAB was one of seven boroughs statewide, and it lasted from 1964 to 1975, when voters chose unification between the GAAB and the city of Anchorage to form the current-day municipality of Anchorage.

In the meantime, Chugiak-Eagle River had gained the distinction of being its own borough through an election in August 1974 but lost it within months because of a lawsuit challenging its constitutionality. Though residents had elected a mayor, a seven-person assembly, and a five-person school board, the Chugiak-Eagle River Borough never got off the ground. Instead, it was absorbed into the municipality of Anchorage.

The oil boom of the 1970s and first half of the 1980s did nothing to help preserve the small-town identity of Chugiak-Eagle River. The boom echoed through the area and caused a rapid expansion in population. Along with it came a spate of new homes and unfamiliar faces, four new schools, and some state-funded capital projects, such as Chugiak High's swimming pool. The bust in 1986 slowed the area's growth but did not reverse it.

The 1990s and 2000s saw continued steady growth, with the landscape being altered by a couple of large chain stores and three new schools, including Eagle River High School, which was completed in 2005.

Chugiak-Eagle River will never be the quiet corner of Alaska it was in the early days. As the saying goes, "You can't close the door," and this particular door has been open nearly 70 years. But as our community grows and takes off in new directions, it is important to know the people and places that make up our history and to let them guide us into the future.

CHAPTER ONE

Founders and Visionaries

The founders and visionaries of Chugiak and Eagle River laid the groundwork for all the later growth in the area. Such people included homesteader Paul Swanson, whose minisettlement encompassed a general store, post office, and cheap housing for the teachers who worked across the road at the Chugiak Territorial School. "Swanee Slopes," as the area was called, allowed people to access what they needed locally, and many ended up putting down roots. The Wallace brothers started and eventually sold Klondike Concrete, one of the biggest employers in the area. Farther south, a farming family named Pippel homesteaded property that through the years morphed into Eagle River's business district. The Pippels' neighbors Glenn and Mary Lou Briggs, also farmers, ended up subdividing their property and building one of Eagle River's original subdivisions as well as its first shopping center and office building. Cloyce and Justine Parks, Rusty Bellringer, and Lee Jordan created the area's first newspapers, while Billie Moore and Polly Kallenberg launched the Chugiak-Eagle River Public Library, now the busiest branch of the Anchorage Public Library System. Some of the area's visionaries are relative latecomers, such as the folks who established the Eagle River Nature Center in the 1990s. No matter when they were laid down, the legacies of Chugiak-Eagle River's founders and visionaries are still being enjoyed by the people who live and visit here.

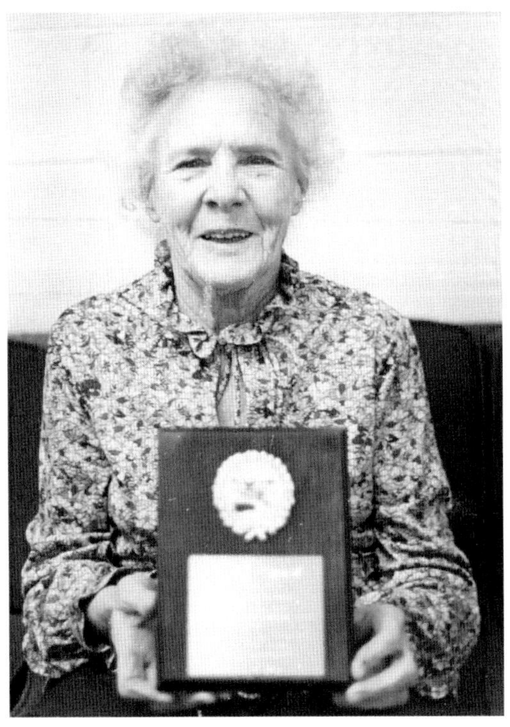

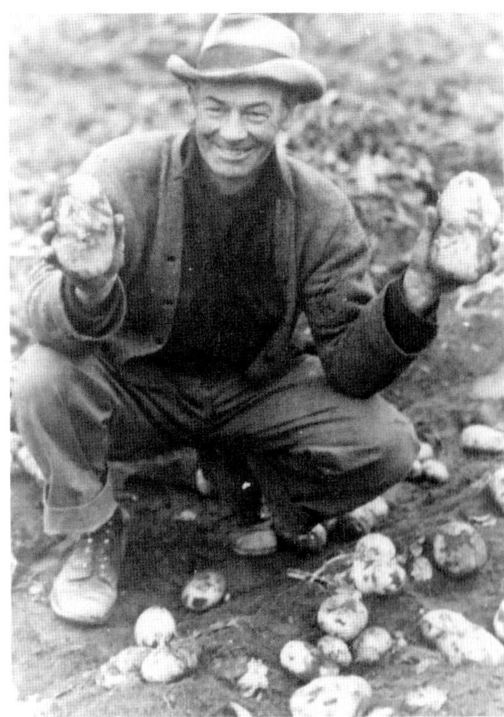

Walter and Melva Pippel

Farming was life for Walter Pippel, who settled in Eagle River with wife Melva and the four youngest of their six children in 1948. The Pippels had farmed as part of the Matanuska Valley Colony Project in the 1930s as well as in their home state of Minnesota. According to Melva, Walter's talent for raising crops was nothing less than artistic. He was 100 percent farmer, she liked to say, and anything he touched would grow. The Pippels cultivated 90 acres, more than half of which contained potatoes. They also grew radishes, turnips, cabbage, lettuce, broccoli, and cauliflower—and they raised hogs. Melva planted wildflowers in their fields and tended a huge garden around their house. The area once known by all as Pippel Field now serves as the Eagle River business district. Below, an unwelcome visitor showed up at the Pippels' pig farm in 1948. (All, courtesy of the Chugiak-Eagle River Historical Society.)

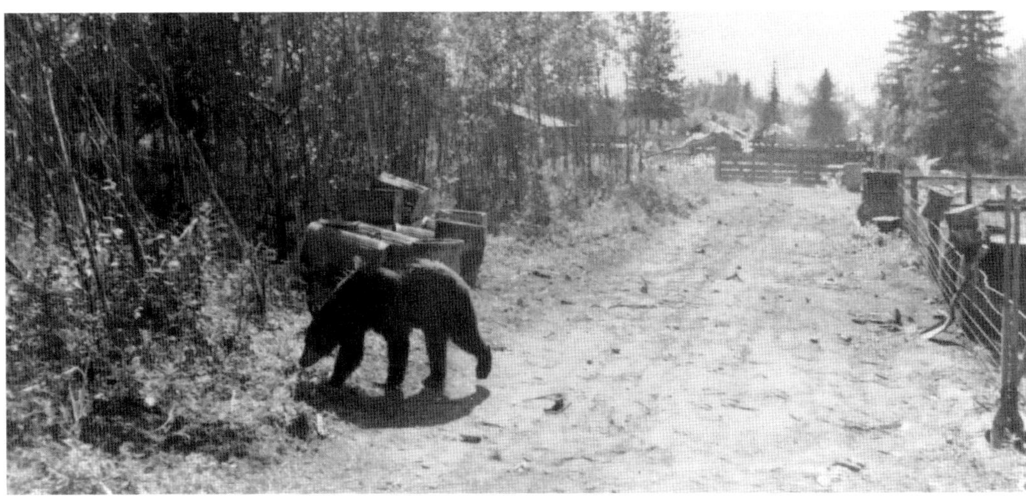

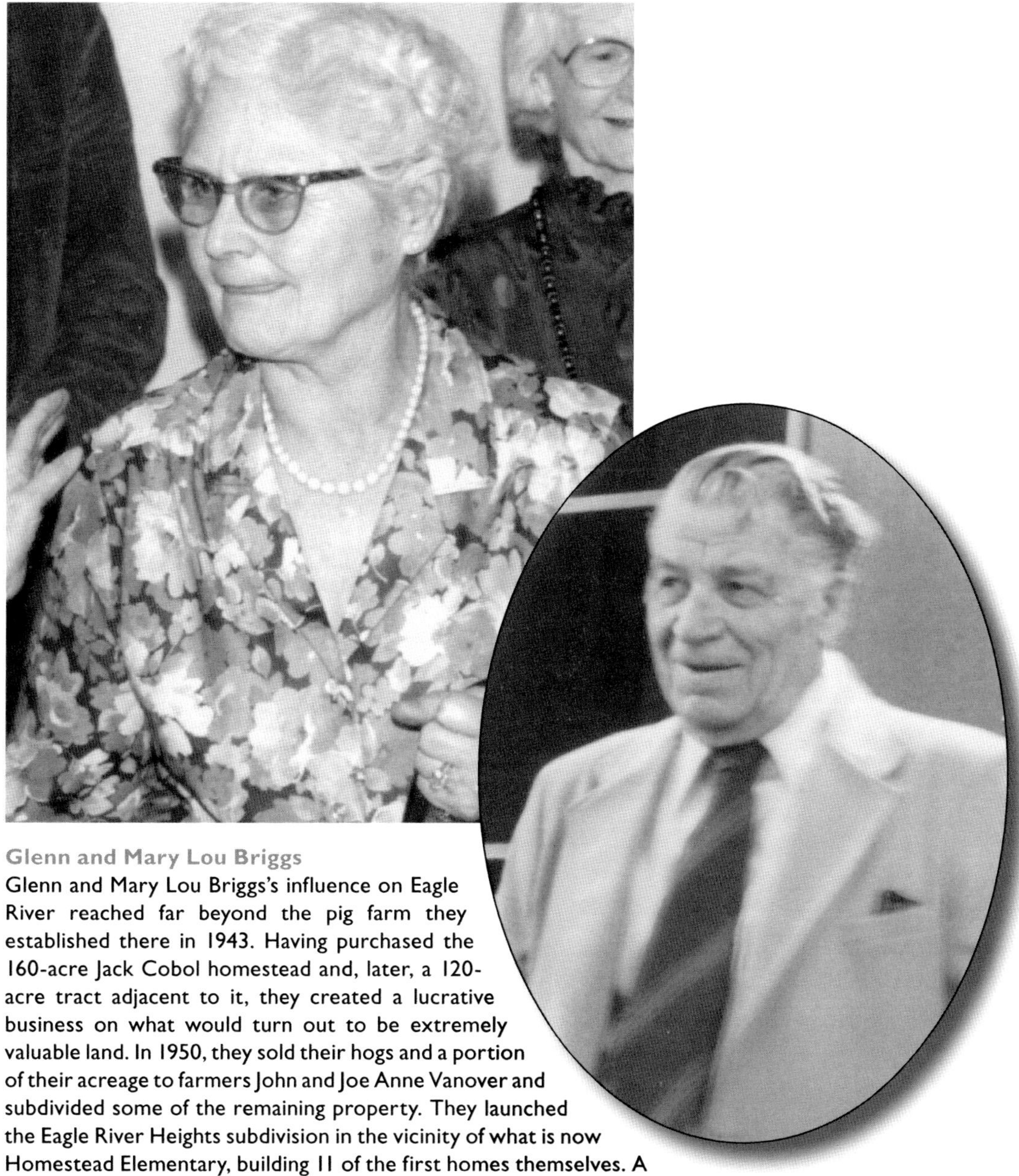

Glenn and Mary Lou Briggs

Glenn and Mary Lou Briggs's influence on Eagle River reached far beyond the pig farm they established there in 1943. Having purchased the 160-acre Jack Cobol homestead and, later, a 120-acre tract adjacent to it, they created a lucrative business on what would turn out to be extremely valuable land. In 1950, they sold their hogs and a portion of their acreage to farmers John and Joe Anne Vanover and subdivided some of the remaining property. They launched the Eagle River Heights subdivision in the vicinity of what is now Homestead Elementary, building 11 of the first homes themselves. A full partner in the business, Mary Lou took pride in designing the homes and performing quality carpentry work. Their development was reportedly among the first to enjoy paved roads and streetlights. Glenn was adamant that Eagle River grow in an orderly fashion, and he pushed for Federal Housing Administration regulations on all new-home construction. The Briggses joined with other local investors in 1955 to build the Eagle River Shopping Center and then the Parkgate Building in 1973. Both structures are still in use. Because of his obvious commitment to the community, Glenn was the first person elected to the now-defunct Greater Anchorage Area Borough Assembly to represent Chugiak-Eagle River. The Briggs Bridge over the Eagle River is named for him. Glenn died in 1990, and Mary Lou died in 2002. (Both, courtesy of the Chugiak-Eagle River Historical Society.)

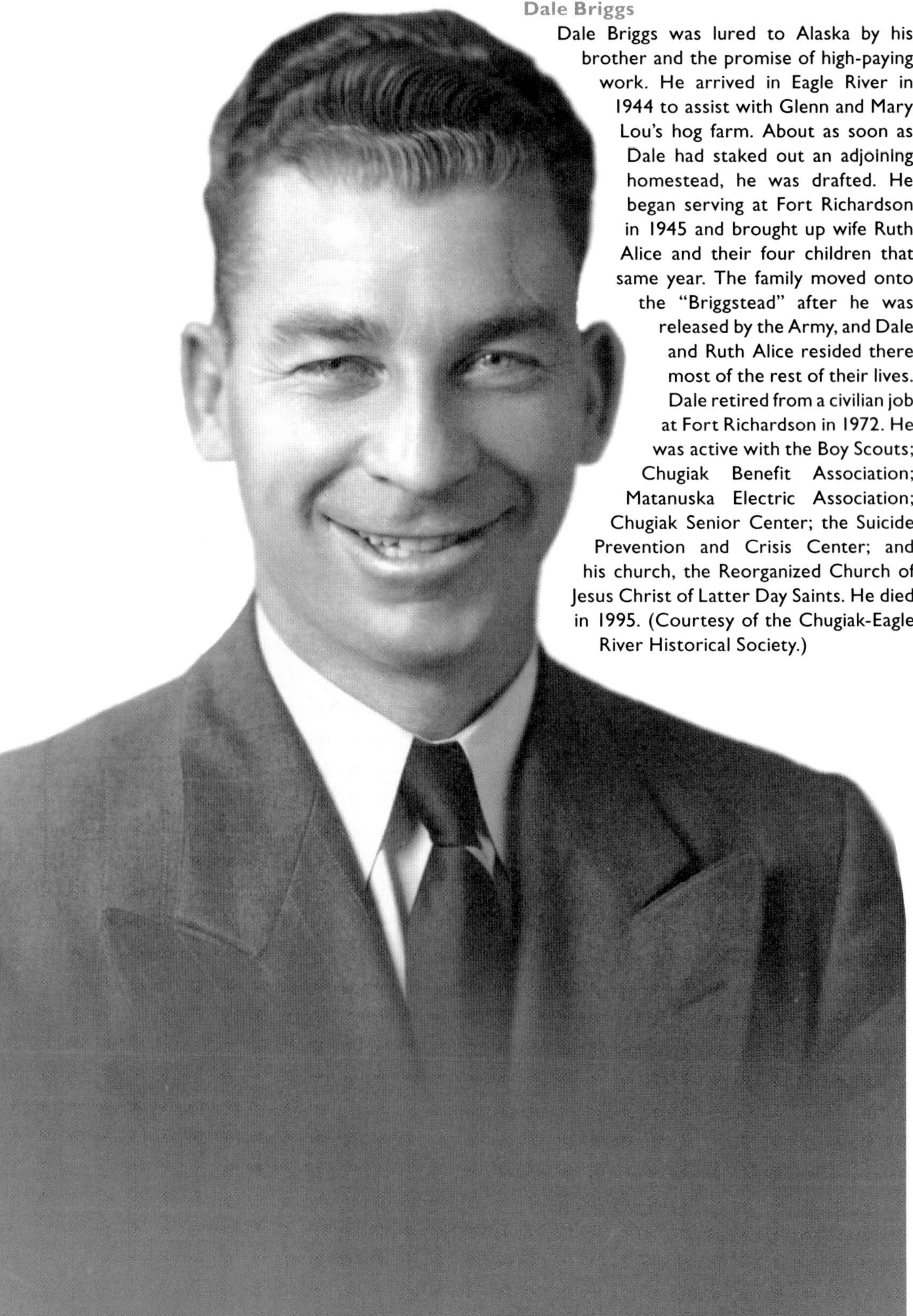

Dale Briggs

Dale Briggs was lured to Alaska by his brother and the promise of high-paying work. He arrived in Eagle River in 1944 to assist with Glenn and Mary Lou's hog farm. About as soon as Dale had staked out an adjoining homestead, he was drafted. He began serving at Fort Richardson in 1945 and brought up wife Ruth Alice and their four children that same year. The family moved onto the "Briggstead" after he was released by the Army, and Dale and Ruth Alice resided there most of the rest of their lives. Dale retired from a civilian job at Fort Richardson in 1972. He was active with the Boy Scouts; Chugiak Benefit Association; Matanuska Electric Association; Chugiak Senior Center; the Suicide Prevention and Crisis Center; and his church, the Reorganized Church of Jesus Christ of Latter Day Saints. He died in 1995. (Courtesy of the Chugiak-Eagle River Historical Society.)

Ruth Alice Briggs

Ruth Alice Briggs had a love affair with music and culture. Beginning in 1948, she hosted a popular radio program on station KENI. Briggs became a charter member of the Anchorage Community (Concert) Chorus in the early 1950s and toured worldwide with the group. She ended her professional career as a public information officer for the state of Alaska, focusing on promoting senior programs through a variety of media. Although she had received an associate's degree in the 1930s, Briggs returned to college, earning a bachelor's degree in music from the University of Alaska Anchorage in 1997. She died in 2005. (Courtesy of the Chugiak-Eagle River Historical Society.)

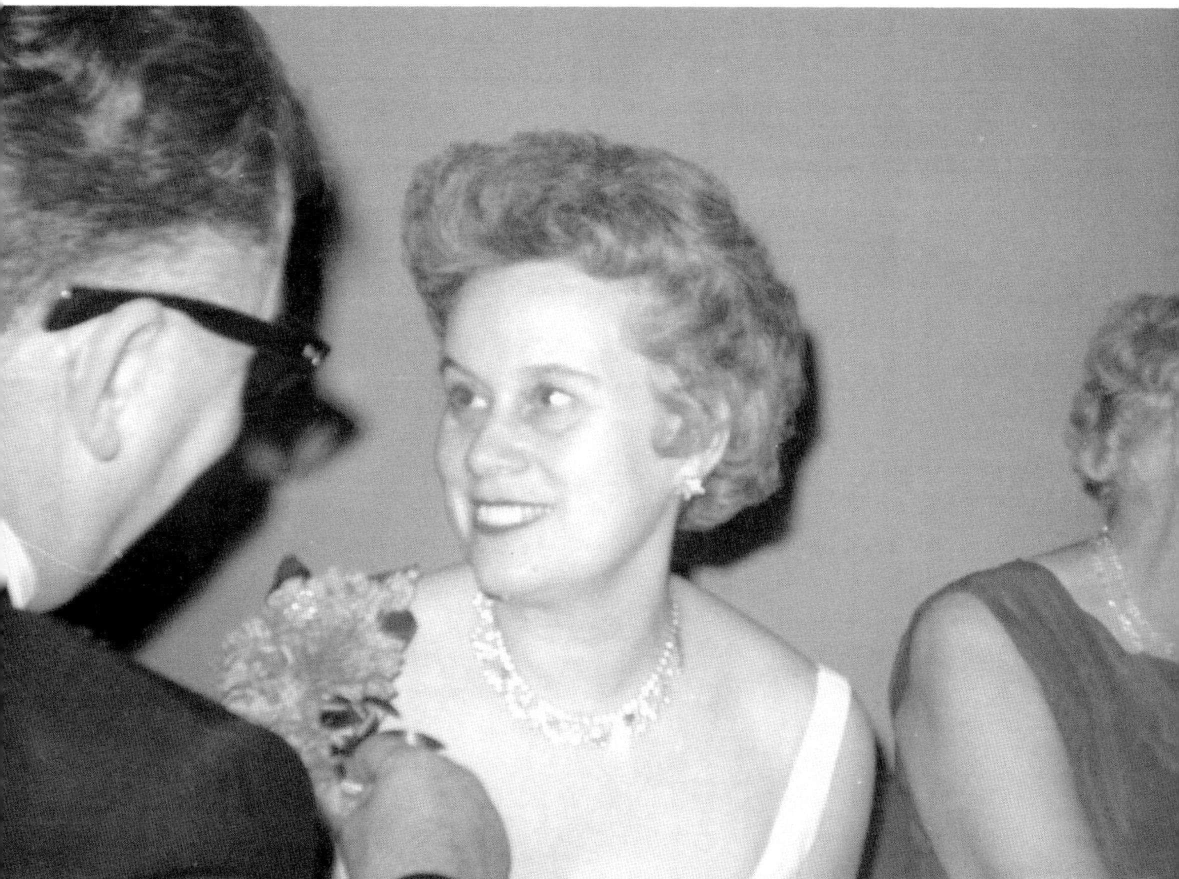

John and Joe Anne Vanover

Joe Anne Vanover can still recall how her husband was dressed when they met in the mid-1940s. The teen was working in a restaurant in Palmer when Johnny Vanover, the middleweight boxing champion of Alaska, walked in wearing cream-colored corduroys and a T-shirt. Joe Anne was smitten, and so, apparently, was Johnny. The couple married in 1947 on Joe Anne's 18th birthday. Having grown up in the Matanuska Colony, she was accustomed to the hard work of farming. This helped in her transition to married life, as John owned a pig farm in Mountain View. The couple sold pork to restaurants throughout Anchorage, to Fort Richardson, and even to Northwest Airlines. They also took time out to play, enjoying a number of social activities in Anchorage. The Vanovers acquired horses to help with the farm work, to ride for fun, and to use in the rodeos they staged for the public. After building a slaughterhouse for the pigs in 1948, they began looking for expansion opportunities. They found one in 1950 when Glenn Briggs wanted to sell his hog farm in Eagle River. The Vanovers moved part of their operations there and in 1953 relocated to a new house nearby with kids John, Jerry, and Julie. The bunkhouse they built for their farmhands also provided a bed for the occasional young person needing a place to sleep, and feeding extra mouths was never a problem. In this way, the Vanovers cared for many Eagle River teens over the years on both a short- and long-term basis. The family expanded operations again, this time in Palmer, in the late 1950s. They exited the farming business in 1972 but continued to live in Eagle River. John died in 2002. (Courtesy of Joe Anne Vanover.)

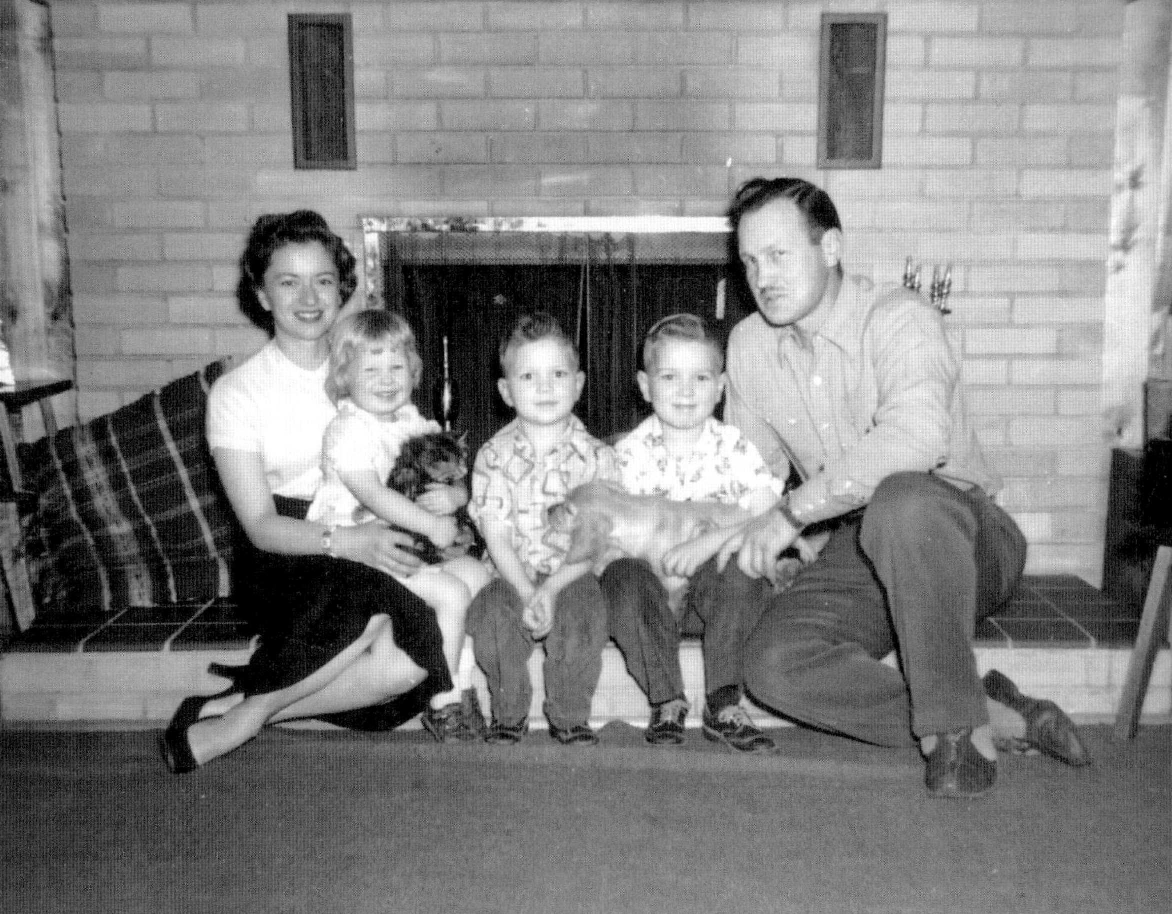

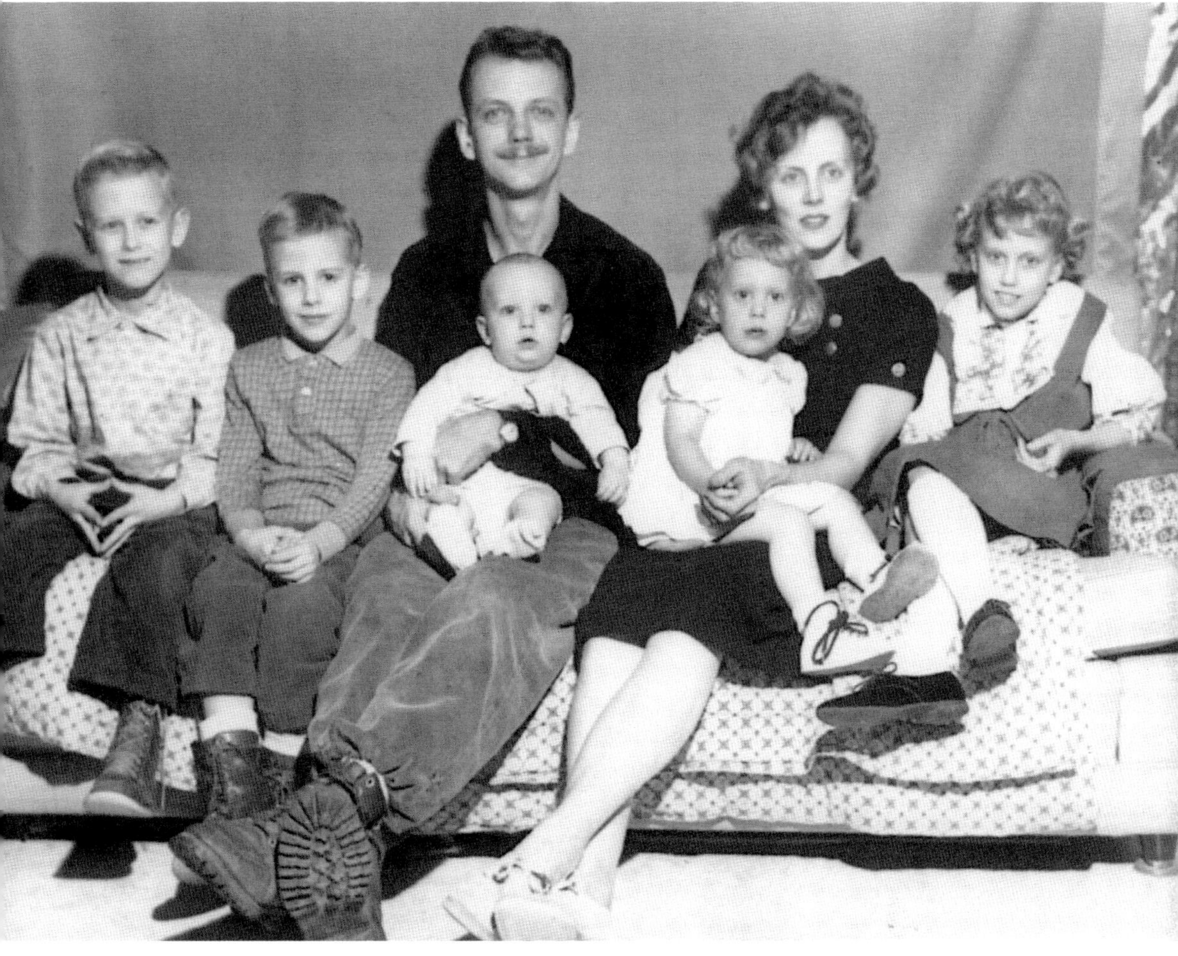

Janke Family

Power—specifically, hydroelectric power—has been on the minds of Eagle River's Janke family for at least 50 years. Parents Joe and Phyllis staked out their homestead in 1961 in part because the South Fork of the Eagle River ran through the property. The couple moved there in 1962 with five of their six children: Joe Jr., Dan, Max, Suzanne, and Patti. (The youngest, Margaret, was born later, and another son was informally adopted in 1971.) The family began proving up the property by cultivating the land and planting their required crops. Cows, pigs, chickens, ducks, turkeys, and goats were soon added to the mix, turning the place into a genuine farm. Living over two miles past the end of Hiland Road, Joe and Phyllis both fought icy or mucky driving conditions on a daily basis—Joe to reach his job as an electrical engineer with the US Army Corps of Engineers, and Phyllis to ferry the kids to and from Eagle River Elementary School. Through the years, Joe and friend Earle Ausman made several attempts to start up a hydroelectric project to no avail. Joe died in 1993, but his dream remained. Phyllis, son Dan, and Ausman formed Southfork Hydro LLC, and in 2012, the company received a $2-million loan from the Alaska Energy Authority to build a plant. It also received a contract from Matanuska Electric Association to purchase the power. The plant has been up and running since September 2013. (Courtesy of the Chugiak-Eagle River Historical Society.)

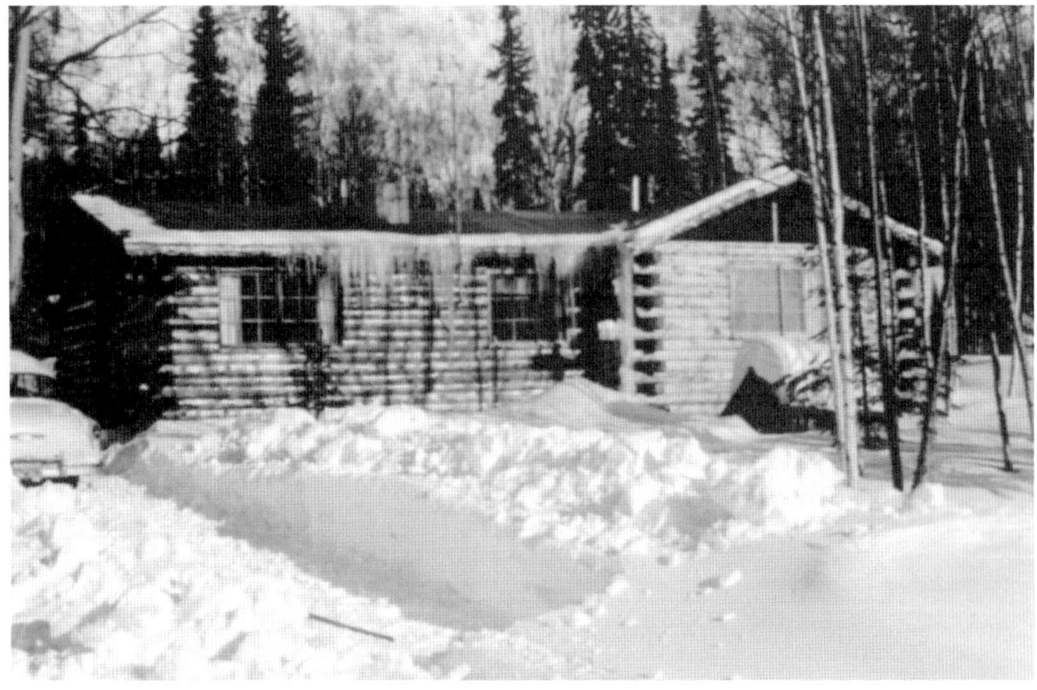

Jack and Phyllis Stewart Home in Earlier Days and Today

Drivers on Eagle River Road cannot help but notice a distinctive log home on the north side of the road at mile three. The house seems too large and ornate to be a homestead dwelling, but it is in fact a gussied-up version of the original Jack and Phyllis Stewart prove-up cabin. The Stewarts arrived in Alaska from Oregon in 1952, and Phyllis stayed with Jack's brother and sister-in-law in Peters Creek while Jack, who had been drafted into the Army, began basic training on Fort Richardson. The couple filed for a homestead in Eagle River and, after basic training was over, set about fulfilling the homesteading requirements. Over the years, they transformed their "habitable dwelling" into a 2,100-square-foot home, raising their three children there. The couple divorced in 1967. Phyllis married Floyd Smith in 1968, and they continued improving the place. Floyd died in 2006 at age 93. Jack married Doris Cairns in 1968 and moved to another location nearby. (Above, courtesy of Phyllis Smith; below, photograph by Chris Lundgren.)

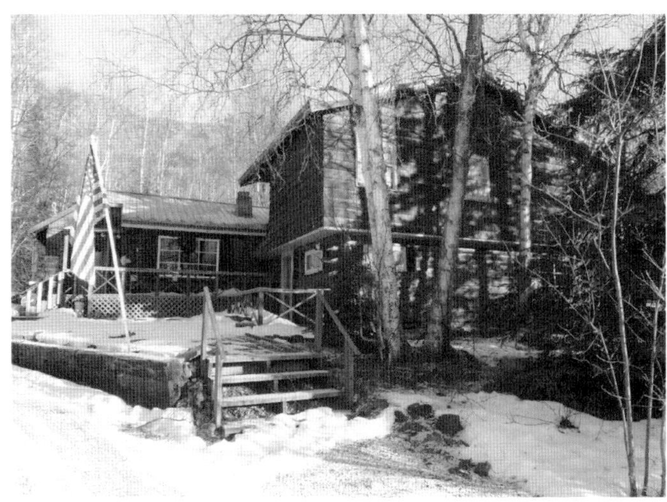

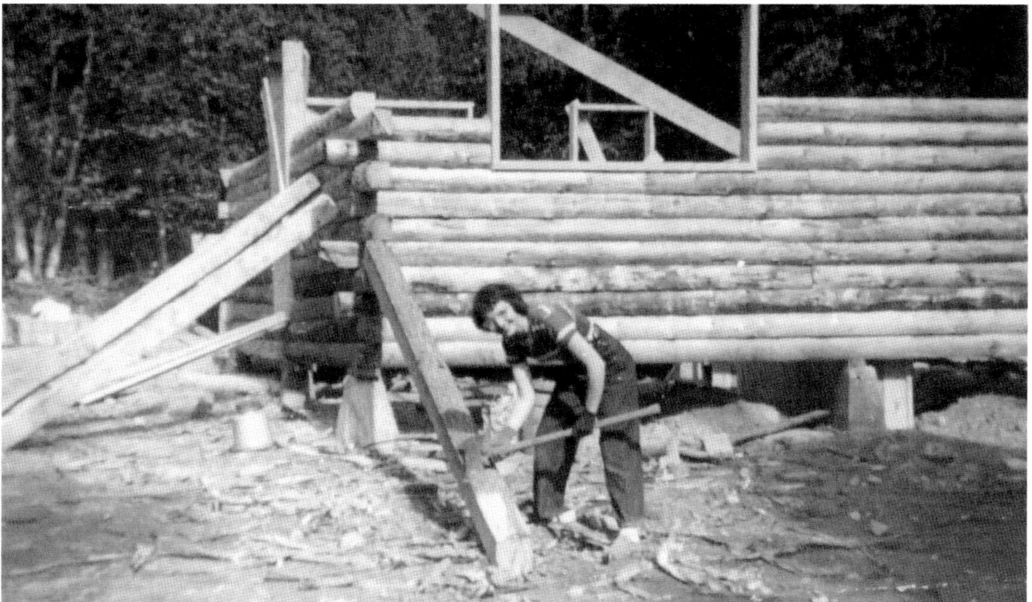

Phyllis Stewart (Smith) and Girl Scout Troop No. 54

Phyllis Smith's impact on Eagle River did not stop with homesteading. Pictured above peeling logs, she was also the area's first Girl Scout leader, founding Troop No. 54 with friend Evelyn Sehm in 1952. Members pictured below, from left to right, are Margaret Davis, Martha Swanson, Barbara Stephens, unidentified, and Linda Hendricks. Smith later studied accounting at University of Alaska, Anchorage, became a certified public accountant, and retired many years later from the Anchorage office of Ernst & Young. She served as a volunteer in a number of capacities, including longtime secretary-treasurer of Knik Little League, longtime treasurer of the Chugiak Benefit Association, youth bowling coach, Chugiak Elementary School Parent-Teacher Association (PTA) president, and member of Operation Chugiak High School, which succeeded in its mission to build a local high school. Smith is the current president of the Chugiak-Eagle River Historical Society. She still lives in the "habitable dwelling" on her homestead. (Above, courtesy of Phyllis Smith; below, courtesy of the Chugiak-Eagle River Historical Society.)

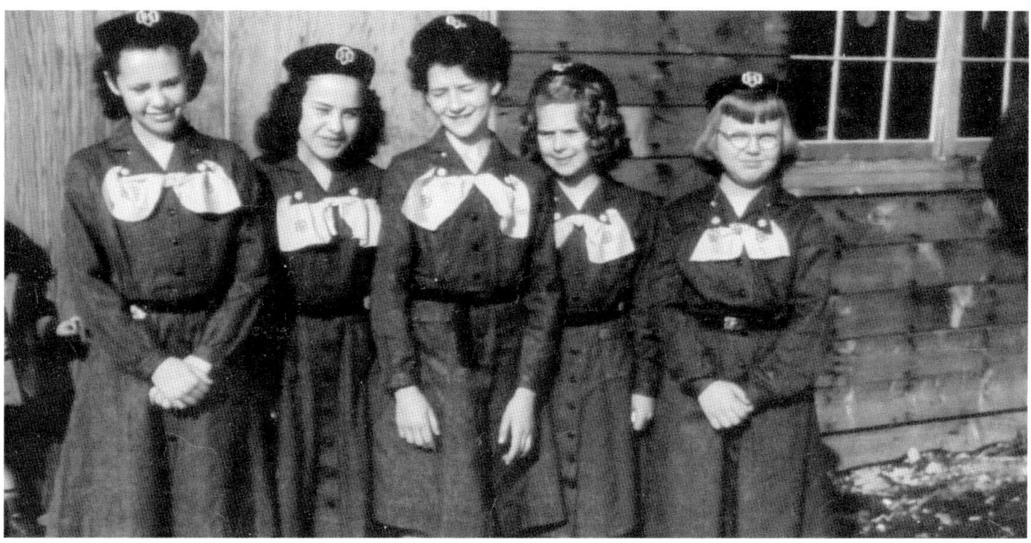

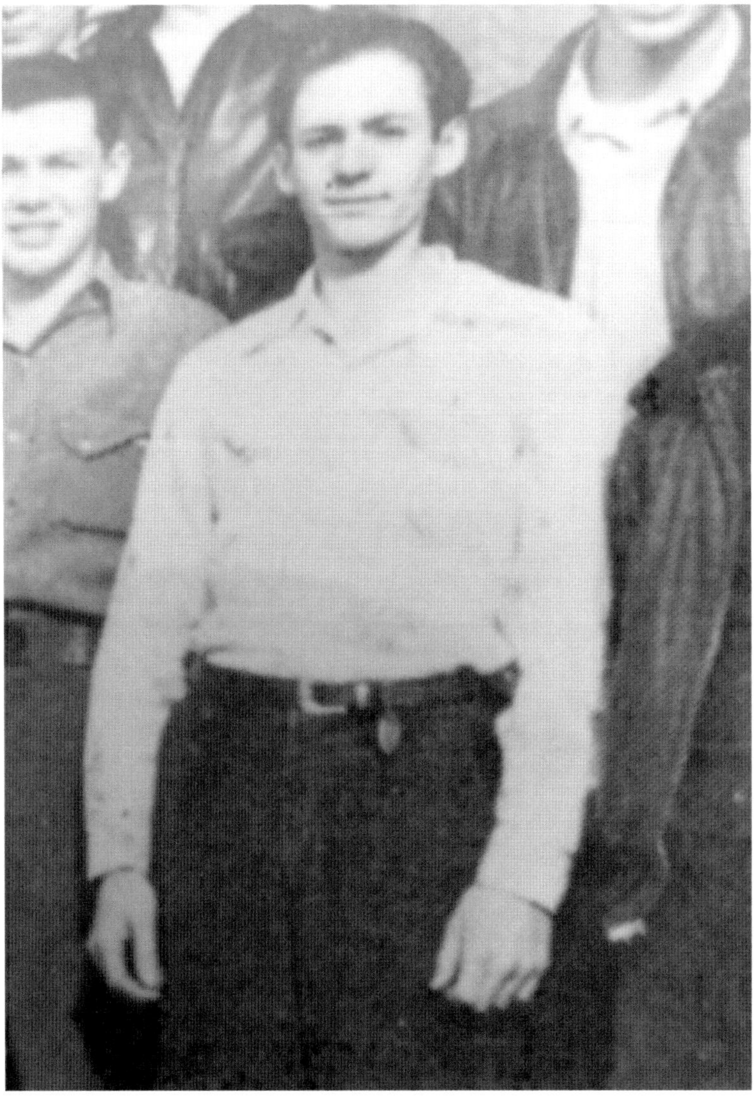

Monte Tedrow

The death of Anchorage High School sophomore Monte Tedrow on September 9, 1950, underscored the need for telephone service and fire protection in Eagle River and Chugiak. The only child of Eagle River homesteaders Ray and Lucille Tedrow, Monte was at home on a windy Saturday when a brush fire broke out. The nearest phone was miles away at the Fort Richardson Army Base, so he got into the family's pickup and headed off. As he approached the Eagle River bridge, his truck swerved left and right before overturning and skidding along its top, dragging him 50 feet. Monte's grief-stricken parents held services for him in Alaska and in his birthplace of Joplin, Missouri. A white cross was added to 12 others memorializing those who had died on or near the Eagle River bridge, and two roads, Monte and Tedrow, were dedicated in his honor. Two years later, residents organized the Chugiak Volunteer Fire Department, though it took until 1957 for telephone service to arrive and until 1959 before Eagle River could claim its own fire department. (Courtesy of the Anchorage Public Library System.)

Lucille and Ray Tedrow
Ray and Lucille Tedrow returned to their Eagle River homestead in 1951 after leaving for several months upon son Monte's death. They built a trailer court and Laundromat on their property and partnered with Glenn and Mary Lou Briggs and Evelyn Sehm to build the Eagle River Shopping Center in 1955. The strip mall housed a comparatively large grocery store along with a hardware store, a gift shop, and a dentist. (Courtesy of the Chugiak-Eagle River Historical Society.)

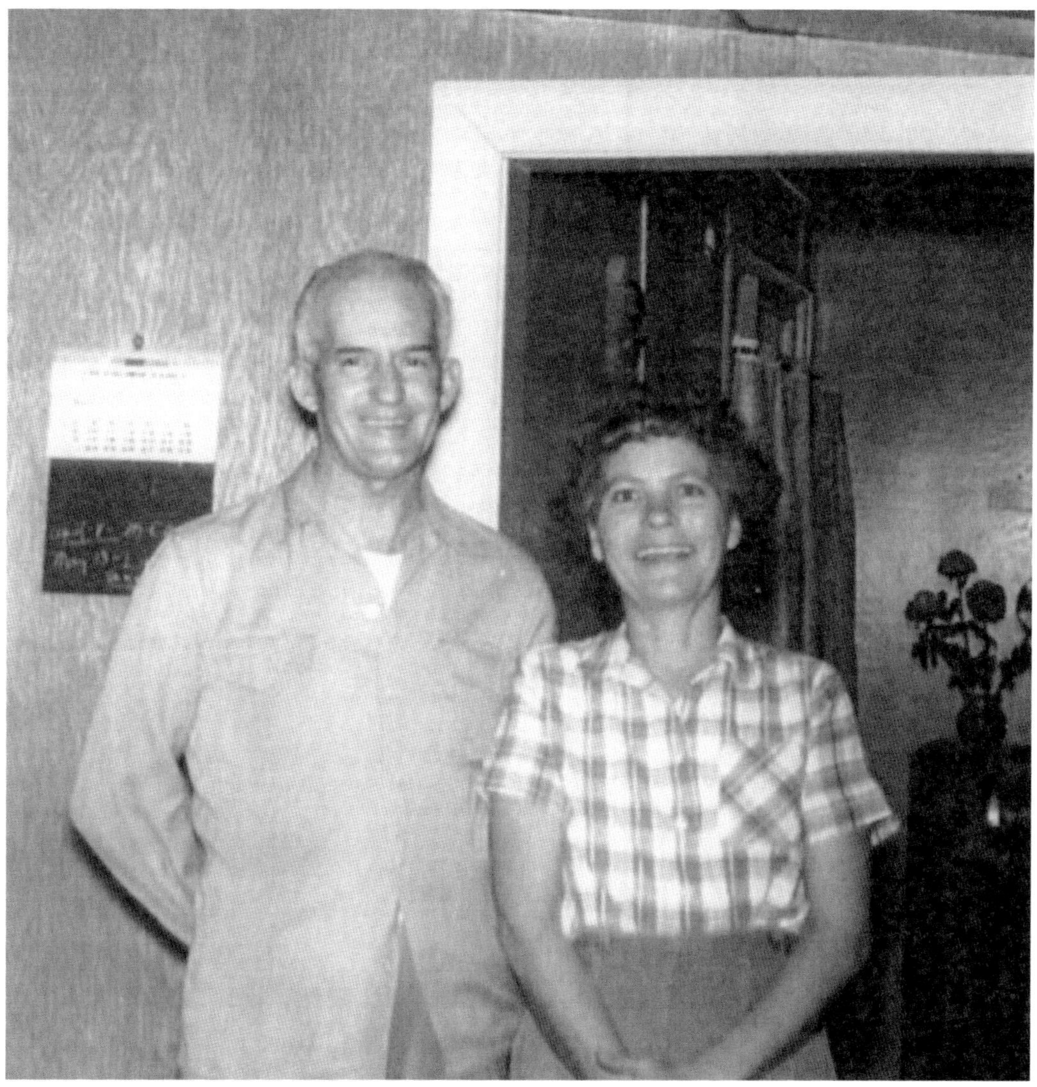

Dan Bell

If the story of Chugiak-Eagle River's early days were made into a movie, Danny Bell would have played the antihero. He and wife, Shirley, homesteaded a 160-acre tract currently occupied by Walmart and the Eaglewood subdivision. Bell was a strong and vocal supporter of the short-lived Chugiak-Eagle River Borough and ran an unsuccessful campaign for borough mayor in 1974. What he is best remembered for, however, is turnips. Eagle River Loop Road originally stopped at the intersection with Eagle River Road. Bell and others believed it should extend down over the river and connect with the Glenn Highway near the entrance to Hiland Road, as it now does. The state disagreed, and in the late 1970s, Bell took matters into his own hands, illegally bulldozing a trail along the edge of his homestead. When forced to revegetate the swath of land, he thumbed his nose at the authorities and planted turnips instead of trees. (Courtesy of the Chugiak-Eagle River Historical Society.)

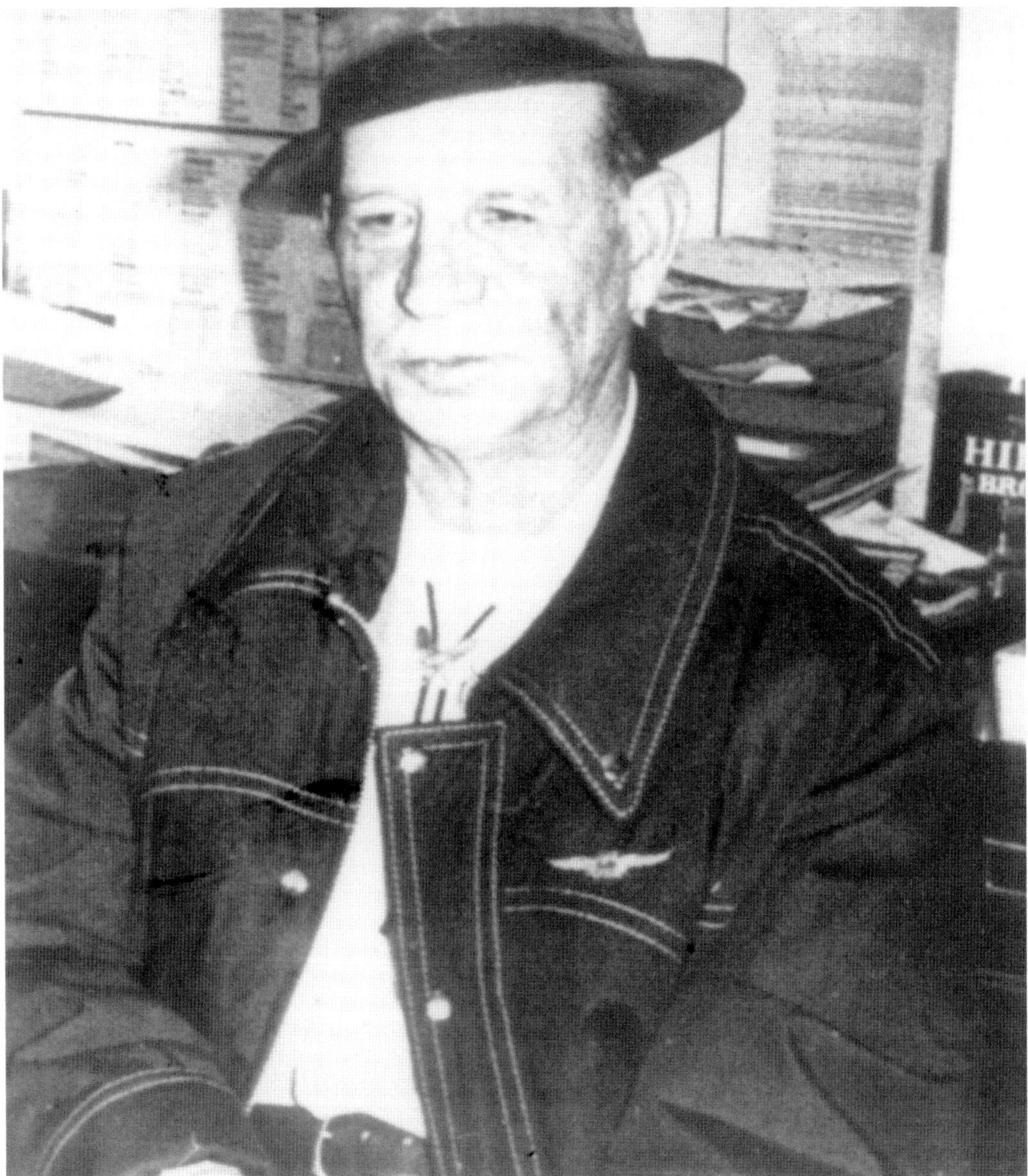

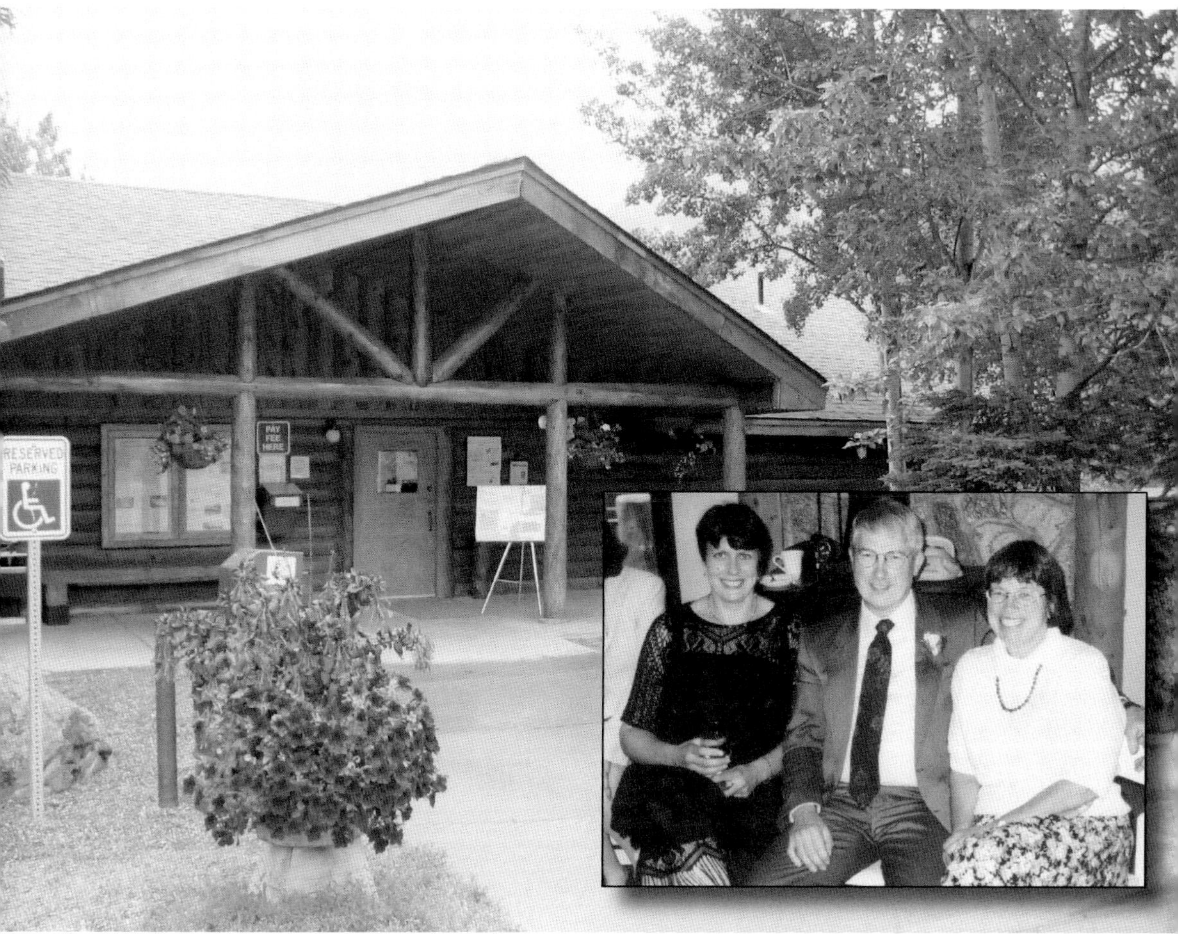

Eagle River Nature Center and Founders Spurgis, Lloyd, and Lloyd
Many hands molded the Eagle River Nature Center into the unique place it is today. The building's history stretches back to the 1960s when homesteader John Barclay opened the Paradise Haven Lodge, a popular bar, grill, and racetrack at the end of Eagle River Road. Getting there was a slippery undertaking during the cold months, and glaciated roads often kept customers away. Barclay sold the property to Alaska State Parks in 1980. Within a year, under the direction of Chugach State Park superintendent Pete Panarese, ranger Dale Bingham, and naturalist Bob Dittrick, the Paradise Haven Lodge was gutted and reemerged as the Chugach State Park Eagle River Visitor Center—a gateway to the Chugach State Park trails behind it. The center, which initially had a deep budget and a staff of five, suffered when oil prices declined in the mid-1980s. By 1995, funding had shriveled, and only one part-time staffer, Asta Spurgis, remained. Even expert naturalist Carole Lloyd was a volunteer. State park officials decided to privatize the visitor center in 1995. Spurgis and Lloyd, along with Lloyd's husband, Dick, created the nonprofit group Friends of the Eagle River Nature Center. The state accepted the organization's proposal to run the facility, and in 1996, the Eagle River Nature Center opened with Dick Lloyd as executive director, Carole Lloyd as naturalist, and Spurgis as operations manager. (The group also has a 12-member board of directors, led by Carl Lundgren since 2003.) Dick spearheaded the building of a public-use cabin just a mile out the Old Iditarod Trail. Before his death in 2004 and Carole's death in 2006, two public-use yurts were erected along the trails; a third was added in 2012. Spurgis remains on staff, now serving as the executive director and overseeing a team of year-round and seasonal employees and an army of volunteers. (Both, courtesy of Asta Spurgis.)

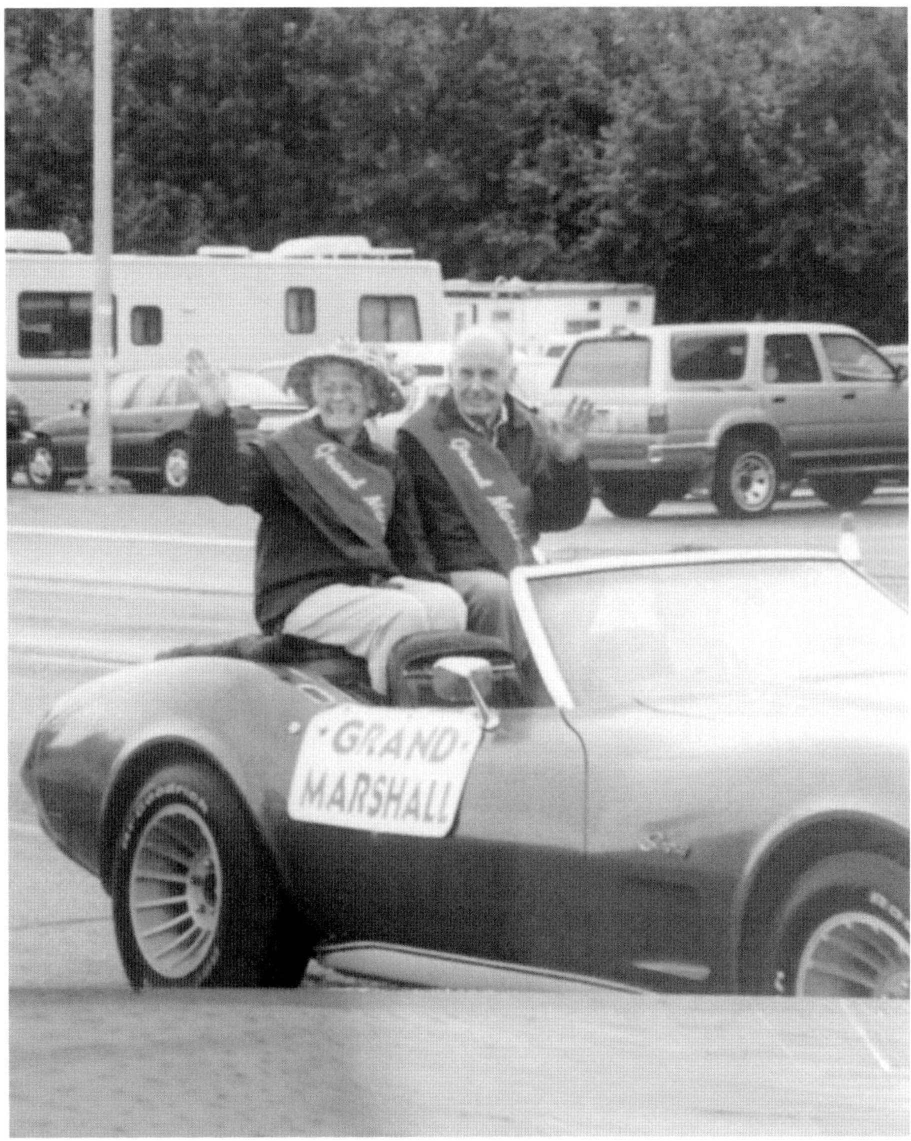

Billie and Vern Moore

The Eagle River School had many fine features when it was built in 1961—bright classrooms, wide hallways, and even a sizable gymnasium. All it lacked was a library. This peeved Billie Moore, a parent and volunteer school nurse. When her fellow PTA members voted to purchase a basketball scoreboard instead of books, Moore took action. She solicited books and funds from the state librarian in Juneau, from officials at Fort Richardson Army Post, and from local families. Bake sale after bake sale brought in waves of pocket change. Soon, the school had its library. It also had a surplus of books, many of which did not suit young readers. Moore refocused her energies on creating a community library. With the help of her husband, Vern; businessmen Glenn Briggs and Ray Tedrow; the Lions Club; and other volunteers, Moore opened the Eagle River Library in April 1965 in a tiny cinder-block building next to the Lazy Mountain Trailer Court. The library moved multiple times as the collection grew, yet no matter the location, Moore drew parents and children in with her obvious love of books and her talent for storytelling. (Courtesy of Katie Mangelsdorf.)

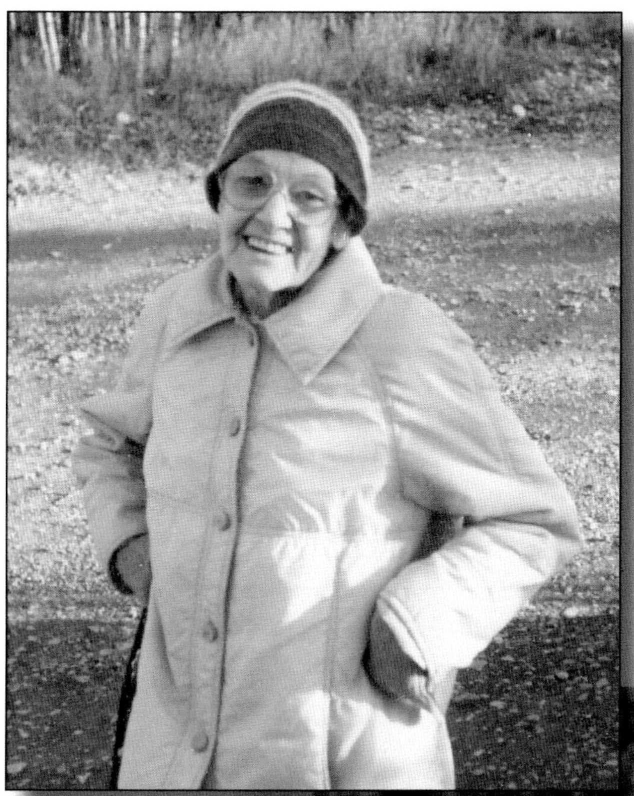

Polly and Bob Kallenberg
One of the first things Polly Kallenberg did when moving to a new community was locate the library. She must have been sorely disappointed when she, husband Bob, and their five children settled in Chugiak in 1963. Although a weathered sign at Swanee Slopes marked the Chugiak Public Library, the little building was empty. The only thing left to do was start over. Kallenberg secured funding from both state and federal sources, cleaned up the small building, and filled it with books. The library opened in the spring of 1965, just a few weeks ahead of Eagle River's. (Both, courtesy of Henry Kallenberg.)

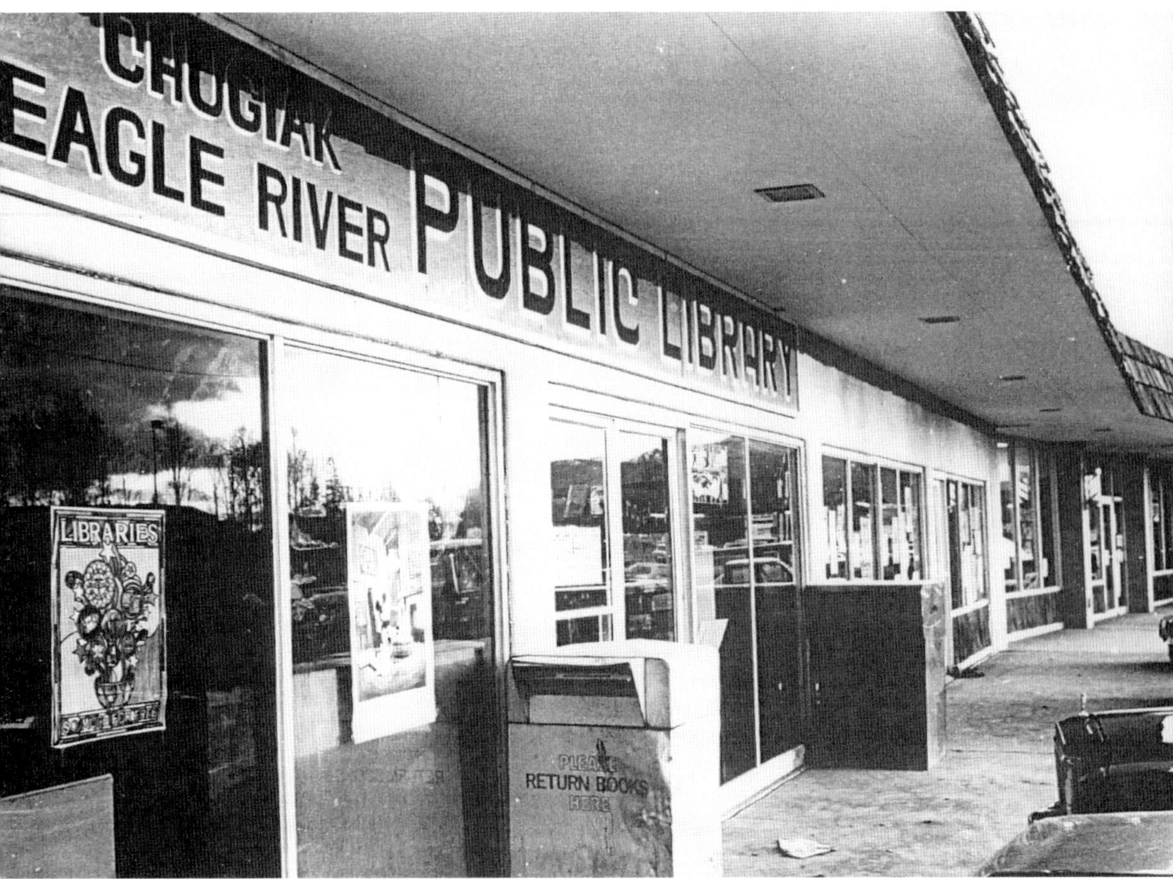

Chugiak-Eagle River Public Library

Polly Kallenberg and Billie Moore were friends and coworkers brought together by their love of books. Each woman opened a library in the spring of 1965—Kallenberg in Chugiak, and Moore in Eagle River. The libraries were combined into the Chugiak-Eagle River Public Library, located in the Eagle River Shopping Center, in 1968. Though both women were outgoing and helpful, Moore most often manned the front desk while Kallenberg worked in back. Kallenberg became an expert at retooling books and opened a book-repair shop upon her retirement in 1981. In 2011, the Children's Section of the Chugiak-Eagle River Branch Library was named for Moore, and the Northern Collection, for Kallenberg. (Courtesy of the Chugiak-Eagle River Historical Society.)

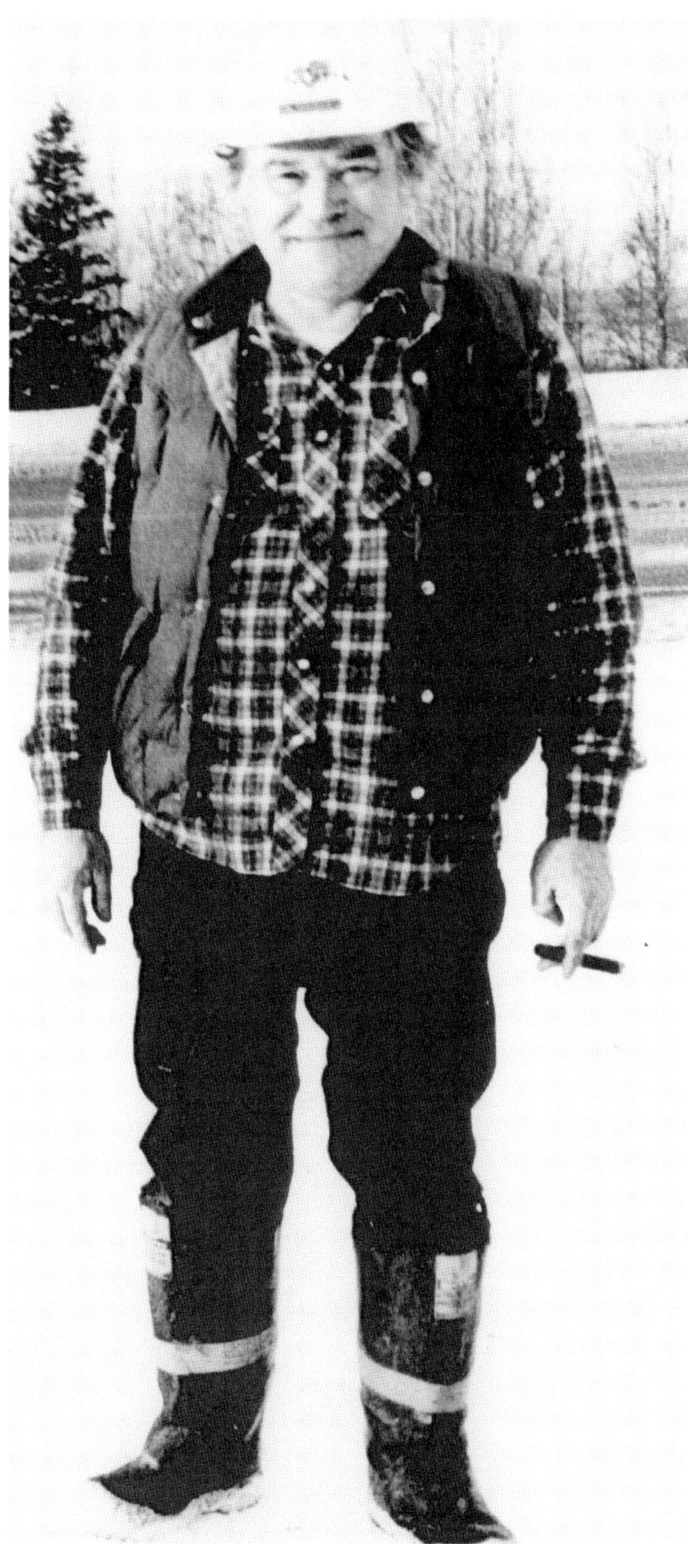

Art Wallace
Art Wallace arrived in Alaska with his younger brother Mike in 1954 after serving in the Marines. He first made his way to Fairbanks to work in the gold fields before coming back south to work on the Eklutna Tunnel Project. In 1955, he settled in the Chugiak-Eagle River area and founded Wallace Economy Concrete Products with his brother Til. In 1964, Art converted the company's headquarters building into Fuji Gifts—a popular shop that became a Chugiak landmark. Wallace served for 30 years on the Chugiak Volunteer Fire Department, four of those years as chief. With Fuji Gifts right across the road from the fire department, Wallace was often the first to respond to an emergency. He retired from the fire department in 1984 but kept Fuji Gifts open for another 25 years. He died in 2010 at age 79. (Courtesy of Til Wallace.)

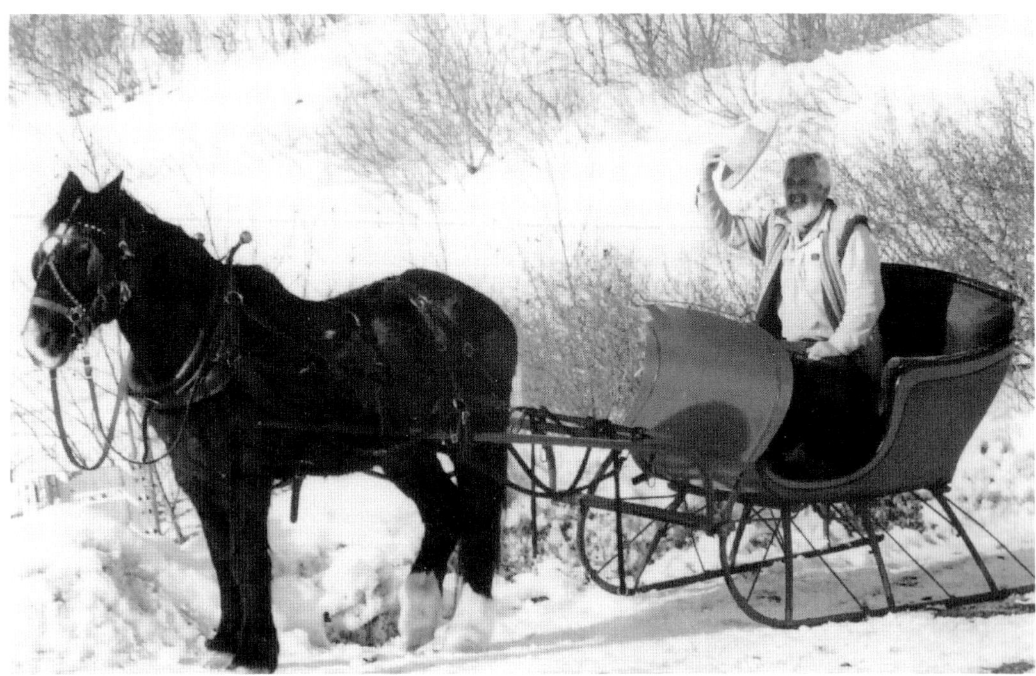

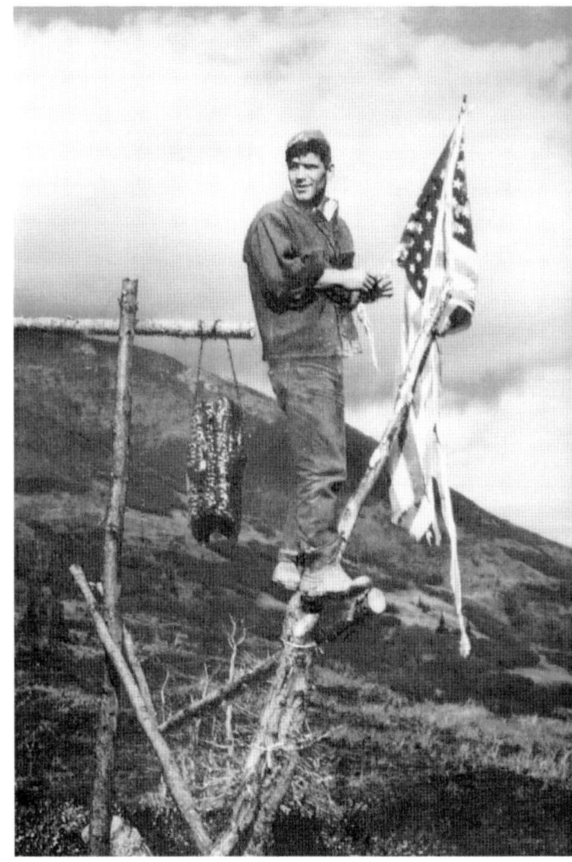

Til Wallace and Mike Wallace

Til Wallace was one of four enterprising brothers from New York who made their way to Alaska in the mid-1950s, three of them settling in the Chugiak-Eagle River area. After serving in the Army Special Forces, Til formed a construction business in 1955 with his older brother Art. Together—by hand—they molded concrete blocks that formed the foundations of many of Chugiak's early commercial buildings. Til (above) and brother Mike (right) built another construction business that became Klondike Concrete, operating it from 1960 until they sold it in 1990. Til and Mike acquired adjoining homesteads abutting what is now Skyline Drive. The 320-acre property, widely used by hikers on their way to and from Mount Baldy, has one of the best views in Eagle River. Til tried to subdivide and sell the property in the 1970s but ran into difficulties with nearby homeowners. Throughout the 1980s, Til acquired 50 horses and about a dozen historical homes from Anchorage and Chugiak. He opened the Wallace Brothers Ranch and lived on the property year-round, giving horse rides and welcoming visitors until the heavy work became too much. Til lives in Chugiak with his wife, Ella. (Both, courtesy of Til Wallace.)

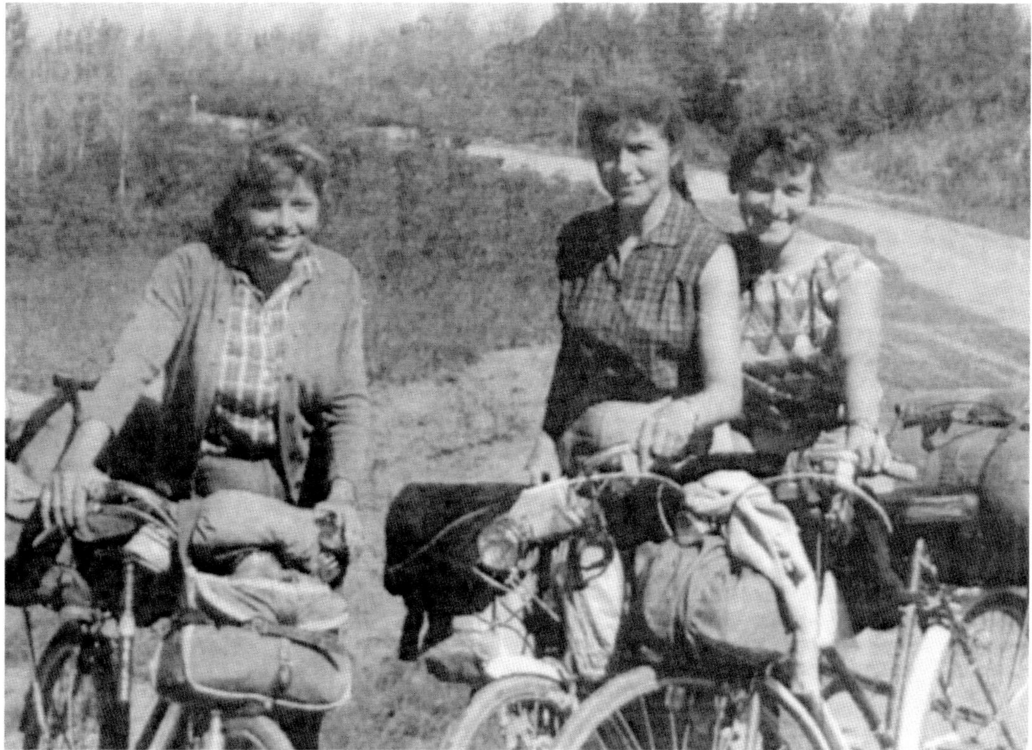

Ella Hitz Wallace and Travel Companions

Ella Hitz Wallace (center) was a natural-born wanderer. Traveling from her native Switzerland with two girlfriends, the 21-year-old traversed Canada in 1957 and 1958, working at different jobs and exploring as time permitted. The women settled in Vancouver but stayed just long enough to save up for bicycles. In the spring of 1959, they undertook a 13-week trek to Anchorage, with knapsacks strapped to their fenders and rubber ponchos to keep out the occasional rain. In Eagle River, they met Til Wallace. As the women made their way down the Seward Highway toward Homer, Til would meet them in their campground and spend evenings with them. Ella and her friends went back to Vancouver to work, and Til got a job in nearby Bellingham, Washington. After Til proposed over the phone on a number of occasions, Ella finally said yes. The two were married in March 1960 and homesteaded in Eagle River. Ella worked in the office at Wallace Construction (later Klondike Concrete) and during winters at Bagoy's Florist in Anchorage. She is now retired. Pictured with Ella are Ruth Gutscher (left) and Sonja Maurer. (Courtesy of Ella Wallace.)

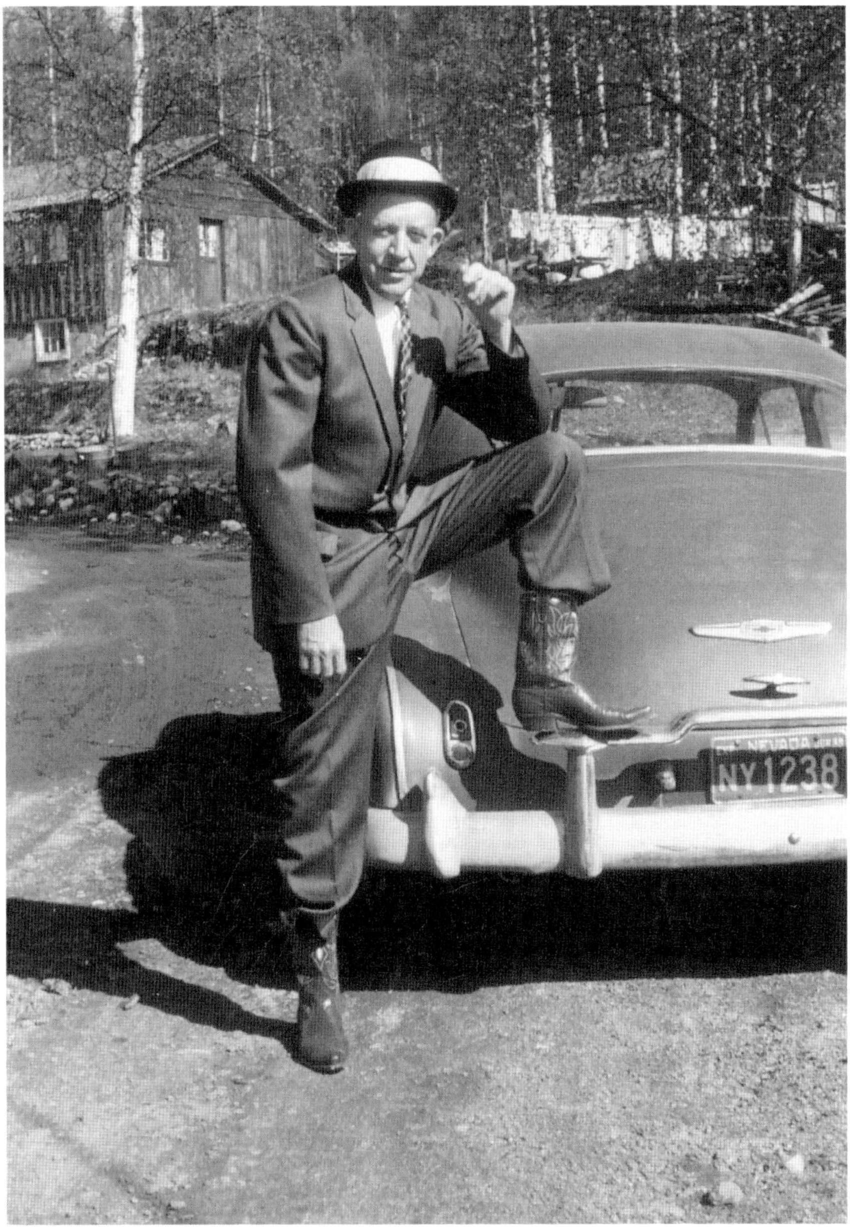

Paul Swanson, Chugiak's Earliest Businessman

Always on the lookout for ways to earn a living, Paul Swanson embodied the homesteader-businessman of early Chugiak. In 1946, he built a $60 house on his 40-acre property using spare wood scrounged from an abandoned Army camp. He did not stop there. Through the years, Swanson amassed an assortment of buildings, trailers, and Quonset huts that at various times housed teachers from the nearby Chugiak Territorial School, supplemental classrooms, pig pens, a church, the Chugiak Library, and the Swansons' general store—which contained the post office (Swanson was Chugiak's postmaster at the time). Nearby residents affectionately dubbed his acreage "Swanee Slopes." Pictured at the top of the opposite page, Swanson mans the counter at his store. Pictured at the bottom, a moose struggles in the snow at Swanee Slopes. (All, courtesy of the Chugiak-Eagle River Historical Society.)

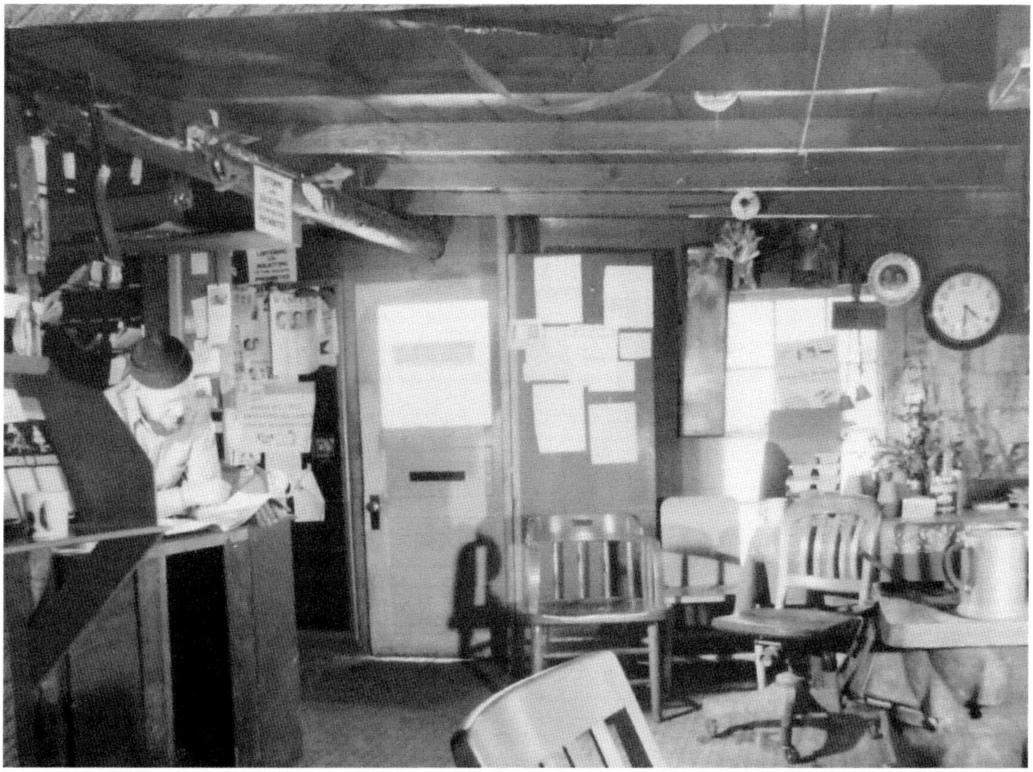

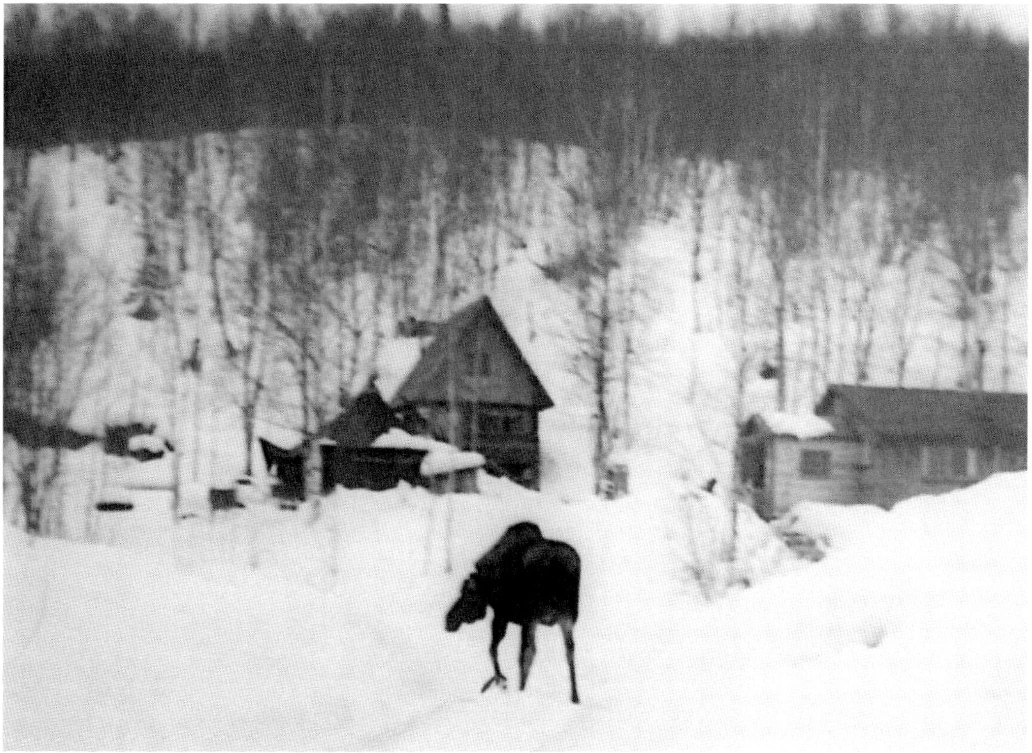

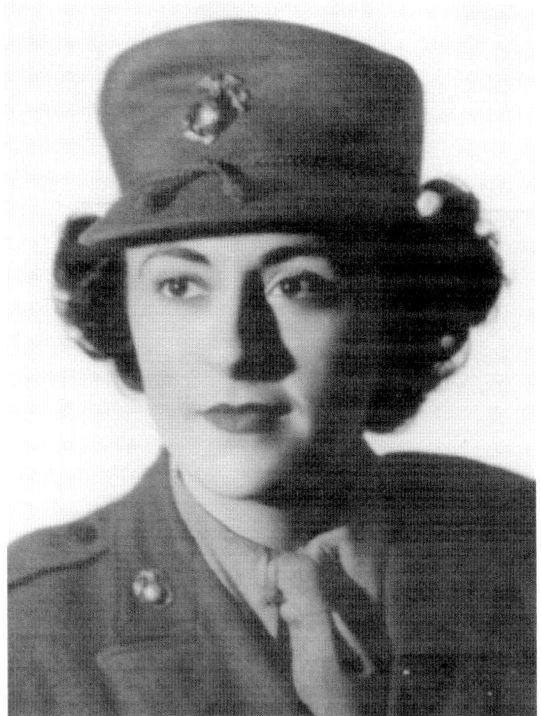

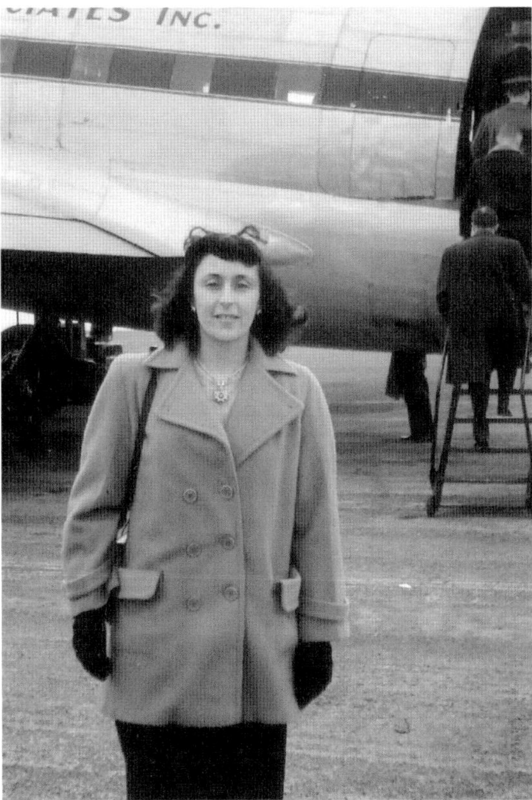

Rusty Bellringer

Harriet S. "Rusty" Bellringer put the final issue of the *Knik Arm Courier* to bed more than 40 years ago, yet people today are still reading the weekly newspaper. Archived at the Chugiak-Eagle River Historical Society, the *Courier* has reemerged as a reliable source of information about the area from 1958 to 1973. Bellringer, a World War II Marine Corps veteran, aircraft-engine mechanic, pilot, wife, and mother, said she never missed a weekly deadline in those 15 years, despite the many challenges involved in being a one-woman operation. Even the 1964 Good Friday earthquake did not stop her. The same focus and determination helped Bellringer earn her bachelor's degree, master's degree, and doctor of philosophy in clinical psychology through the 1970s and 1980s, and she went on to open a private counseling practice. A 53-year resident of Peters Creek, Rusty passed away at age 81 in 2003. (Courtesy of the Chugiak-Eagle River Historical Society.)

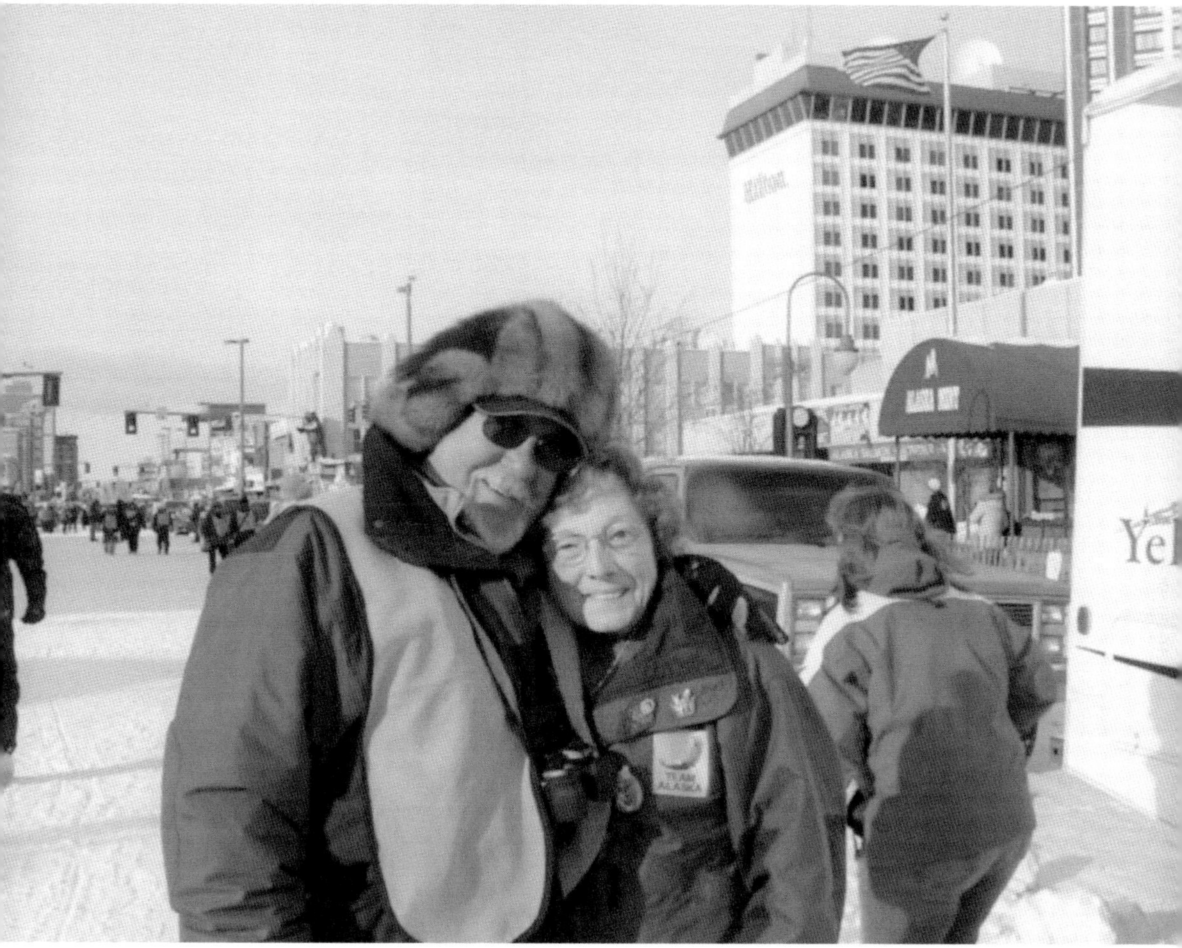

Bill and Dixie Waddell

A passion for dog mushing connects many of the enterprises Bill and Dixie Waddell have undertaken in the past 30 years. The couple met in 1984 in Dixie's hardware store, Peters Creek Supply, and they married three years later. When Dixie introduced Bill to mushing, he embraced the sport and took to the animals. It was dog food, in fact, that triggered the idea for their general merchandise store, Rural Discount Center (RDC). Bill opened RDC in 1984 after learning that Costco was discarding perfectly good kibble in slightly damaged packaging. He began reselling pet food and other salvaged products, operating the store with Dixie for 20 years before they sold it to longtime store manager and friend Randy Lemmens. Outside of work, the Waddells have donated thousands of volunteer hours to a variety of organizations, some mushing-related and some not. They include Arctic Winter Games-Team Alaska, Chugiak Dog Mushers Association, Alaskan Sled Dog & Racing Association, Chugiak-Eagle River Historical Society, Chugiak Benefit Association, and Chugiak Area Business Association. Lately, the Waddells have turned their attention to the Chugiak-Eagle River Chinooks baseball team, and they housed two of the young players in 2013. They also held a huge cookout for team, the host families, and a party-crashing bear that hung around for photographs. Bill took charge of the team's concessions that same year, grilling endless hot dogs and hamburgers at home games and extinguishing his appetite for all food served on a bun. Today, the couple is busy plotting their next adventure. (Courtesy of Mary Lou Raychel.)

Lee and Barbara Jordan

The seed for Chugiak-Eagle River's longest-running newspaper was planted in 1949 when Lee Jordan arrived in Whittier with the US Army Signal Corps. He was assigned to the Alaska Communication System (ACS) in Anchorage, which provided long-distance telephone and telegraph service throughout the territory. Jordan worked a late shift at ACS and also found time for a day job as a printer with the *Anchorage Daily Times*. He ultimately opened his own print shop in Anchorage. In 1962, he and wife Barbara and their children moved to Chugiak and immersed themselves in the community. Jordan felt his new hometown was being overlooked by the Anchorage papers, and he had a solution: on January 14, 1971, the first issue of the *Chugiak-Eagle River Star* slid off Jordan's printing press. Coverage of local news and community events, sports news, feature stories, and the publisher's down-to-earth editorials attracted readers to the weekly paper. Jordan himself became part of the news in 1974 when he was elected mayor of the short-lived Chugiak-Eagle River Borough. The Jordans sold the *Star* to Morris Communications in 2000. It is still being published. (Courtesy of Lee Jordan.)

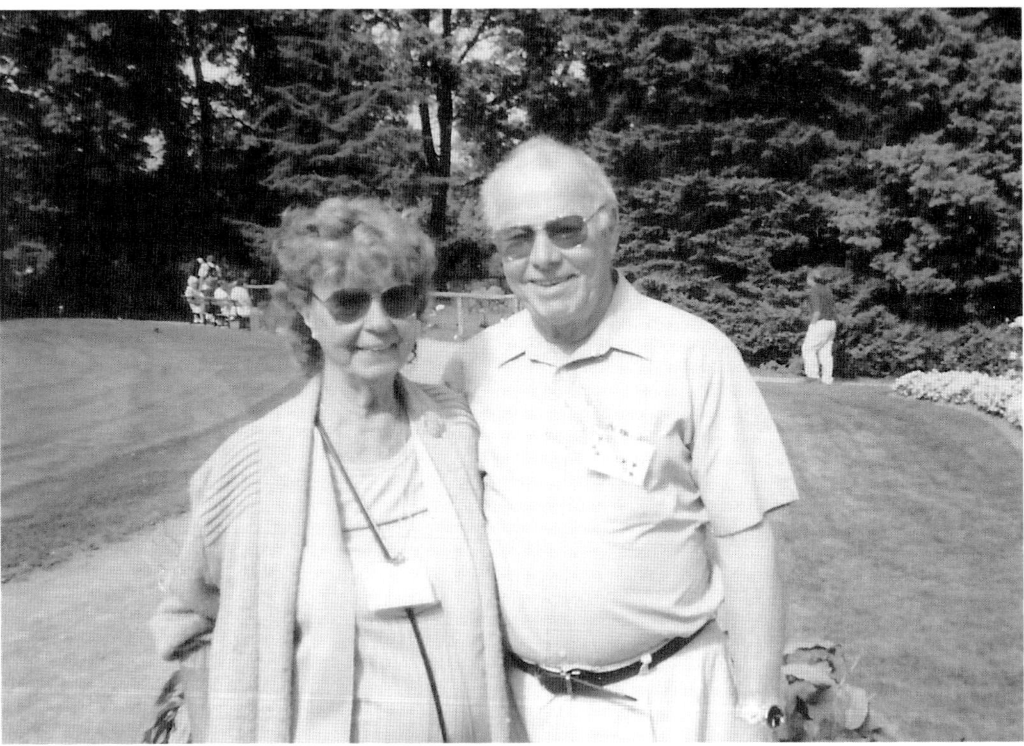

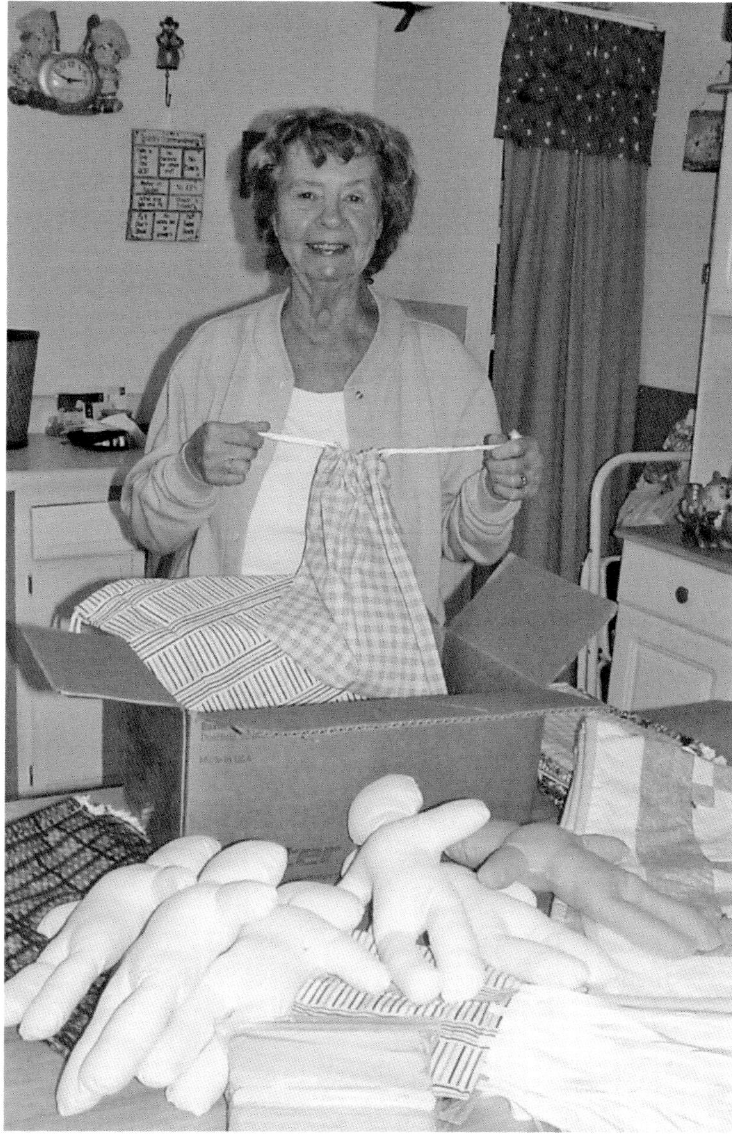

Barbara Jordan

Barbara Erickson Jordan, pictured here helping with a project for Operation Smile, was only six in 1939 when she arrived with her mother, father, and two of her siblings in the territory. Traveling aboard the S.S. *Alaska*, the family landed in Seward. Her father began working at the Eklutna Power Plant, and the family settled into a nearby cabin in the small complex of homes for employees. Jordan's memories are of the *Little House in the Big Woods* variety, attending a school taught by two mothers (including her own), using buckets to scoop salmon out of the streams for dinner, and having a body of water—Lake Barbara—named after her. The family moved to Spenard within a few years. Jordan met husband Lee while waiting tables at Lu's Cafe in Anchorage during her senior year of high school, and the couple married soon after graduation in 1951. They had four children and owned print shops in Anchorage and Eagle River. After helping Lee open the *Chugiak-Eagle River Star*, Jordan bought Frontier Fabric & Craft and ran the store for 30 years. She outlasted several other fabric shops, including a large chain store, before finally closing doors in 2001. (Courtesy of Lee Jordan.)

Les and Dottie Fetrow and Chugiak Players

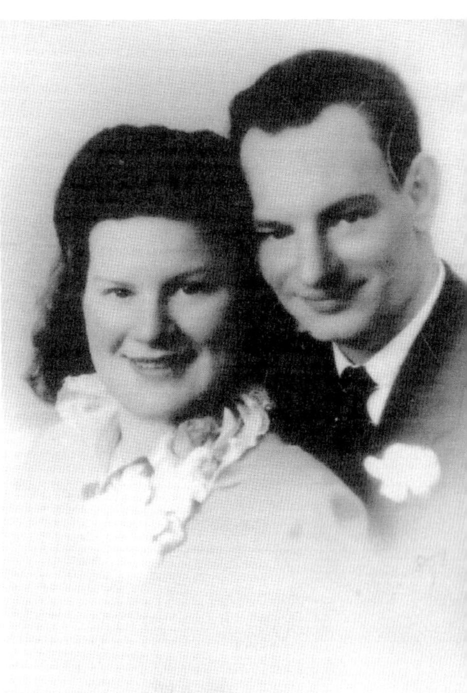

Homesteaders Les and Dottie Fetrow were regular fixtures around Chugiak from their arrival in 1947 until their retirement from public life in the 1990s. Many people remember Les by his involvement with the Chugiak Players theater group, where he was an actor, director, publicist, ticket salesperson, and anything else that was needed. Yet his involvement in the community went much deeper. Les was instrumental in establishing necessary amenities in Chugiak, such as fire protection, electricity, and phone service. When the Chugiak Community Club sponsored the area's first Boy Scout Troop in 1949, he became the troop's institutional representative. A veteran of the Seabees, Les worked on Fort Richardson Military Post as a civil servant with the Army from 1946 to 1977 and later served as a supply manager for the Chugiak Senior Center. Les and Dottie both received several certificates of recognition for their contributions to the center. The couple had six children. Below, Chugiak Players performing the play *Ladies of the Jury* are, from left to right, Les Fetrow, Bonnie Flint, Dee Steeby, Lois Rydell, Joe Anne Vanover, and Rusty Bellringer. (Both, courtesy of the Chugiak-Eagle River Historical Society.)

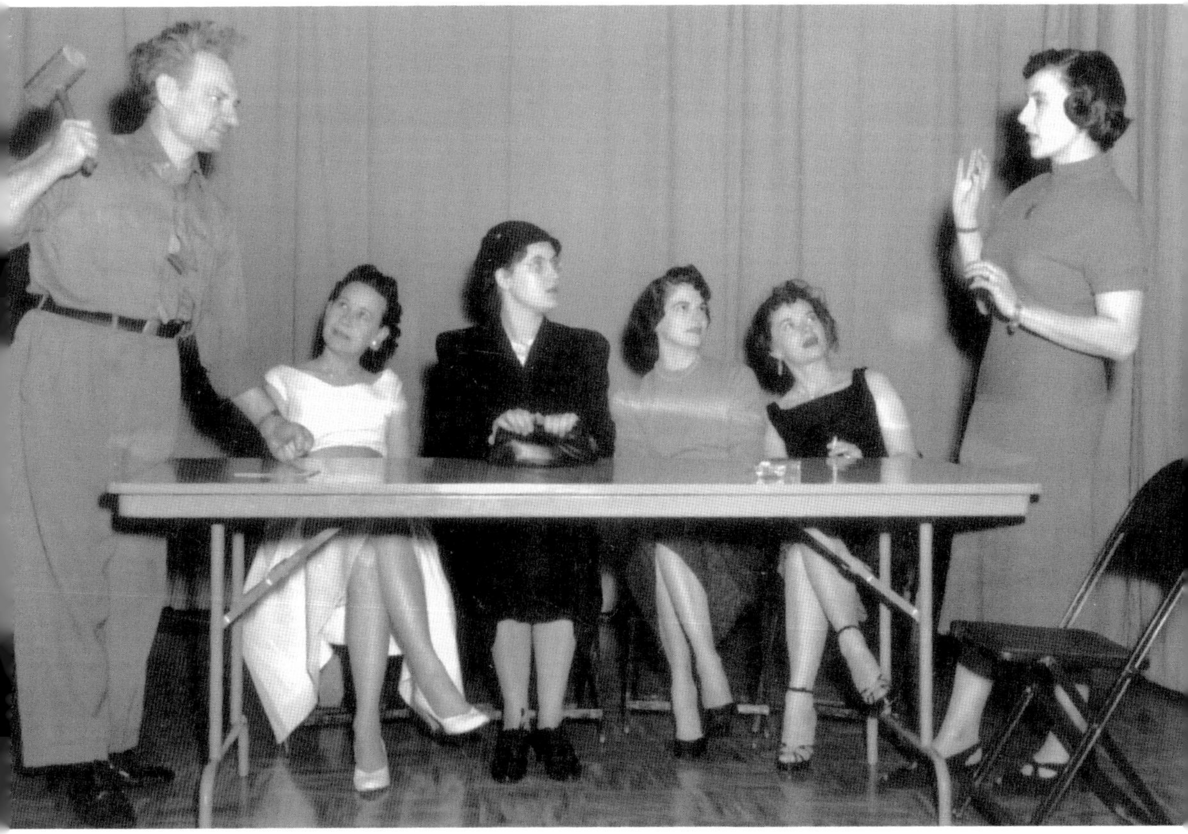

CHAPTER TWO

Entrepreneurs and Business Professionals

Some of Chugiak-Eagle River's earliest businesses simply supplied residents with the basics—food, shelter, gasoline, and heat. Tom Slanker's Far North Service and Far North Fuel and Bill Stephens's Peters Creek Fuel were such businesses. Jim and Marie McDowell's Moose Horn, a conglomeration of trading post, public laundry, and showers, drew customers from the far corners of Chugiak and Eagle River. Yet some of the other best-remembered establishments are the ones that offered last-frontier–style luxury in the wilderness. Stories circulate about the Chugiak Candy Kitchen, where Nora Collett's chocolates were flavored with local berries and her spicy commentary was part of the buying experience. Tony and Betty Bockstahler's Alaska Woodcraft was a furniture-and-gift shop in which all the wares were made from Alaska wood. The community also remembers fondly many of the area's ice-cream shops, such as the Dari Delite in Peters Creek and Eagle River's Tastee-Freez. Full-scale restaurants like the Spring Creek Lodge were wildly popular from the 1940s into the 1960s. However, the lodge, like countless other businesses, lost customers after the Glenn Highway (originally called the Palmer Highway) was rerouted in 1969, and it closed doors in the early 1970s. Around the same time, George Malekos opened the North Slope Restaurant in Eagle River, a place that earned a loyal, long-term following. Nowadays, though Chugiak-Eagle River is still very much a bedroom community to Anchorage, it has a variety of restaurants and shops, including a few chains. People still cherish small, specialty businesses, however, and many heed the call to shop and eat locally.

Cloyce and Justine Parks's Chugiak Coffee Shop

Nebraskans Cloyce and Justine Parks acquired a homesite at mile 19.5 of the Palmer Highway in 1945, expecting only to build a cabin for themselves and their two teenage children. Justine (pictured) soon realized she could put her talents to work baking pastries and brewing coffee for the visitors who stopped by to see the family and check out their pet, a wolf-dog hybrid named Wolf. In May 1947, Justine opened the Chugiak Coffee Shop, and a year later, Cloyce installed a gas pump adjacent to the building. The area became known as "Parksville." A neon sign, which provided the only light between Anchorage and Palmer, beckoned customers. Parksville served as an informal community center, and it was a natural place to start up a newspaper. The couple published and mimeographed the biweekly *Chugiak Calendar* for several years beginning in 1953. (Courtesy of the Chugiak-Eagle River Historical Society.)

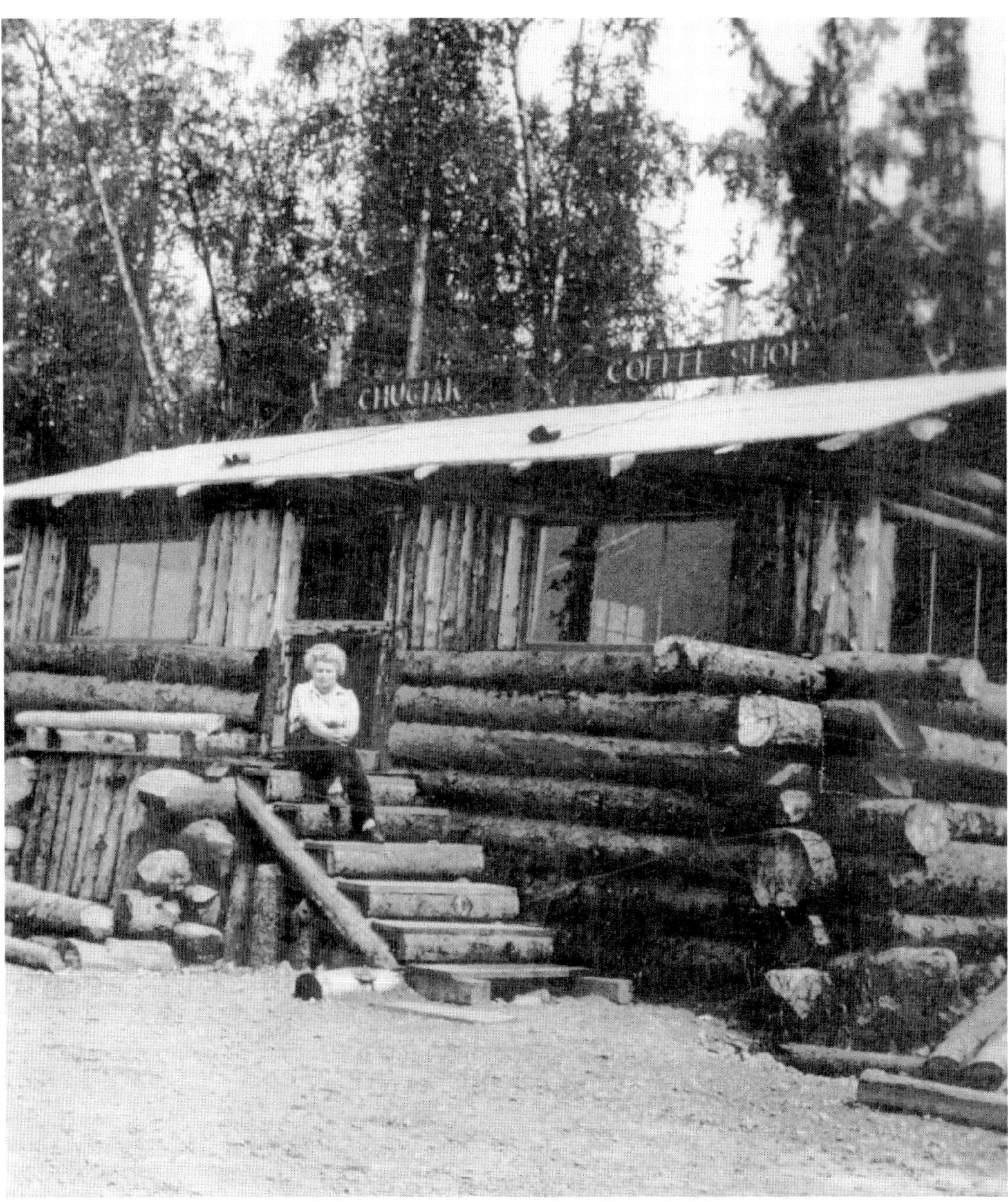

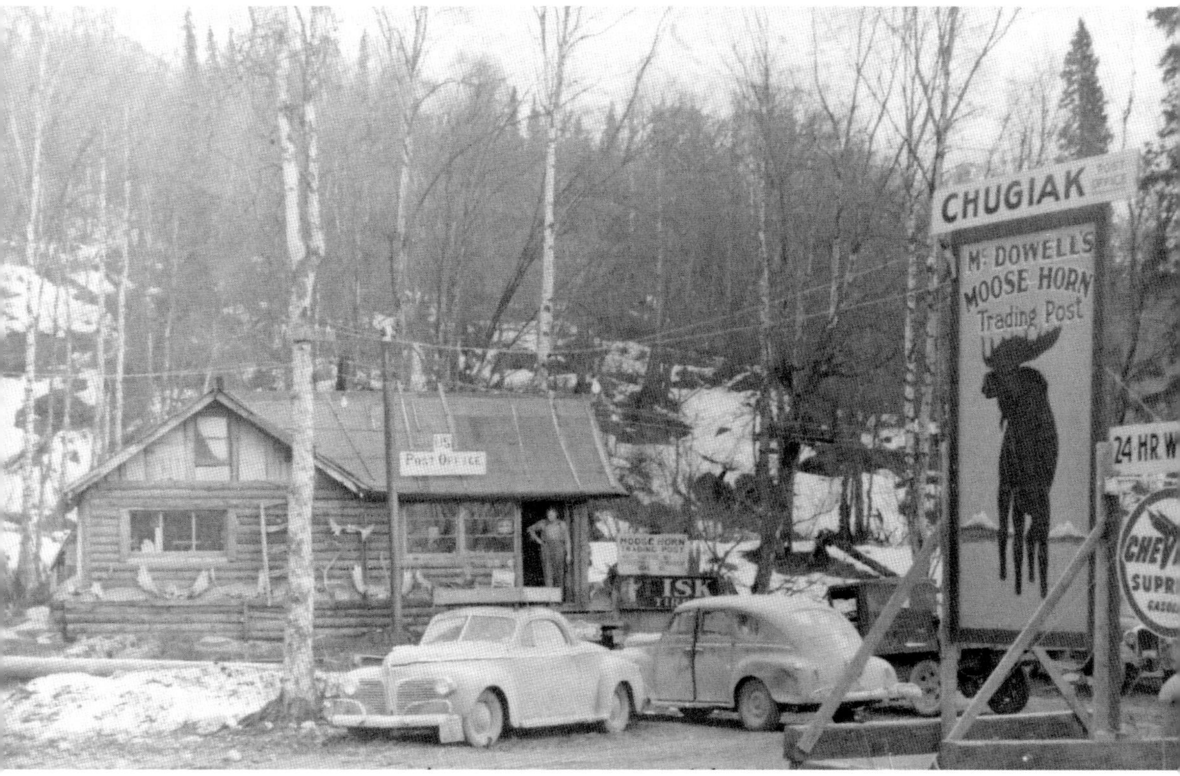

McDowell's Moose Horn Trading Post

A giant "Moose Horn" sign marks the spot of Jim and Marie McDowells' former business homesite along the Old Glenn Highway. It refers to the trading post, public laundry, and showers the McDowells built soon after their arrival in 1946. (Jim McDowell was a lumberjack from Washington who was displaced when logging ceased during World War II.) The Moose Horn property has changed hands over the past 65 years, reemerging variously as a gas station, bus barn, and apartment building. Beginning in 1947, the land also included the first Chugiak Post Office, with Marie McDowell as postmaster. (Courtesy of the Chugiak-Eagle River Historical Society.)

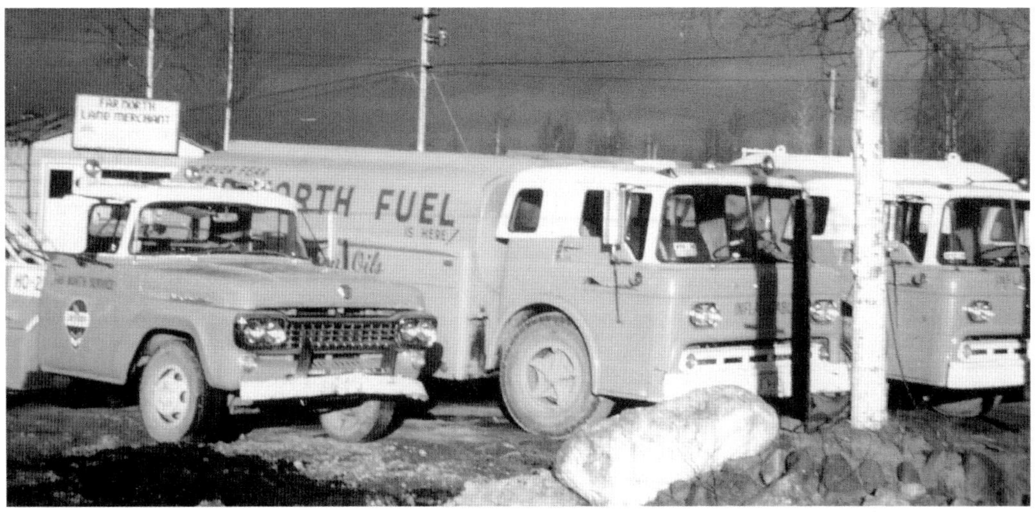

Tom Slanker's Far North Fuel

Tom Slanker was stationed at Fort Richardson and moonlighting as a gas station attendant in Anchorage when he learned of a good business opportunity. In 1955, he bought Far North Service in Eagle River, which sat next to Tony Bockstahler's Alaska Woodcraft just off Artillery Road. Slanker's purchase included a trailer court and a single gas pump, the latter of which he expanded into a full-scale garage. After running out of fuel oil to heat the place, he envisioned a new direction in which he could grow. He bought a 1,000-gallon truck and started Far North Fuel, delivering heating oil to homes in and around Eagle River. Over time, Slanker developed his property into what is now a commercial hub near the Eagle River exit to the Glenn Highway. The Slanker Building houses Pizza Man and Vibe Salon. Slanker is pictured below at the Chugiak Spring Carnival in the late 1950s. (Both, courtesy of the Chugiak-Eagle River Historical Society.)

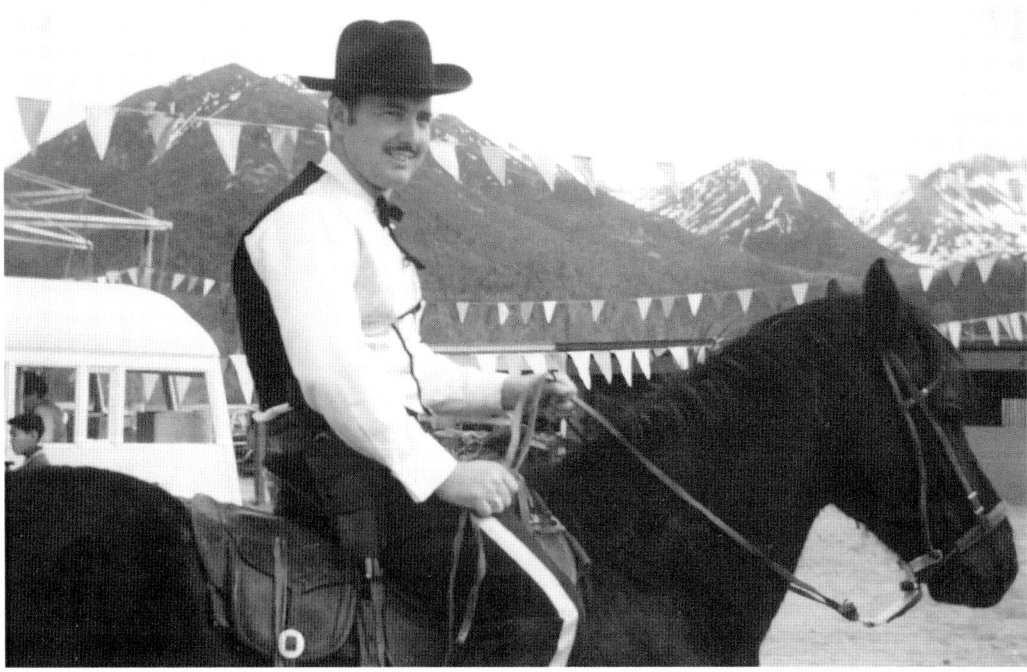

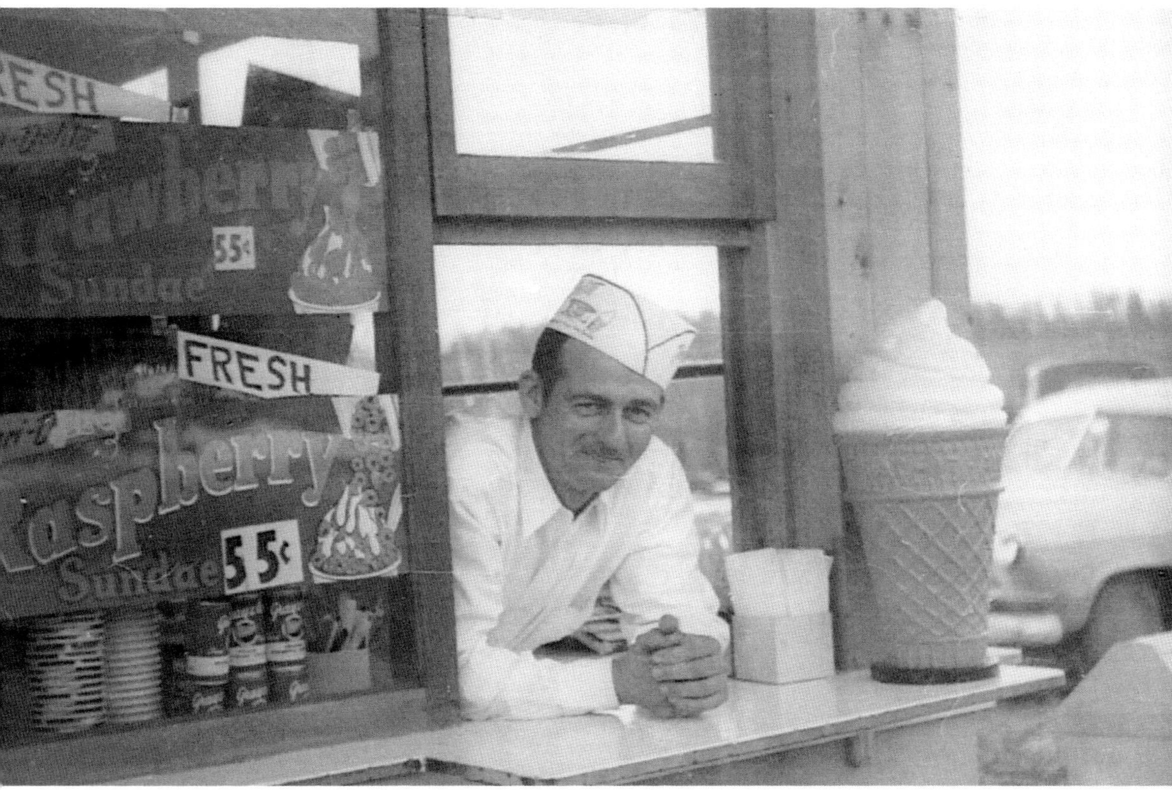

Bill Stephens at the Dari Delite

After a handful of false starts that bounced them between Washington and Alaska, Bill and Cleda Stephens and their growing family settled in Peters Creek in 1950. Stephens and family friend Grace Tatro built the Dari Delite drive-through in 1954 and ran it for the next several years. Situated at mile 21.5 of the Glenn Highway (now the Bella Vista Restaurant site), the Dari Delite was a popular hangout for locals and also attracted highway travelers. Stephens opened a gas station and Peters Creek Fuel in 1959, delivering fuel oil to homes throughout the area. The gas station and Peters Creek Trading Post stayed in the family for many years and still operate on property south of the old Dari Delite. Stephens retired and sold the fuel oil–service business in 1973. He died in 2001. (Courtesy of the Chugiak-Eagle River Historical Society.)

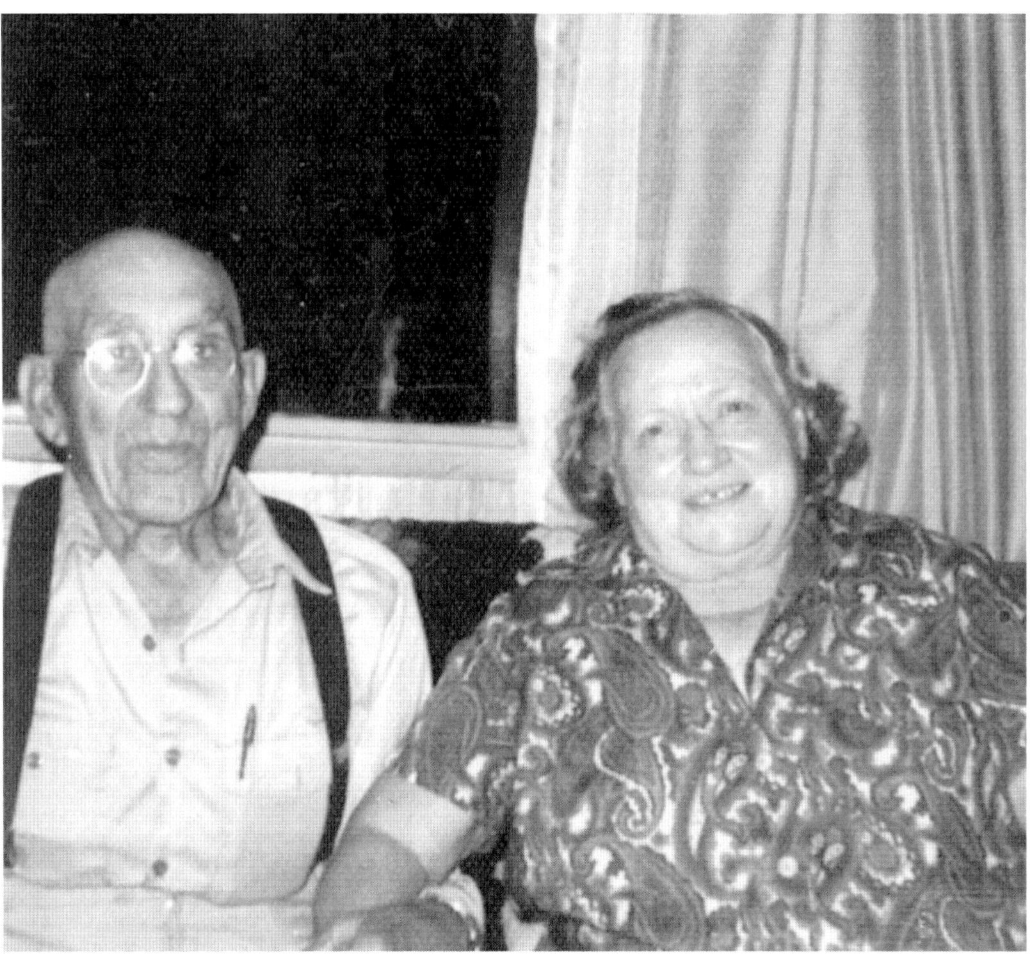

Reese and Grace Tatro

In 1946, newlyweds Reese and Grace Tatro moved into a tent on their 130-acre homestead in Peters Creek. The property encompassed Mirror Lake, then known as Bear Lake, and turned out to be a suitable place to raise geese. They established a poultry farm, calling it Quanta La Goose Farm, a parody of the catchy 1940s song, "Cuanto le Gusta." In addition to geese and chickens, the Tatros grew potatoes, grain, cabbage, and even daisies. They built the Dari Delite with Bill Stephens in 1954. (Courtesy of the Chugiak-Eagle River Historical Society.)

John and Bernie Stockhausen and Daughters

John and Bernice Stockhausen and their two small daughters, Nancy (left) and Darlene, arrived in Peters Creek in 1947 in a camper the couple had forged out of a trailer. The former Wisconsinites acquired a homestead between Peters Creek and Mirror Lake where they planted oats and potatoes and raised chickens and a few pigs. Entrepreneurs at heart, the couple opened Bernie's Liquor Store, which they expanded to include a bar (now the site of American Legion Post 33). Daughter Darlene grew up to write a book describing the family's time on the homestead. (Courtesy of Darlene Halverson.)

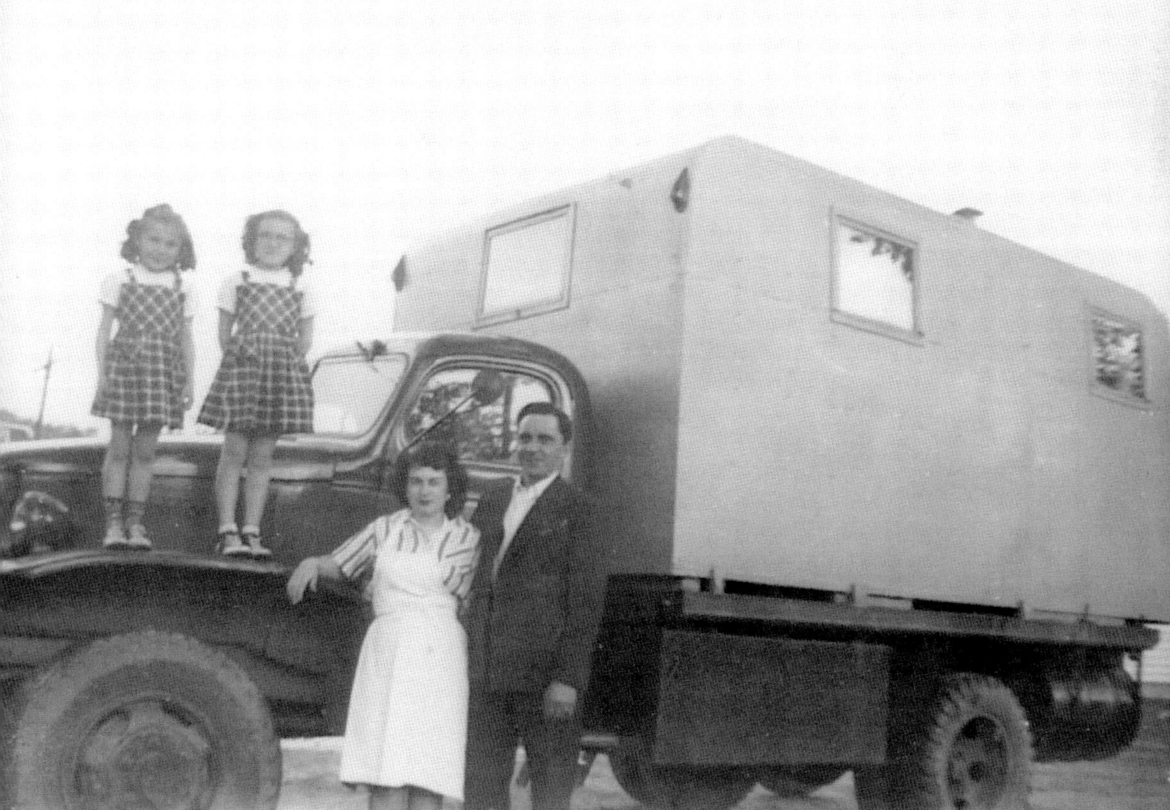

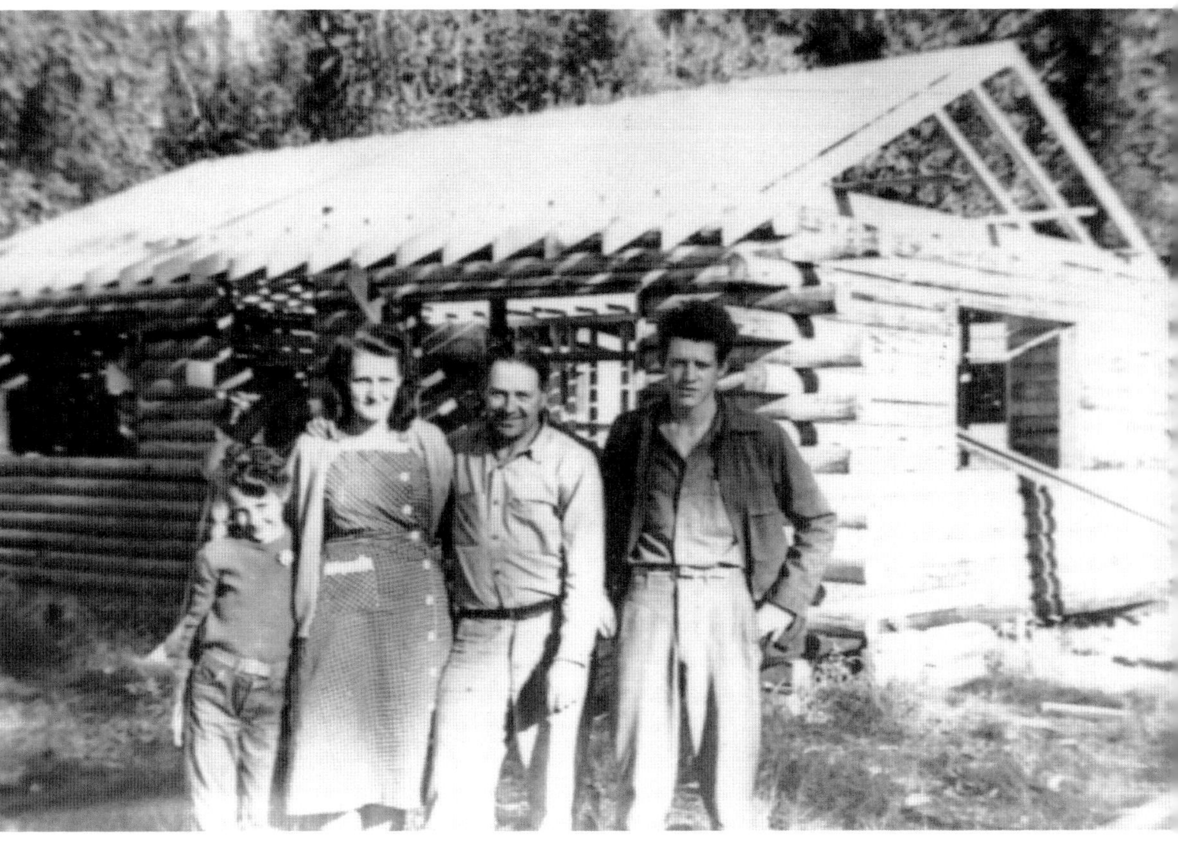

Vernon and Alma Haik (ABOVE AND OPPOSITE PAGE)

The second time was the charm for Vernon and Alma Haik, pictured above with children Beverly and Vernon Jr., when they struck out for Alaska in 1946. The would-be farmers had tried to homestead in the Matanuska Valley a decade before, but land had been unavailable. This time, just after World War II, they took advantage of a construction boom on Fort Richardson Army Post near Anchorage, and Vern became a surveyor. Frustrated by a housing shortage in Anchorage, the Haiks followed the lead of another Fort Richardson surveyor, Paul Swanson, and staked a claim just north of Swanson's land in 1947. On May 30, 1949—Memorial Day—the Haiks opened the Spring Creek Lodge restaurant, despite having no electricity. They used a tiny gas stove that Haik described as "apartment-sized," lanterns and candles for lighting, and a crock submerged in the creek for cold storage. Electricity arrived in 1950, and the Haiks were able to update the restaurant. Alma's banana cream pies became widely sought after, and customers traveled in from Anchorage to the south and Palmer to the north to have their fix. The Haiks expanded the business to include a full bakery, and by the mid-1950s, they regularly supplied grocery stores throughout the area with Spring Creek Lodge home-baked bread. They sold the business in 1962 and moved out of state. (All, courtesy of the Chugiak-Eagle River Historical Society.)

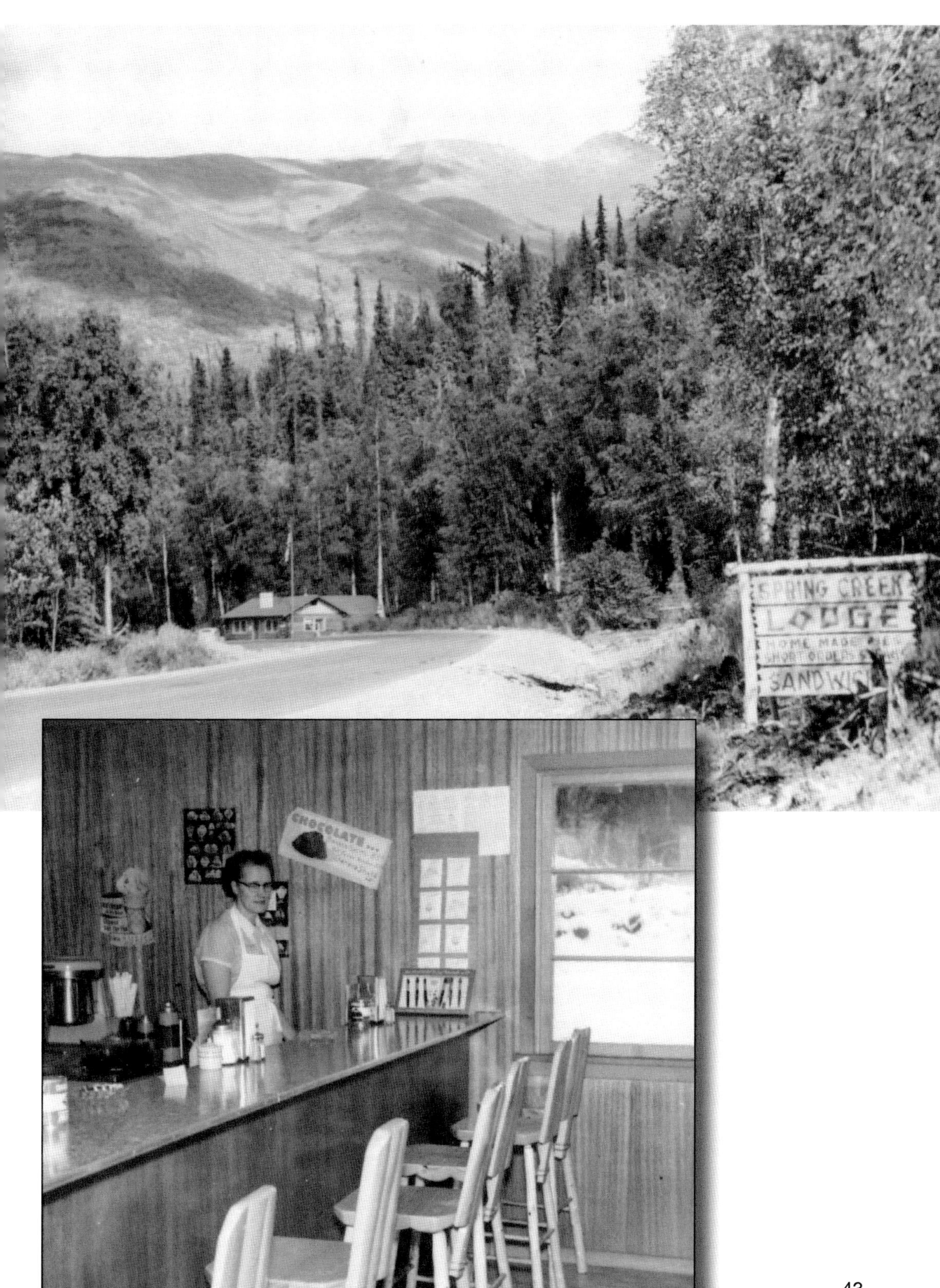
SPRING CREEK
LODGE
CHOCOLATE

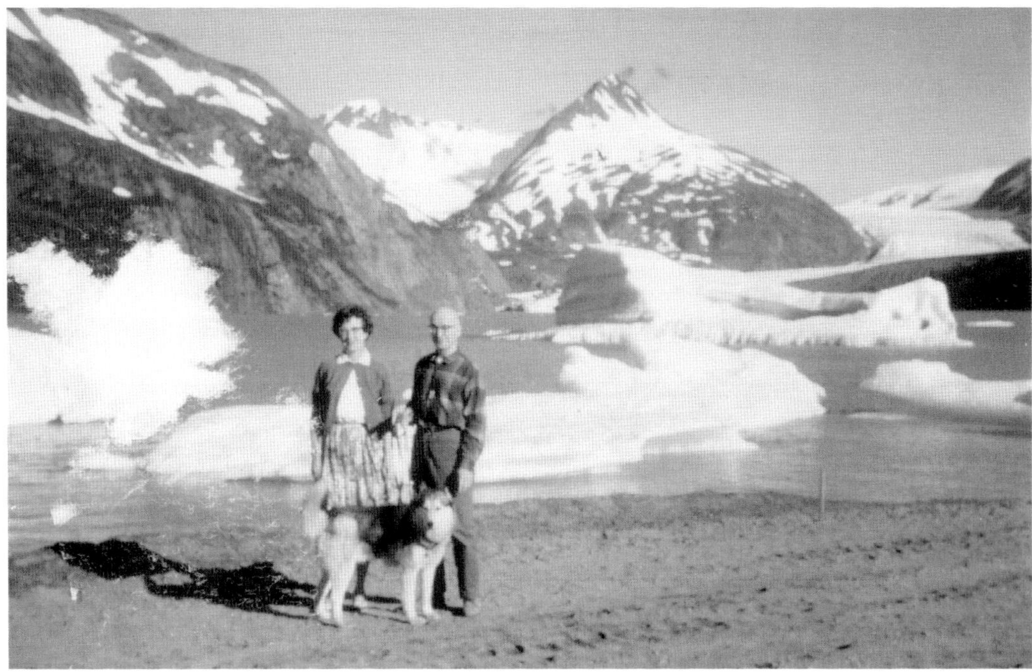

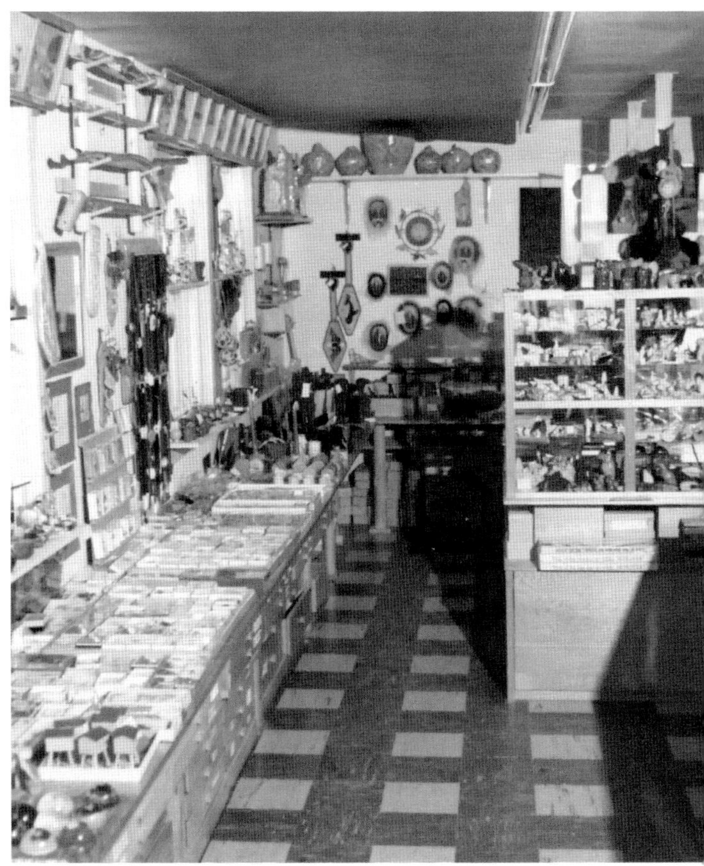

Bockstahlers at Portage Glacier and Alaska Woodcraft
Tony and Betty Bockstahler operated Alaska Woodcraft in Eagle River for about two decades beginning in 1953. For most of its life, the furniture-and-gift shop was located on Artillery Road between what are now the Glenn Highway and the Old Glenn Highway. A food cache adjacent to the business provided an unmistakable landmark. Tony handcrafted all of the merchandise from Alaska wood, and customers responded. Locals bought tables, chairs, cabinets, and specialty pieces. Visitors seeking high-quality souvenirs arrived on tour buses. The couple sold the four-acre property around 1970 to Tom Slanker, who was expanding Far North Service. The Bockstahlers continued operating out of their house on their Eagle River Valley homestead for a few more years. (Both, courtesy of the Chugiak-Eagle River Historical Society.)

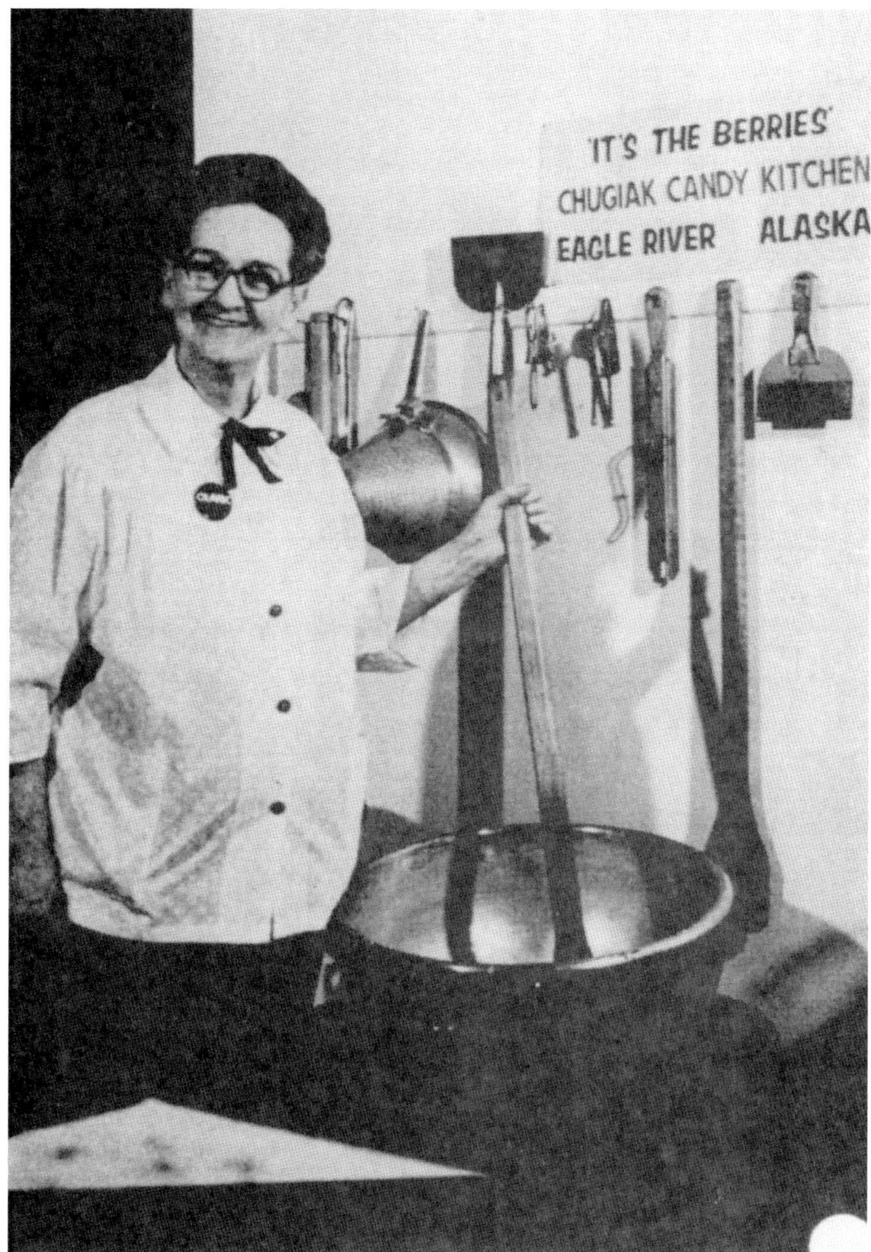

Nora Collett Stirs the Pot

Until she opened her mouth, Nora Collett was routinely mistaken for the grandmotherly type. Her gray-streaked hair was fastened into a bun, and she wore a starched white smock and an apron. The Chugiak Candy Kitchen, which she had owned and operated since 1948, was a magnet for children. Her language, however, was not sweet, nor was it suitable for all ages. Collett spoke like the former truck driver she was, and colorful opinions flowed as freely as melted chocolate. Soon, her personality became part of the candy-buying experience, and customers swapped tales of what had transpired in her shop. This and, more importantly, the candy itself kept them coming back, despite several location changes. Collett retired in 1985 and passed away in 1997. (Courtesy of the Chugiak-Eagle River Historical Society.)

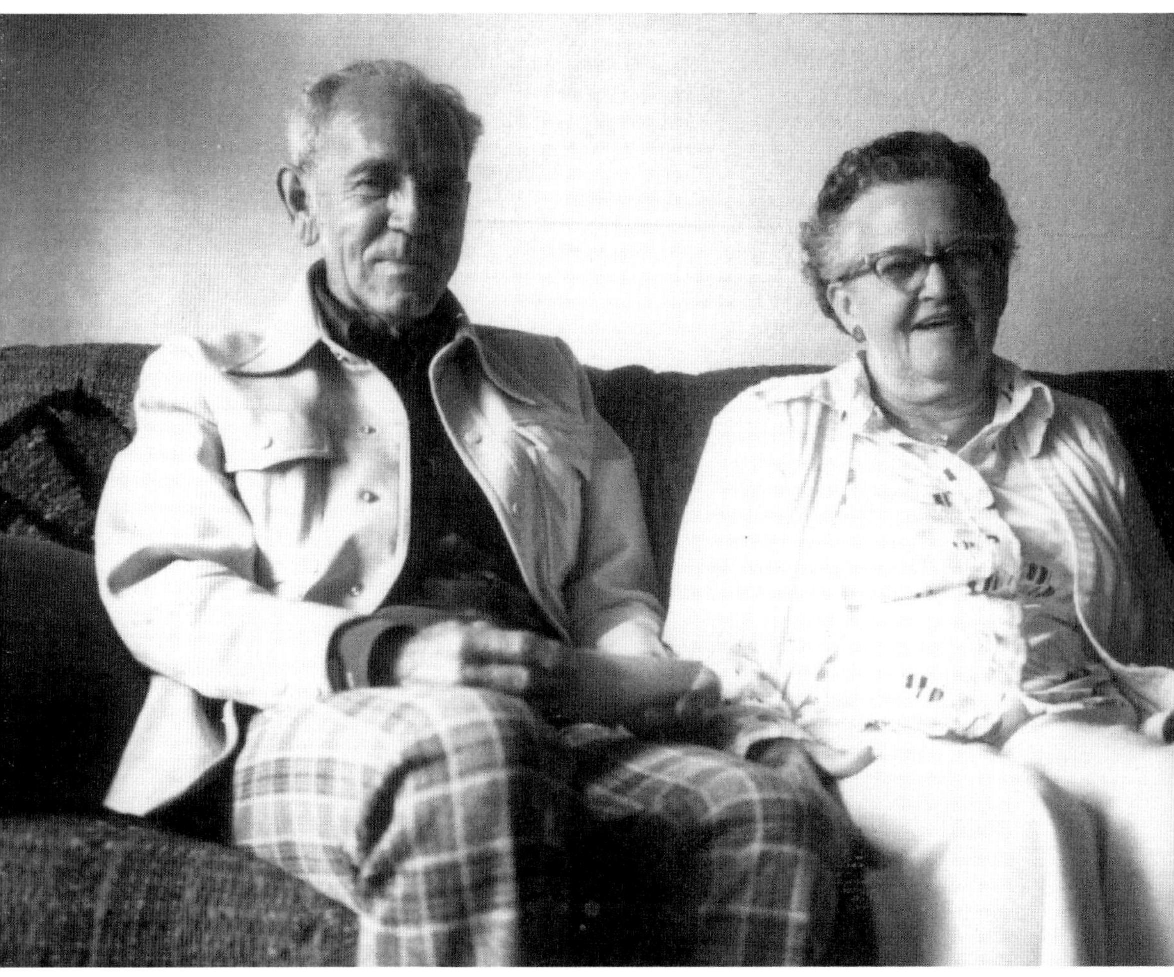

Gene and Lucille Fly

Ray Tedrow's niece Lucille Fly and her husband, Gene, accompanied the Tedrows to Alaska when the Tedrows returned after son Monte's funeral (see pages 18 and 19). The Flys bought an 80-acre homestead east of (Old) Glenn Highway. They constructed Lugene Lane, a combination of "Lucille" and "Gene" to access their land. In 1956, they leased a section of the new Eagle River Shopping Center and opened the Knik Knak Shop, which carried gifts, magazines, and drugstore products and also offered dry-cleaning services. Later, they added a soda fountain. (Courtesy of the Chugiak-Eagle River Historical Society.)

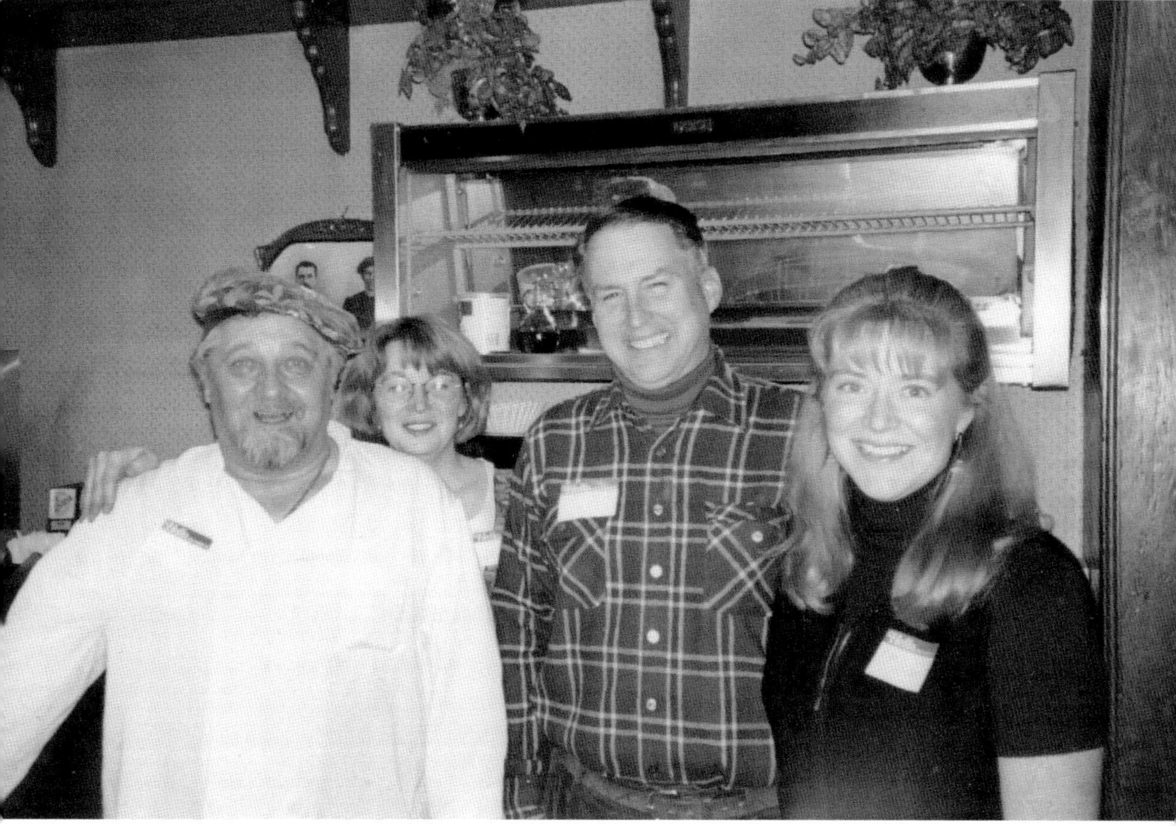

Malekos and Halford Host Old Timers Dinner

George Malekos earned his kitchen cred on Alaska's North Slope, where he served as head chef for workers on the Discovery Well in Prudhoe Bay in the late 1960s. He opened the North Slope Restaurant in Eagle River in 1972, serving out of the same mobile kitchen he had used on the job. The North Slope was among Eagle River's first dining establishments and was also the longest lasting. Remodeled and expanded through time, the restaurant ended up with a homey interior and a gold rush–style facade. Patrons could order breakfast anytime, omelets being a universal favorite. Malekos could be contentious, but this was overridden by his sense of humor and good works. He hosted a number of spaghetti feeds for those in need and, in 1997, set in motion the annual Old Timers Dinner with wife Susan and friend Rick Halford. As a founder of the Chugiak-Eagle River Chamber of Commerce, Malekos proudly opened his doors to the chamber and other community groups for their regular meetings. He sold the North Slope in 2004, and the restaurant continued operating through 2007, when it closed its doors and went into foreclosure. Malekos died in 2008 at age 67. Pictured from left to right are George and Susan Malekos and Rick and Rona Halford at the Old Timers Dinner at the North Slope Restaurant in 1997. (Courtesy of the Chugiak-Eagle River Historical Society.)

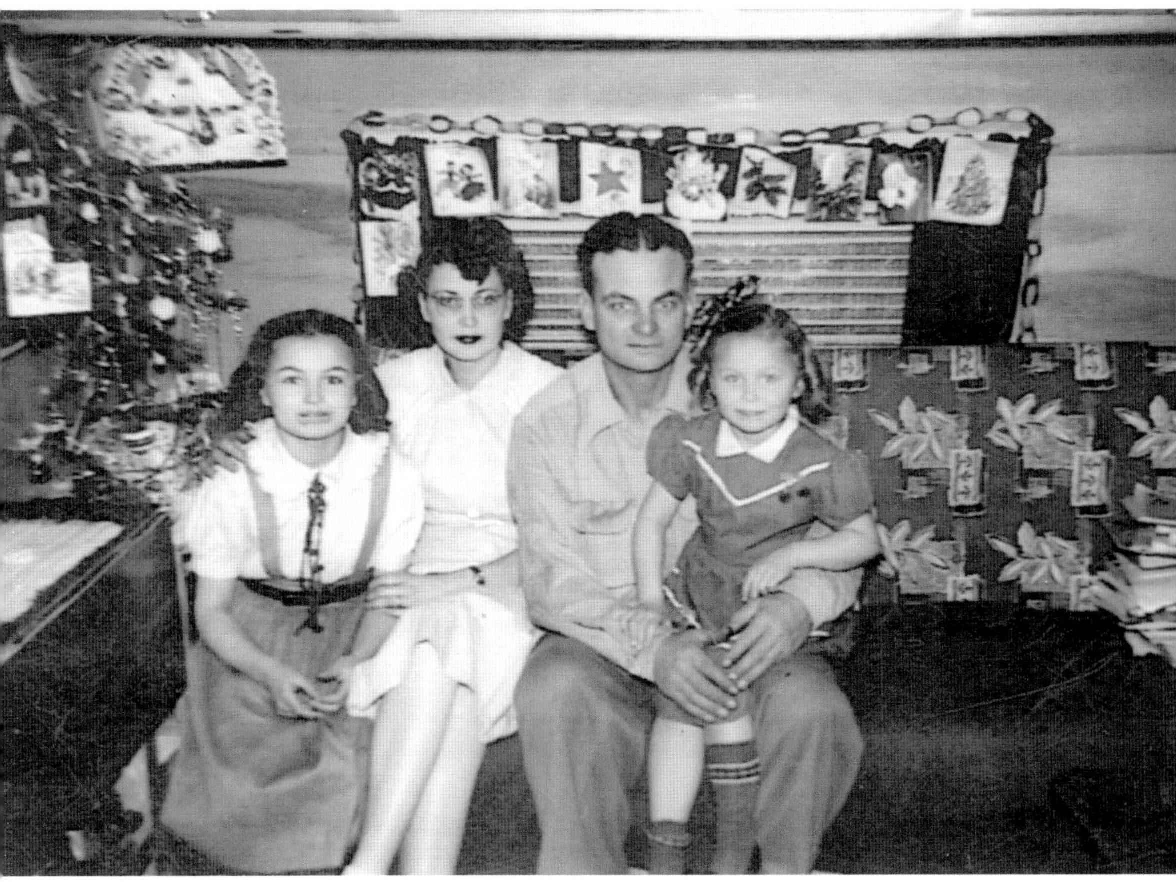

Bernie and Elnora Stewart

Bernie Stewart was perhaps best known throughout the Eagle River Valley for his Ice Palace bar and restaurant, which operated off Hiland Road in the early 1970s. The Ice Palace's defining feature was a speedway Stewart had built across the way. People came to race all manner of motorized vehicles, and the racket echoed up and down the valley. After neighbors complained, Stewart shut down the track and sold the building to Volunteers of America for a residential treatment center. However, the Ice Palace was far from Stewart's only venture. As an original homesteader in the South Fork Valley in

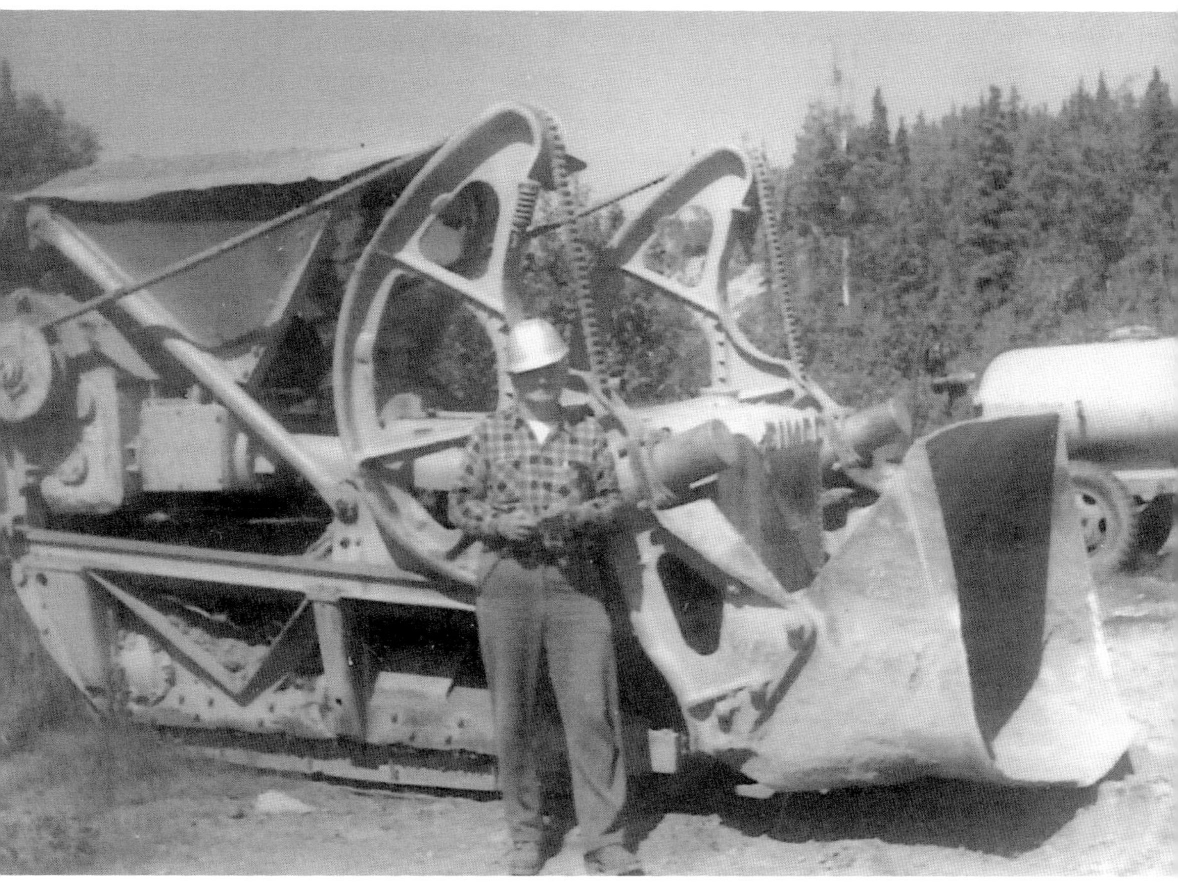

1958, he constructed the first few miles of Hiland Road out from what was then the Glenn Highway. On the homestead, the Stewart family—which included wife Elnora, daughters Sylvia (left) and Sandy, and sons Stacey and Steven Dennis—raised a sizable garden and a herd of goats. The Stewarts took in many foster kids over the years. Bernie, who had established an excavating business in the late 1950s, continued to drive his dump trucks, backhoes, and tractor equipment until a year before his death in 2010 at age 92. (Both, courtesy of the Chugiak-Eagle River Historical Society.)

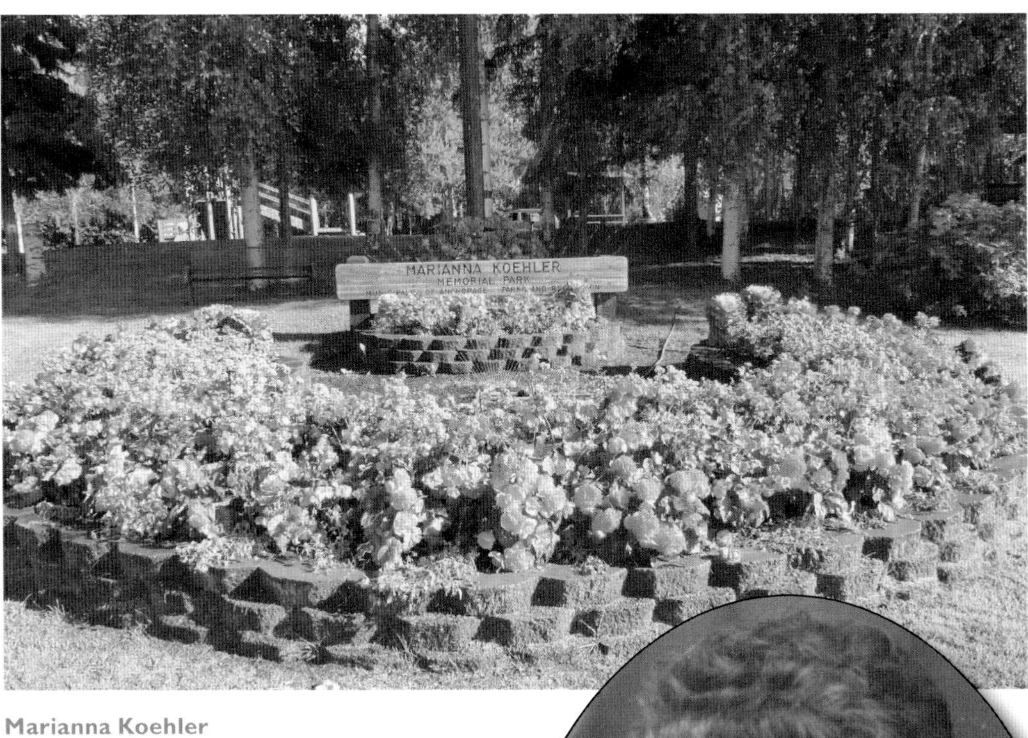

Marianna Koehler

Realtor and entrepreneur Marianna Koehler was known as much for her kind disposition as for her business savvy. Through time, she owned two area agencies—Great Land Realty and Today's Real Estate. Stories still circulate about how she waived her own commission to help buyers who were unable to afford it. Koehler co-owned the Eklutna Lodge motel and campground with husband Bill. She was also a founding member of the Chugiak-Eagle River Chamber of Commerce and helped develop the Chugiak Area Business Association. Generous with her time, Koehler taught many real estate classes and workshops. She served on at least a dozen community-service organizations throughout her adult life. When she died in a house fire in 1991, her family donated the Peters Creek property to the Municipality of Anchorage for a recreation area. Marianna Koehler Park is a small, flower-bedecked playground by the Old Glenn Highway. (Above, photograph by Chris Lundgren; right, courtesy of the Chugiak-Eagle River Historical Society.)

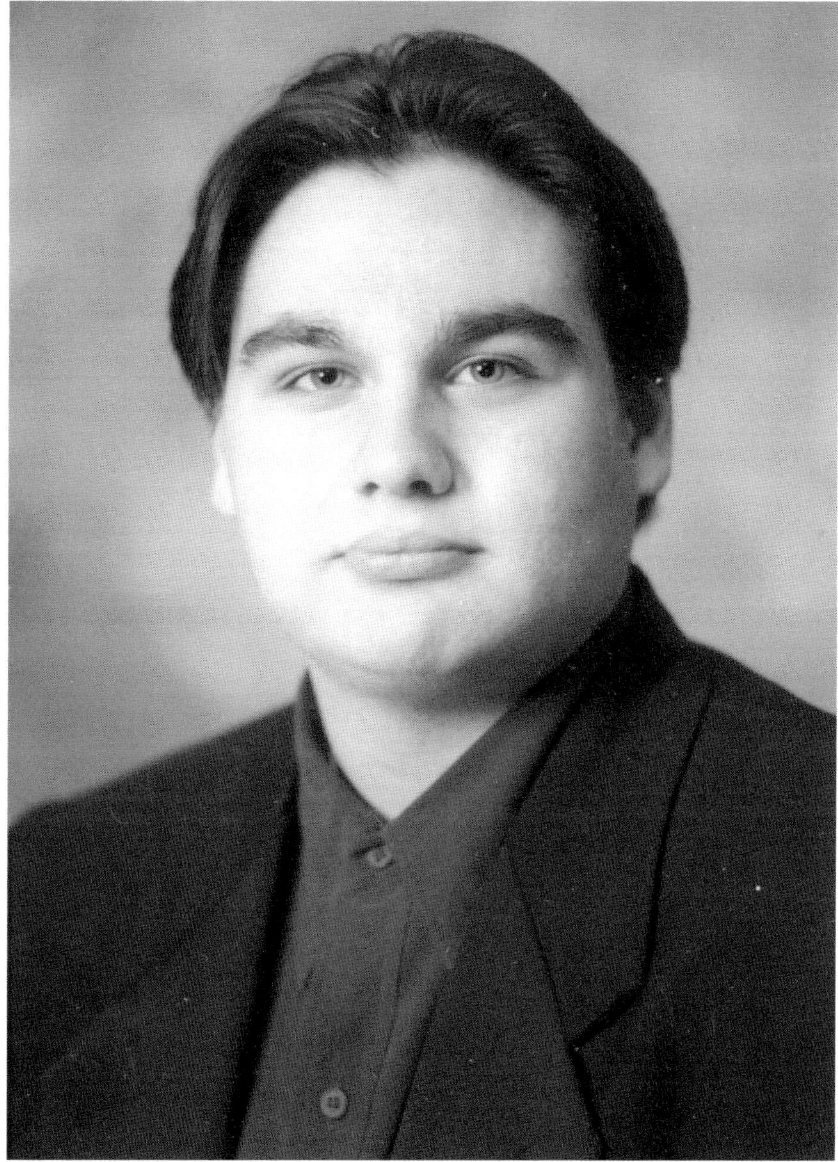

Mike Dunckle of Mike's Music

When sixth-grader Mike Dunckle announced he needed a $10,000 violin back in 1993, his parents suggested he find a way to earn the money. A few options were open to the young orchestra student—snow shoveling, yard cleanup, pet sitting, and the like—but he made an unexpected choice. With his parents' backing and the help of orchestra teacher Philip Burch, Dunckle purchased and refurbished 10 violins and violas and rented them out to other students. His top bunk served as a storehouse for a time until he informed his parents he needed to expand. By the time Dunckle was a seventh-grader at Gruening Middle School, his retail store, Mike's Music, had moved into rental space on the west side of the Old Glenn Highway. By his freshman year at Chugiak, Dunckle had bought the specialty violin he had wanted in sixth grade. Mike's Music moved two more times and landed at its current location in the Eagle River Mini Mall in 2008. Although Mike moved away and is no longer at the helm, mother Sharon has taken over and continues to run the store according to his vision. (Courtesy of Sharon Dunckle.)

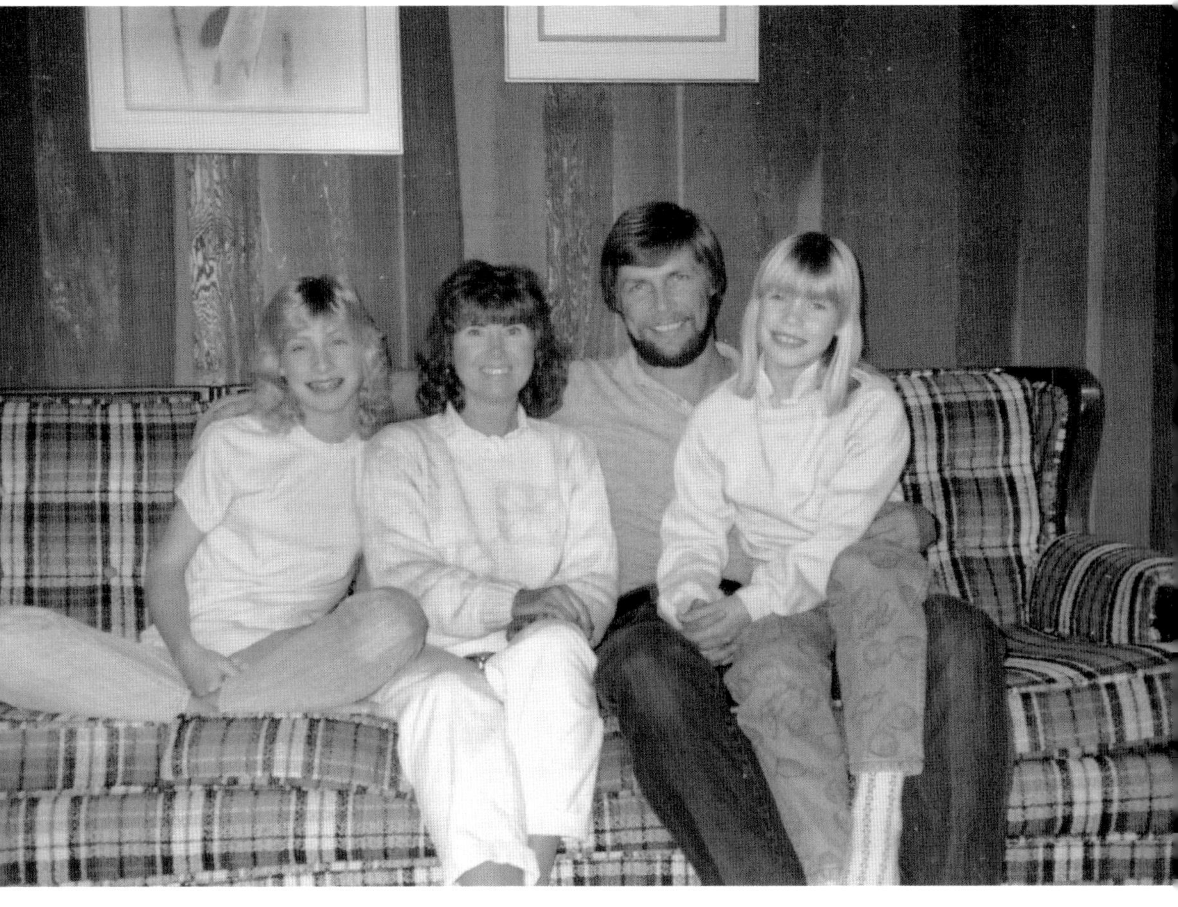

The Family Behind Picture This and Jitters

Minnesotans Dennis and Linda Johnson arrived in Anchorage in 1968. Three years later, they moved to Eagle River, where Johnson taught fifth- and sixth-graders at Homestead and Fire Lake Elementary Schools and Linda acted as head secretary at Fire Lake. Their now-grown daughters, Briana Theis (right) and Shanda McDonald, have taken on many of the business responsibilities at Picture This and Jitters. (Courtesy of the Johnson family.)

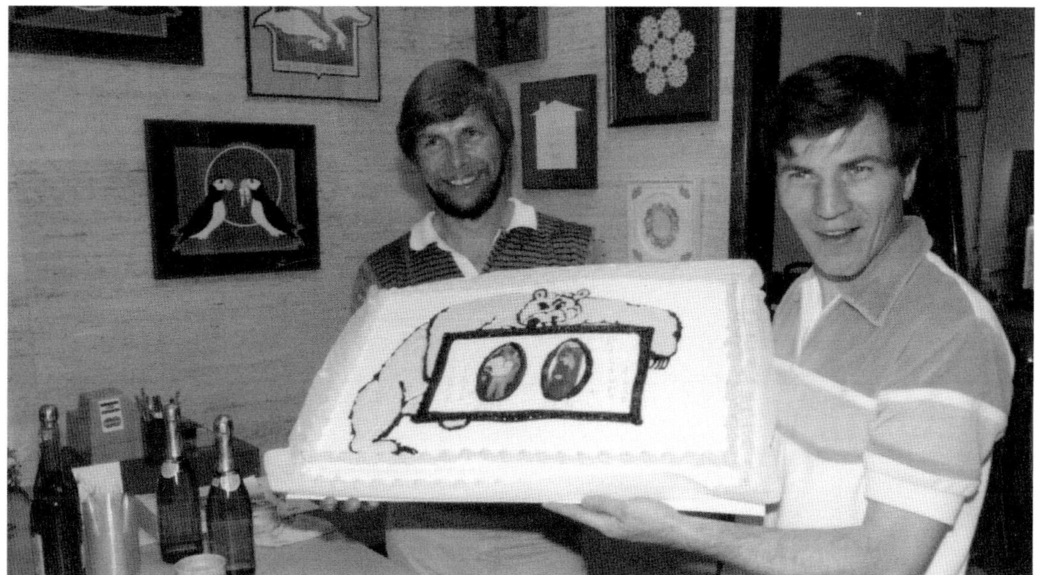

Picture This

Dennis Johnson (left) refers to his store, Picture This, as "a hobby gone astray." The onetime elementary school teacher began shooting photographs as a sideline and framing them to sell at Christmas bazaars and art shows in the early 1980s. Word got out that he was a framer, and suddenly he had customers. From there, all it took was a vacancy in the Eagle River Shopping Center. Johnson and Fire Lake Elementary principal Jim Starry opened their art-and-framing shop in June 1984. Johnson bought out Starry, becoming sole owner in 2000. (Courtesy of Dennis Johnson.)

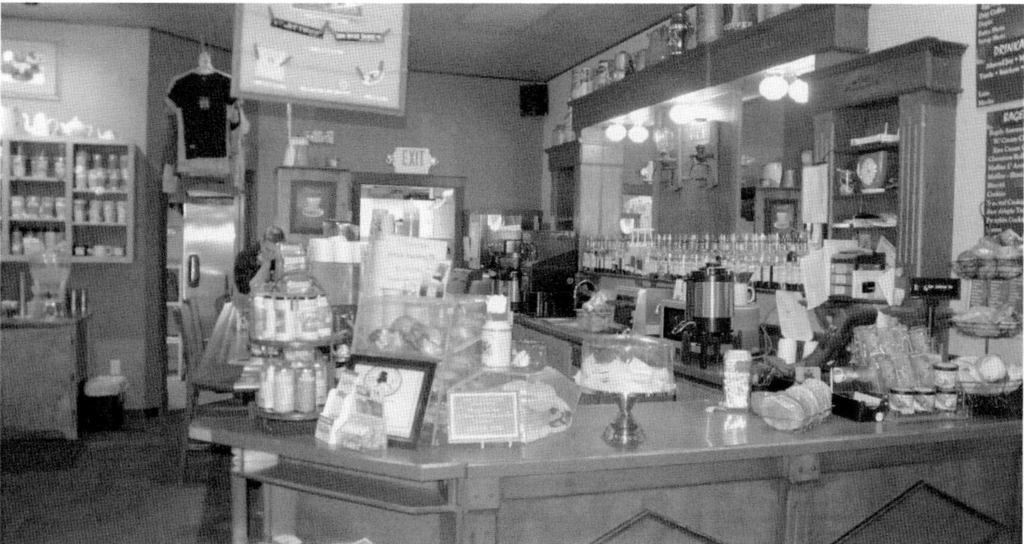

Jitters

A decade after opening Picture This, Johnson felt another bite from the entrepreneurial bug. A storefront next door had become available, and he believed Eagle River could use a coffee shop with space for local musicians to perform. Jitters Coffeehouse welcomed its first customers in February 1994. It continues to be a popular meeting place with an eclectic clientele. (Photograph by Chris Lundgren.)

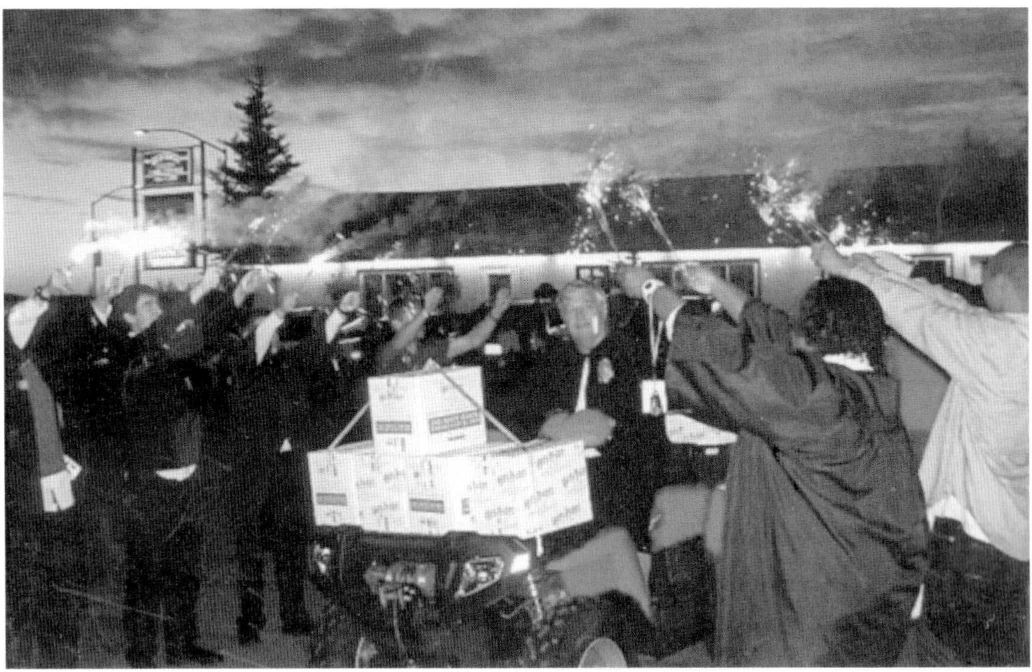

The Book Shelf

By happy coincidence, the Book Shelf bookstore opened in Eagle River in 1998, just as the Harry Potter craze was sweeping the country. Owners Bob and Kim Pakney—along with store mascot Jacob—were ready to supply fans with the books they craved. The Pakneys preordered the latest Potter installments for their customers and hosted midnight release parties when the books arrived. The store appealed to more than just wizard fans, though, with a customer base heavy on the romance and mystery readers. Jacob, a German shorthaired pointer, served as the customer-loyalty program. The Pakneys sold the Book Shelf in 2011 to longtime manager Cindy Montgomery, who was in place to celebrate its 15th anniversary in 2013. Montgomery has continued to foster the friendly, small-town atmosphere of the shop. (Both, courtesy of The Book Shelf.)

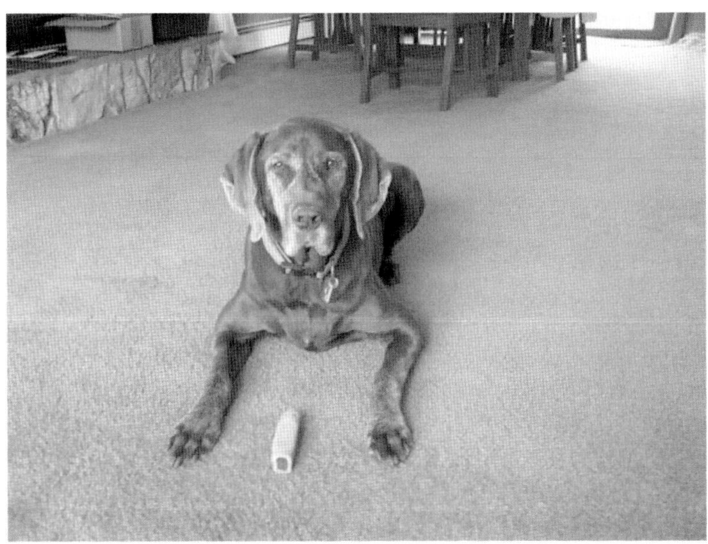

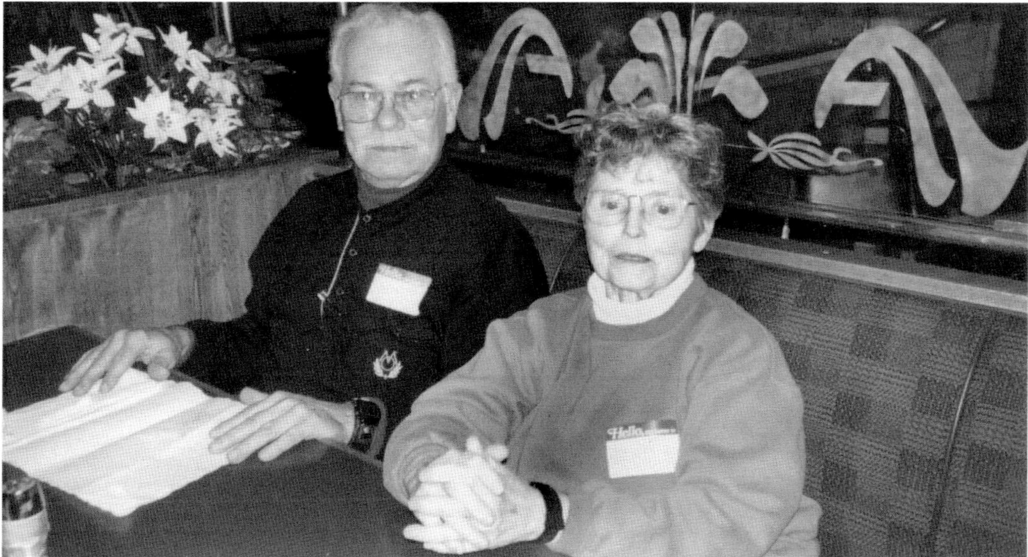

Jesse and Nella Wooten and the Eagle River Tastee-Freez

Jesse and Nella Wooten opened Eagle River's first and only Tastee-Freez in 1960, and the public responded. Little League teams swarmed the place after games, military men grabbed a burger between shifts, and travelers from Anchorage treated themselves on their way to and from the Matanuska-Susitna ("Mat-Su") Valley. Back then, an ice-cream cone cost 5¢, and a burger was just 35¢. Nella, who manned the grill and oversaw all operations, prided herself on paying an hourly wage of $1.50, while other nearby businesses were only paying $1 an hour. Yet the work was hard. Employees—mostly teenage girls—were expected to serve crowds of customers quickly, lift five-gallon buckets of ice cream and pour them into the soft-serve machine, and take apart and sterilize equipment each evening. The Tastee-Freez stayed open from April through September each year until the Wootens shuttered it in 1987, the year Jesse retired from his job with the city of Anchorage and the couple took up traveling. (Above, courtesy of the Chugiak-Eagle River Historical Society; below, courtesy of the Wooten family.)

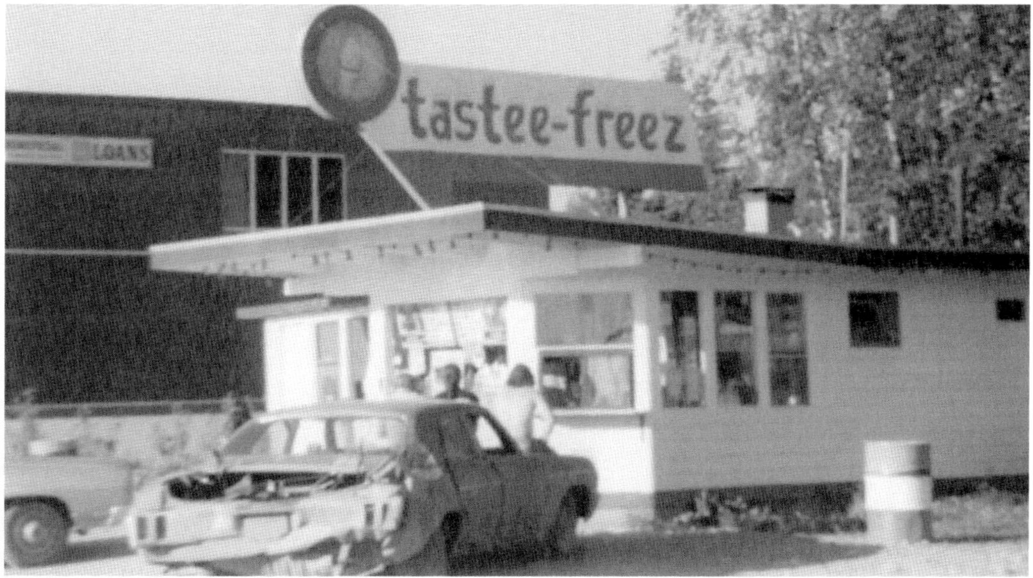

Susie Gorski

Susie Gorski and Merry Braham have worked so closely together for so many years, they like to joke that they share a brain. Instead, what they really share is a dedication to all things Chugiak-Eagle River. Gorski, the executive director of the Chugiak-Eagle River Chamber of Commerce, has been in place since 1989, when the chamber was smaller, far less organized, and did not yet have nonprofit status. A careful listener and natural-born connector, Gorski expanded the board to include not only local and Anchorage business owners but also standing positions from the police and fire departments, military base, school district, Anchorage Assembly, and landholder Eklutna, Inc. The result is a collaboration among people who have the area's best interests at heart. Gorski is pictured here at the installation of the town clock in Eagle River's Chief Alex Park. (Both, courtesy of the Chugiak-Eagle River Chamber of Commerce.)

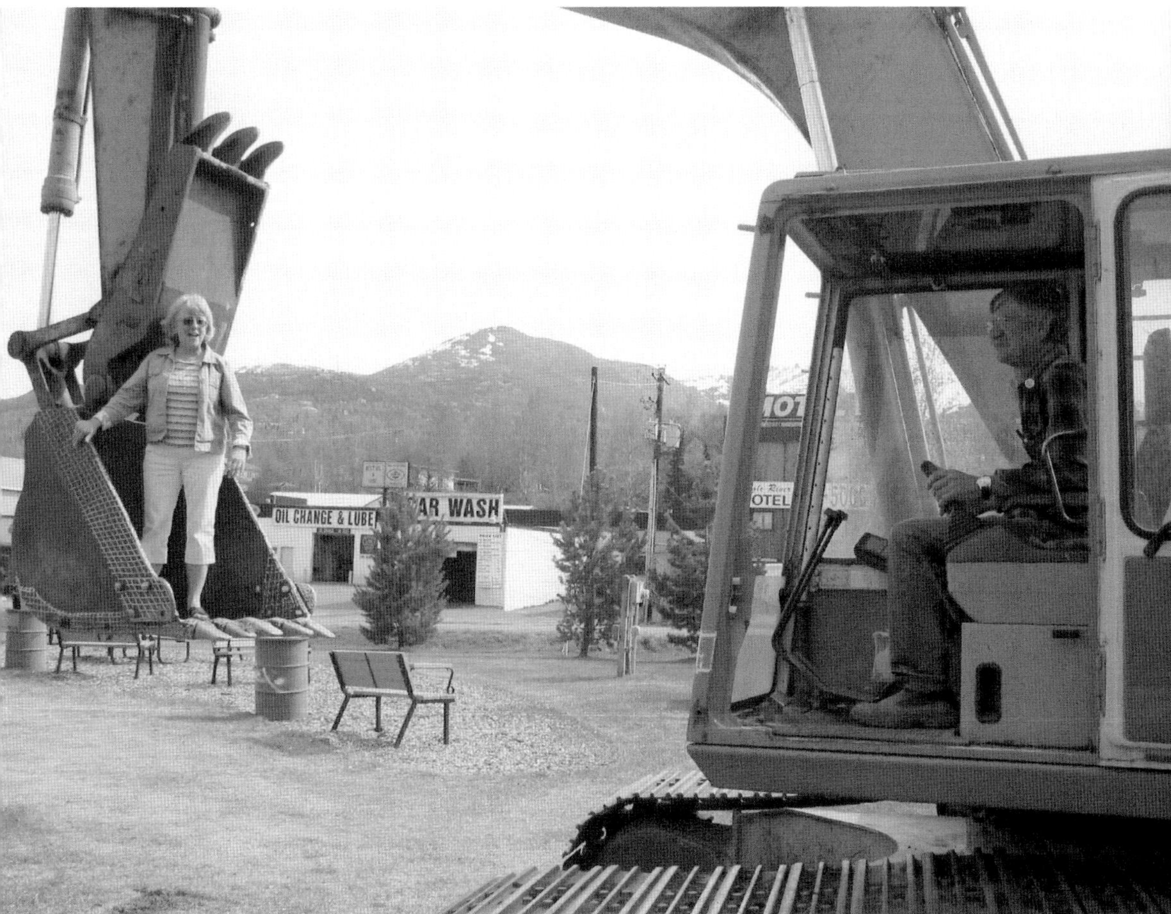

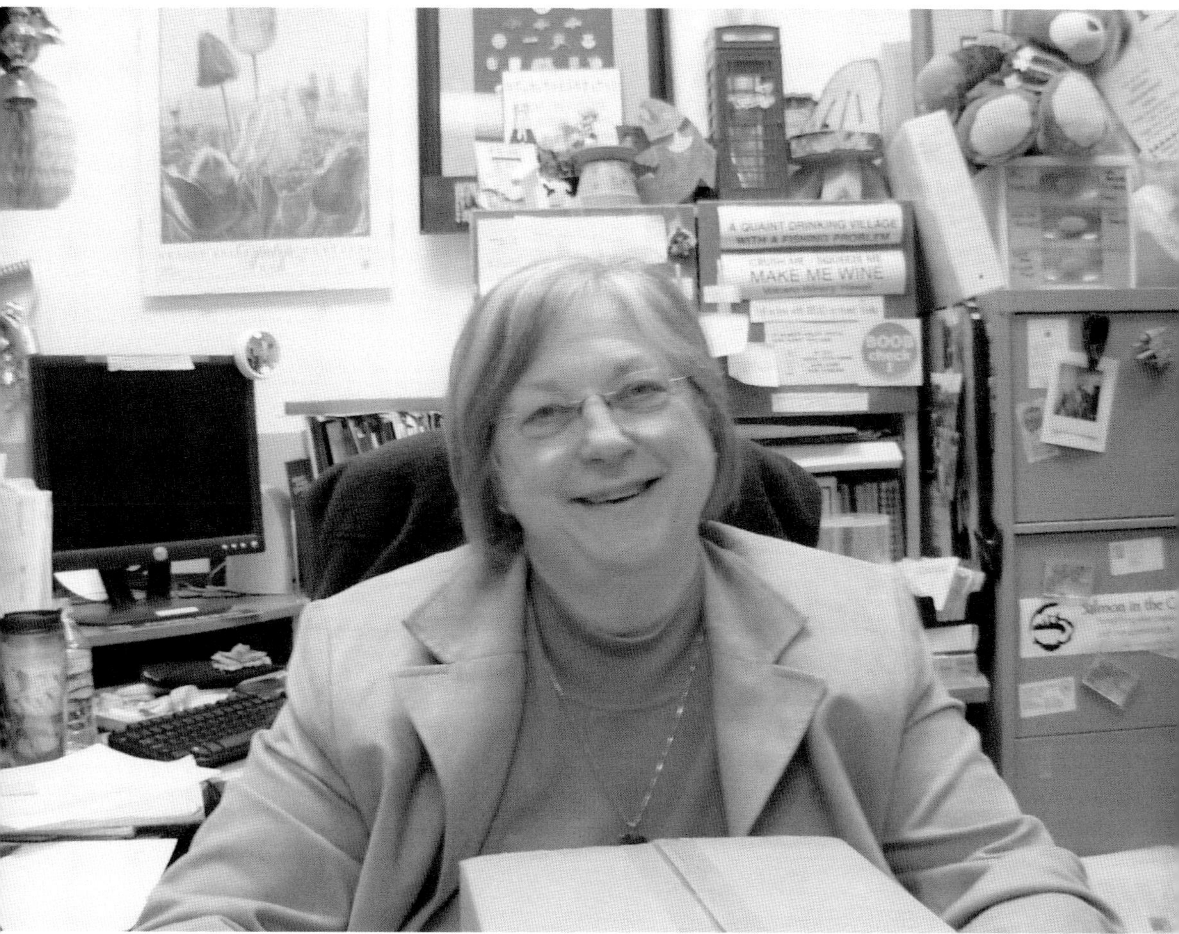

Merry Braham

Merry Braham, the events director and creative heartbeat of the Chugiak-Eagle River Chamber of Commerce, owned a gift shop in Eagle River from 1984 to 1998 and has been active in the chamber for 30 years. Braham was one of the driving forces behind Eagle River's annual Bear Paw Festival and continues to shape and manage it. (Courtesy of the Chugiak-Eagle River Chamber of Commerce.)

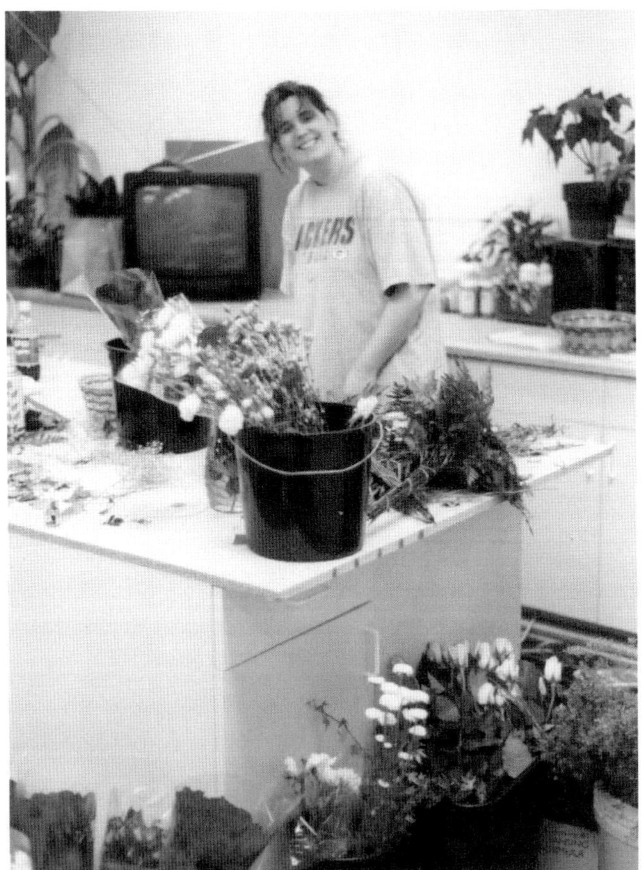

Meredith Abbett
Oopsie Daisy joined three other independent flower shops in Eagle River when Meredith Abbett opened it in May 1998. Now, it is the only one. Abbett, a former Army brat, relishes the close ties she has made in her adopted hometown. Customers here, she has found, are loyal and committed to supporting small businesses. Oopsie Daisy participates in Eagle River's Bear Paw Parade each July. (Both, courtesy of Meredith Abbett.)

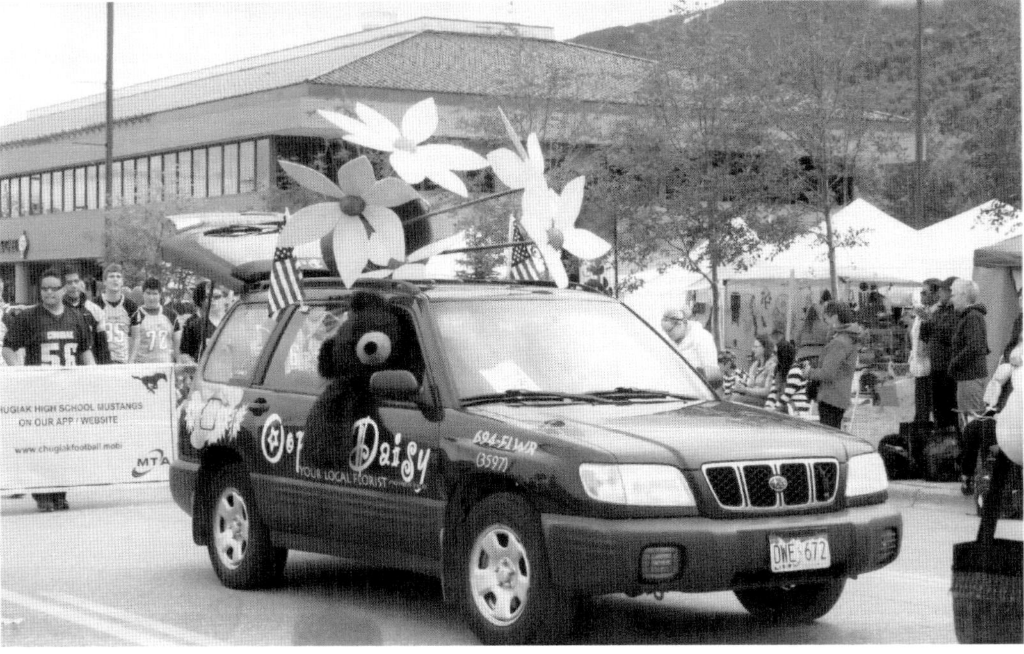

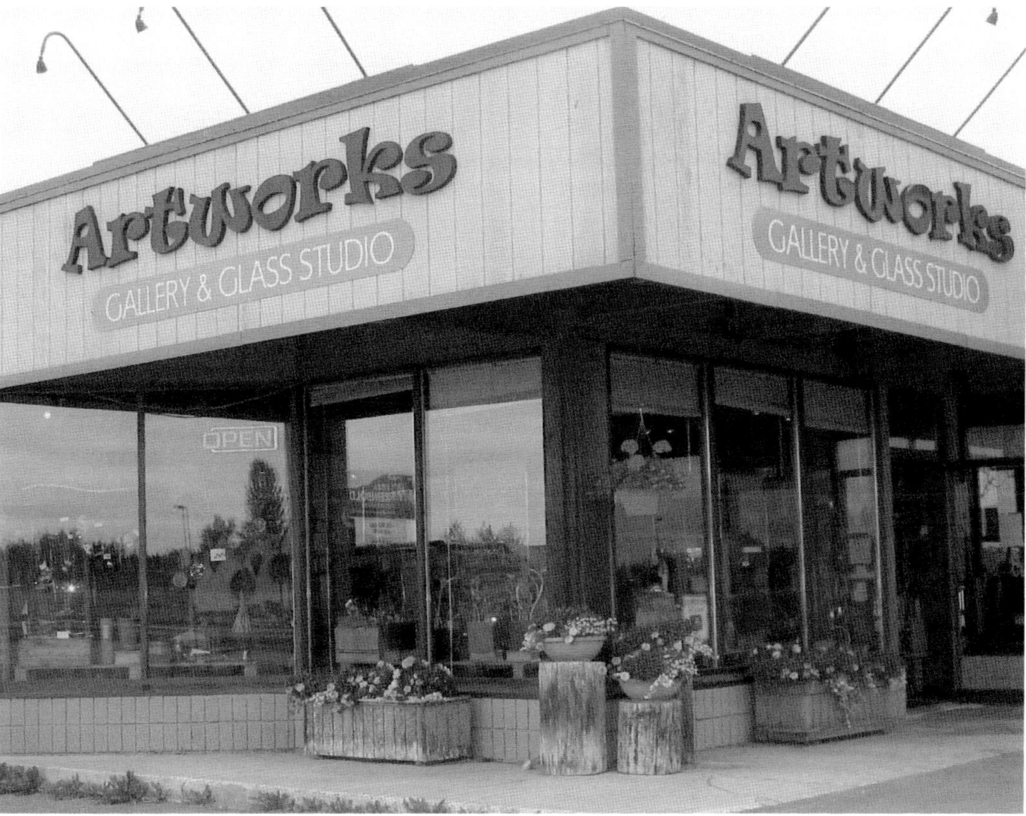

Artworks
When mother-daughter artists Iris Vail and Heidi Banach bought a stained glass shop in Eagle River back in 1999, they assumed they would simply sell supplies and offer classes. Yet Artworks Gallery & Glass Studio has blossomed far beyond its origins, and it now includes a gift shop full of whimsical pieces by North American artists, including stained glass by Banach. The owners strive to make the Old Glenn Highway store a fun and colorful place. They take turns teaching stained glass and fused-glass classes, and both maintain studios in their homes. (Courtesy of Heidi Banach.)

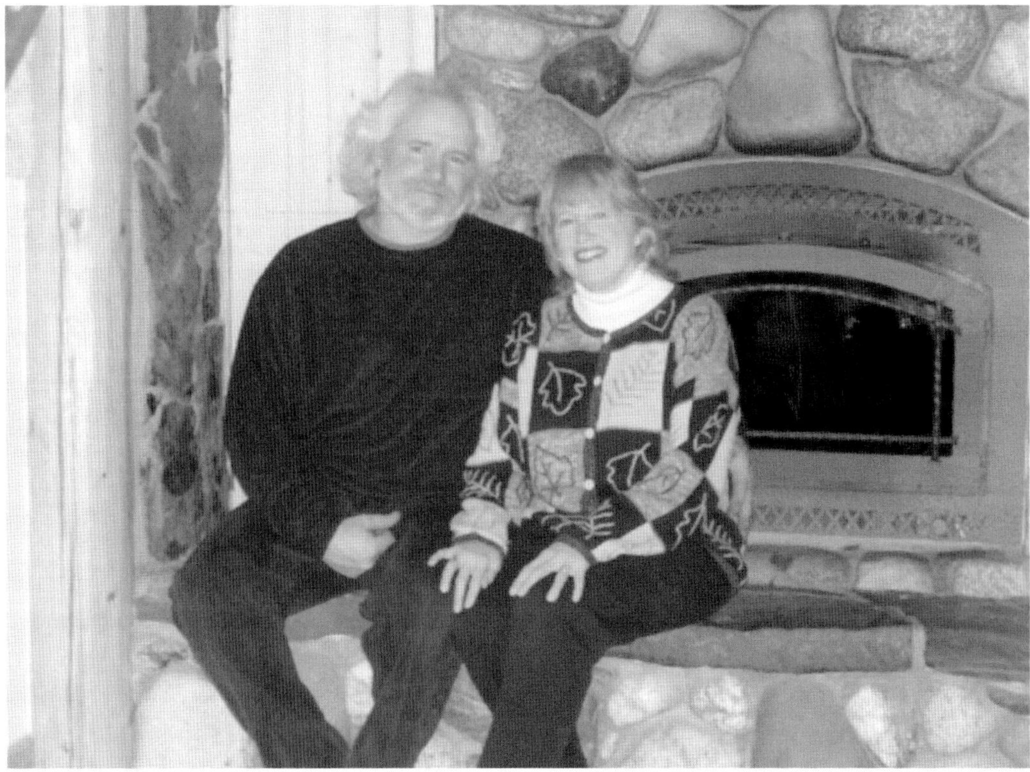

Texas "Gail" and Lee Raymond and Sleepy Dog Coffee Co.

Texas "Gail" and Lee Raymond opened Sleepy Dog Coffee Co. in March 1993 to an Eagle River public eager for a hometown coffee shop. At a time when most commuters beelined it to Anchorage for their morning coffee, the Raymonds offered a reason to stop. Then as now, customers filled the store's tables and booths, enjoying an old-fashioned ambiance with lighthearted touches. Six wooden "doggoyles" carved by Lee overlook the shop's back room—also known as the "Dog House," and three of them have been dedicated to famous mushers. Gail decorated the store with coffee- and dog-related antiques, including a sign that instructs customers to "tie dogs in the rear." Sleepy Dog has special acoustic features that allow for quiet conversations even when the place is at capacity. Despite their commitment to the shop, both Raymonds have full-time careers. Gail, a former science-curriculum coordinator and 27-year veteran of the Anchorage School District, works as a mentor for first- and second-year teachers in the Alaskan Bush. Lee owns Lee's Custom Designs, a construction company specializing in log homes. In early 2014, he was featured on the reality-television show "Building Alaska" on the DIY network. (Courtesy of Texas Gail Raymond.)

CHAPTER THREE

Humanitarians, Advocates, and Educators

Humanitarians, community advocates, and educators are a special breed of people who commit themselves to bettering others' quality of life. Teachers are featured heavily in this chapter, particularly music teachers. Chugiak High's Ron Lange and the late Philip Burch as well as Mirror Lake Middle School's Travis Harrington have all elevated the musical IQ and performance abilities of their students while providing highbrow entertainment for concert audiences. Mirror Lake's Emily Blahous, who teaches piano-keyboarding/music-exploratory classes, runs a video-news team at the school that creates a daily newscast and weekly radio broadcast. Blahous takes students on performing arts field trips as often as time and budget will allow. The late Elsie Oberg was heavily involved in children's education as a mother of six, substitute teacher, and member of the school board of the short-lived Chugiak-Eagle River Borough. Other elected officials figure into the chapter because they are some of the community's most ardent advocates—as are the volunteers who buttress the dozens of community organizations throughout the area. Some volunteers—the likes of Shirl Mauldin, Christa Burg, and Betty Hand—operate solo. Without the commitment of these generous humanitarians, community advocates, and educators, Chugiak-Eagle River would not be the place it is today.

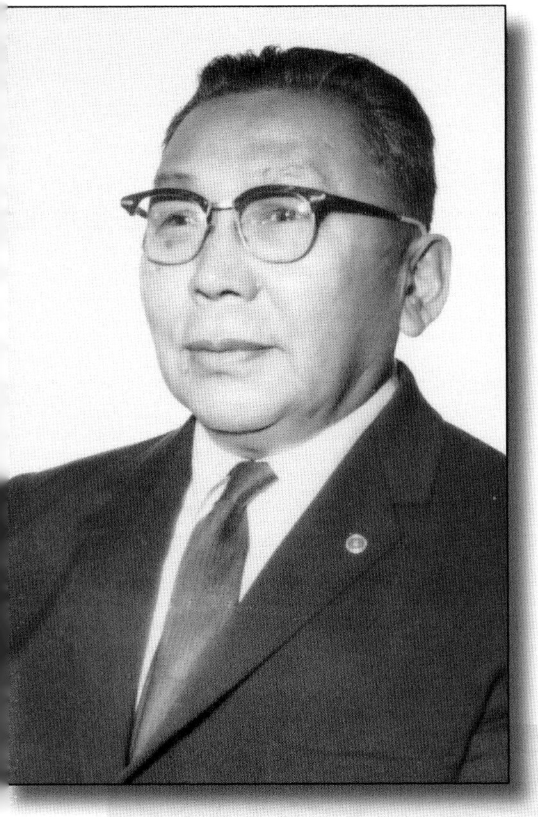

Mike Alex

During his life, Mike Alex was known as the best fisherman in the Cook Inlet. He was also a skilled carpenter who restored the 140-year-old St. Nicholas Russian Orthodox Church in Eklutna Village with his sons, completing construction on a new church building in 1962. Alex was a 28-year veteran of the Alaska Railroad, where he was a section foreman, and the father of 13 children with wife Nellie. Most importantly of all, Alex was the last traditional chief of the Dena'ina Athabaskans, and he tried to organize his fellow villagers to fight against the encroachment on their land by the federal government. Chief Alex Park, adjacent to Eagle River Elementary School, commemorates him. He died in 1977 at age 70. (Both, courtesy of the Chugiak-Eagle River Historical Society.)

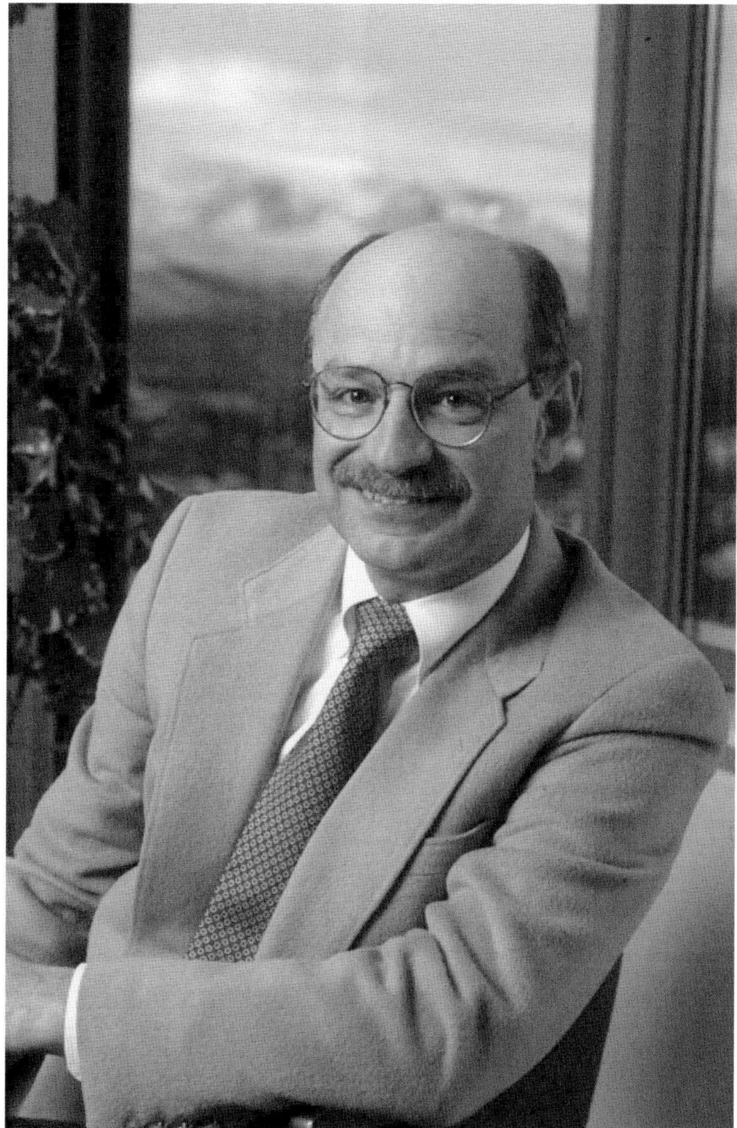

Jim Palmer

Eagle River's Jim Palmer is a businessperson, public servant, and philanthropist. After retiring from an 18-year career in senior management at BP, he opened the Palmer Group, an Anchorage-based government and public affairs consulting firm in 2003. That same year, he became the first person from Chugiak-Eagle River to receive the William A. Egan Outstanding Alaskan award from the Alaska Chamber of Commerce. Palmer's private-industry experience is bookended by public service: he worked for US senator Mike Gravel in Washington, DC, for most of the 1970s and served as deputy chief of staff for Alaska senator Lisa Murkowski from 2011 to 2013. Considering his high profile professionally, Palmer is a quiet philanthropist. His good works generally take place behind the scenes as he empowers others to make things happen. In addition to his many volunteer endeavors past and present, Palmer is currently president of the Chugiak-Eagle River Foundation, which provides grants to community organizations and student scholarships, and president emeritus of the Chugiak-Eagle River Chamber of Commerce. (Courtesy of Jim Palmer.)

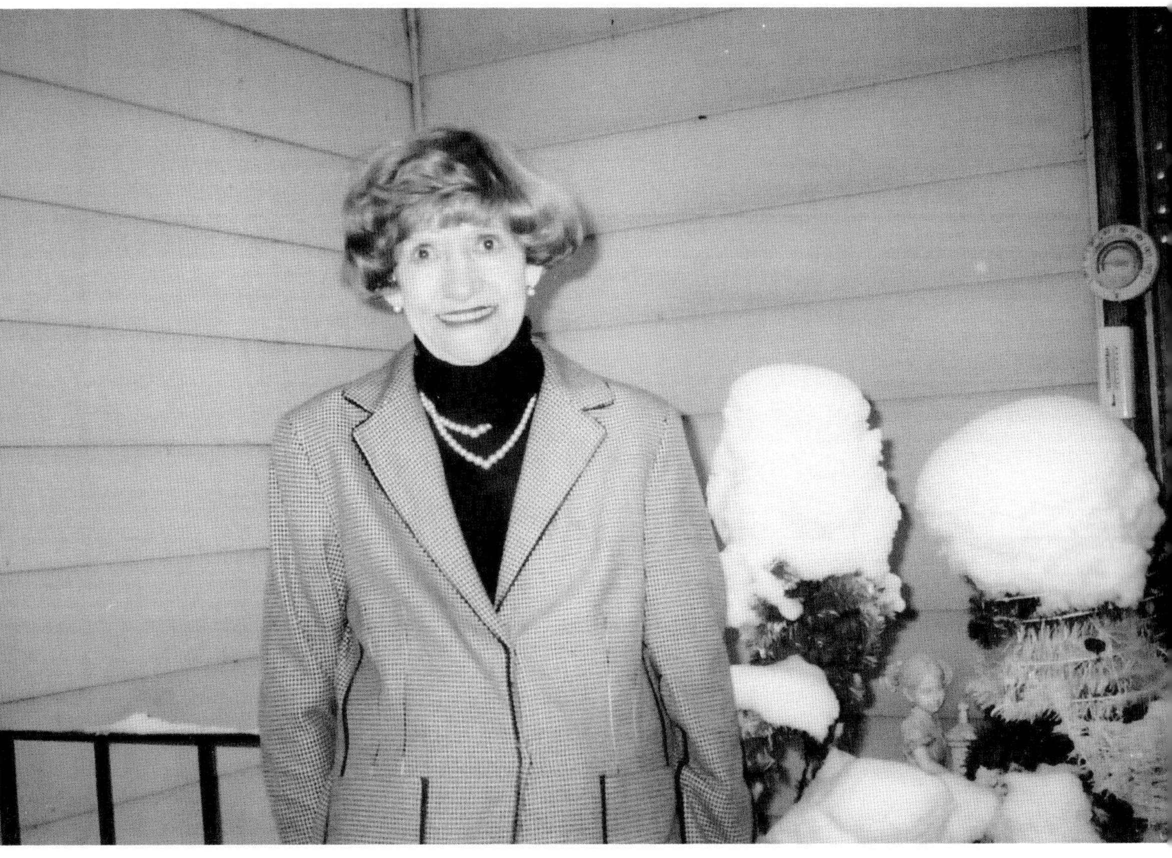

Ruth Callan

During the last two decades of her life, retiree Ruth Callan was known as a dedicated fundraiser for the Chugiak Senior Center. She won the Outstanding Volunteer in Philanthropy award from the Association of Fundraising Professionals in 2002 for her efforts on behalf of the center and other local beneficiaries. Back in 1992, she established the ongoing Walk for Seniors, which helped fund a new Meals on Wheels truck and provide seed money for the Denali View Senior Housing Project that was built next to the center in 2003. She equipped the center's gift shop with unique merchandise that sold well. But Callan's efforts were not limited to helping seniors; she was active with several community organizations, including the Ladies Auxiliary of the Fraternal Order of Eagles in Chugiak. Serving as the auxiliary's first president, Callan drew on her long career as a union organizer for hotel, restaurant, and camp workers. Sometimes, her philanthropic efforts hit closer to home. After her sister Marianna Koehler died in a house fire in 1991, Callan and other family members deeded Koehler's Chugiak property to the Municipality of Anchorage and saw that it became a public park. Callan died at age 84 in 2012, but the family still gathers to plant flowers in Koehler's honor. (Photograph by Chris Lundgren, courtesy of *Chugiak-Eagle River Star.*)

Loretta French

Loretta French has made a lasting impact on Chugiak-Eagle River residents young and old. As the owner of the first licensed day-care facility in the area, French was tapped to help launch a Head Start program in the 1960s. She collaborated with others to get the facility up and running at the United Methodist Church of Chugiak. In the 1970s, while working as a counselor with the Alaska Department of Health, she wrote the first grant to get the Chugiak-Eagle River Senior Center going. French later assisted in the raising of between $15 and $20 million in additional grants for the facility. Loretta French Park and Sports Complex—an expansive public space that stretches out behind the center—pays tribute to her behind-the-scenes advocacy. (Courtesy of Betty Powell.)

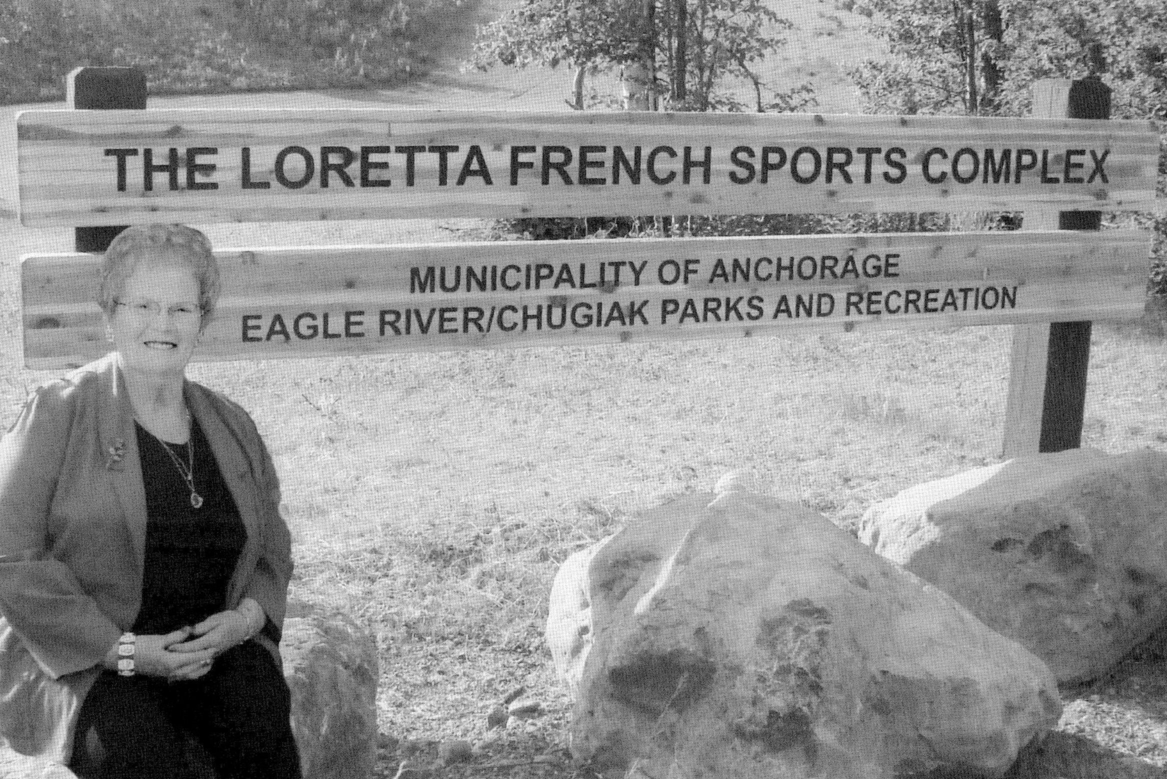

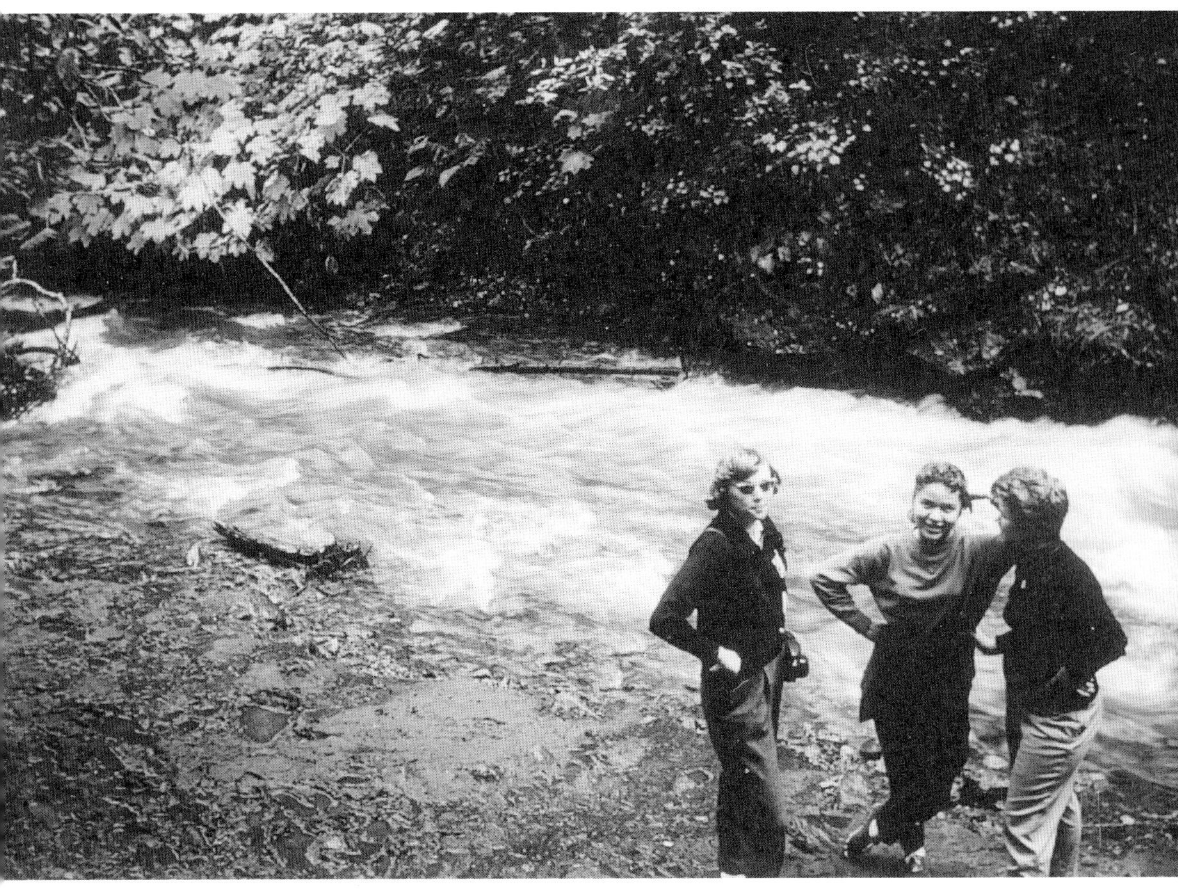

Donna McGladrey

After serving as the very first music teacher at the Dillingham Territorial School during the 1958–1959 school year, 24-year-old Donna McGladrey migrated to Chugiak, a place she found comparatively modern and welcoming. She embraced her new community, forming fast friendships with other young teachers at the elementary school, such as Zona Miles Dahlmann and Dorothy Thompson, and signing on as the choir director and pianist at the United Methodist Church of Chugiak. After Christmas 1959, McGladrey's on-again, off-again fiancé Richard Newton, a plumbing contractor and student pilot whom she had met in Dillingham, offered to fly her back to her old community to visit friends and celebrate New Year's Eve. She accepted. The couple took off in Newton's Cessna 175 mid-afternoon on December 30 and encountered a heavy snowstorm and darkness. They crashed south of Dillingham, and the wreckage was not found until the following June. More than 40 years later, McGladrey's niece published a book on her life. McGladrey is pictured (left) with Zona Miles Dahlmann (center) and Dorothy Thompson at Eklutna River. (Courtesy of the Chugiak-Eagle River Historical Society.)

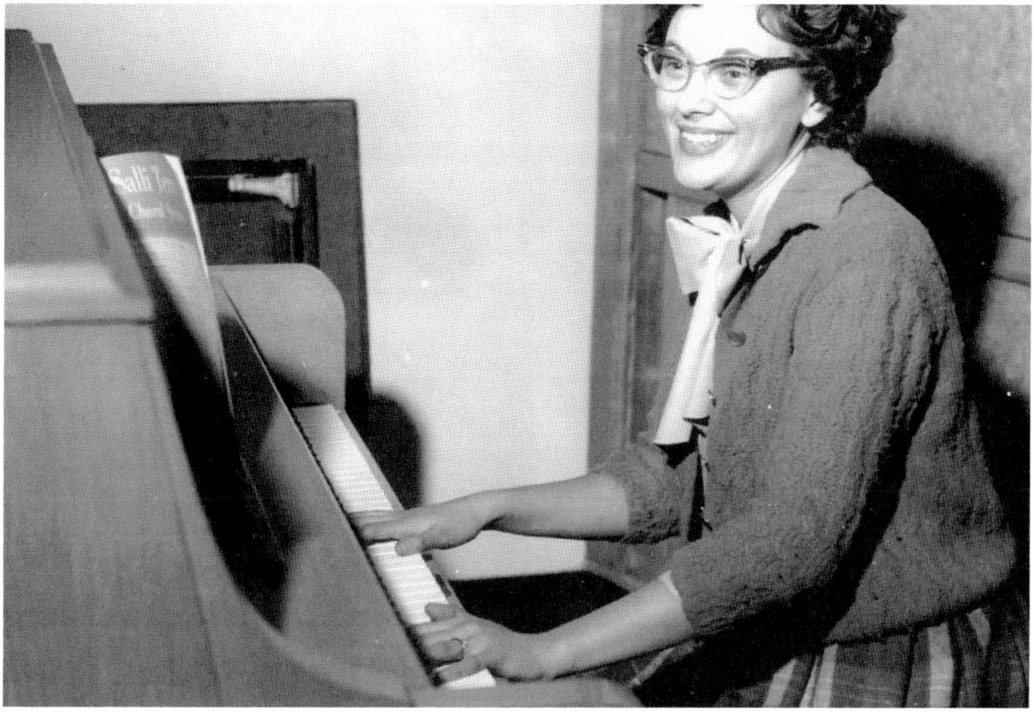

Natalie Haskell Brooks

When Natalie Haskell Brooks arrived in Chugiak in 1960, the community was still grieving the loss of Donna McGladrey. Yet Brooks took on her role as the elementary school's new music teacher with appropriate amounts of solemnity and enthusiasm. She also signed on as choir director, pianist, and organist at the United Methodist Church of Chugiak, where she remained for 30 years. She was a founding member of Chugiak Children's Services and the Chugiak-Eagle River Historical Society, serving as the society's first president. In 1975, she began teaching piano, directing a choir, and helping facilitate visitation and outreach at Hiland Mountain Correctional Center, which she continued for nearly three decades. Brooks passed away unexpectedly on New Year's Day 2008. Two music practice rooms at the correctional center were dedicated to her in 2009. The Chugiak Territorial School is pictured below in 1958. (Both, courtesy of the Chugiak-Eagle River Historical Society.)

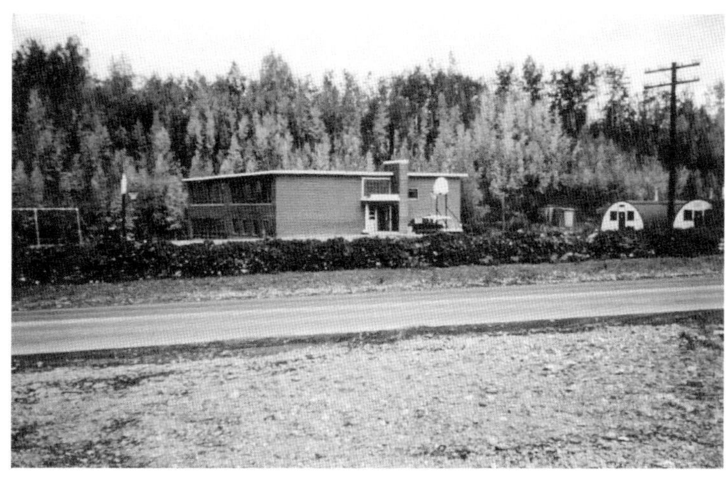

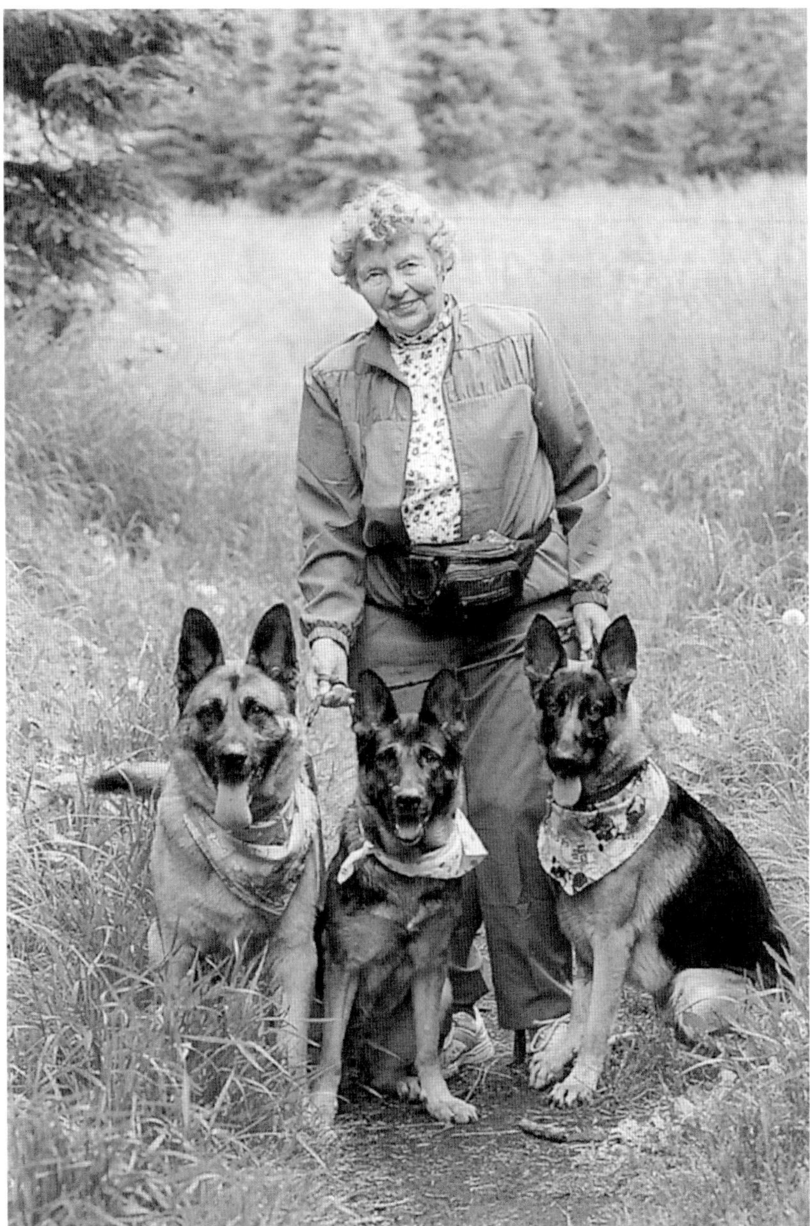

Christa Burg

Thousands of German shepherds and their offspring across the state have Christa Burg to thank for a long and purposeful life. Burg, who immigrated to Anchorage in 1952 from Nuremberg, Germany, with one of the state's first shepherds, moved to Chugiak with husband Richard in 1954. The couple raised two sons and many dogs there, and in 1966, Burg started the Obedience Training Club of Chugiak, a nonprofit group that is still active today. Burg's own shepherds won title upon title in obedience trials until 1986, when she turned her attention to more altruistic pursuits. She joined the fledgling German Shepherd Dog Rescue Group of Alaska, revamping its record-keeping practices, seeking donations, and then taking over and turning it into a nonprofit. To date, the group has placed almost 1,300 dogs in stable Alaskan homes. (Courtesy of Christa Burg.)

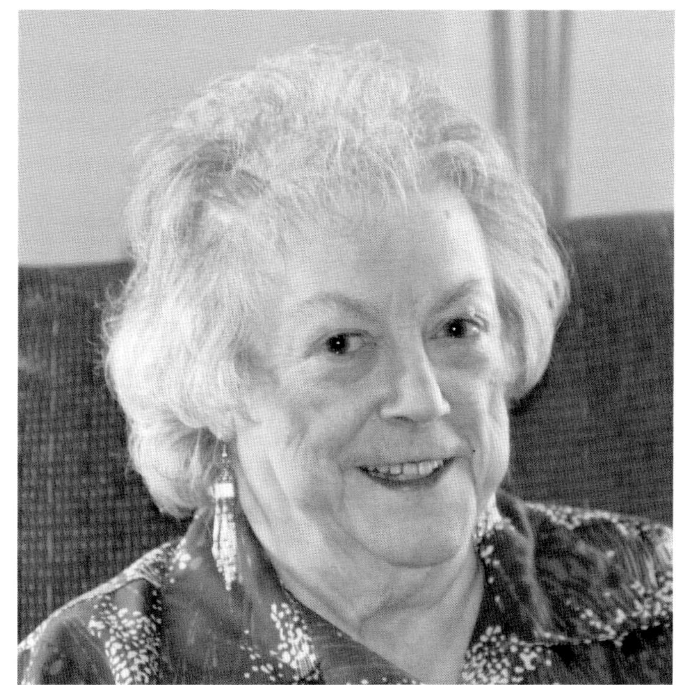

The "Eagle Lady," Betty Hand

Betty Hand has kept the "Eagle"—hundreds of them, in fact—in "Eagle River." She is widely known as the "Eagle Lady" who feeds the raptors in the parking lot of Veterans of Foreign Wars Post 9785 each winter. The retired Anchorage School District employee has lovingly performed this duty for over 20 years, cutting up donated meat and fish and scattering it across the icy lot. The gliding, swooping, and landing of eagles provides an unforgettable show. (Right, photograph by Eric Lundgren; below, photograph by Chris Lundgren.)

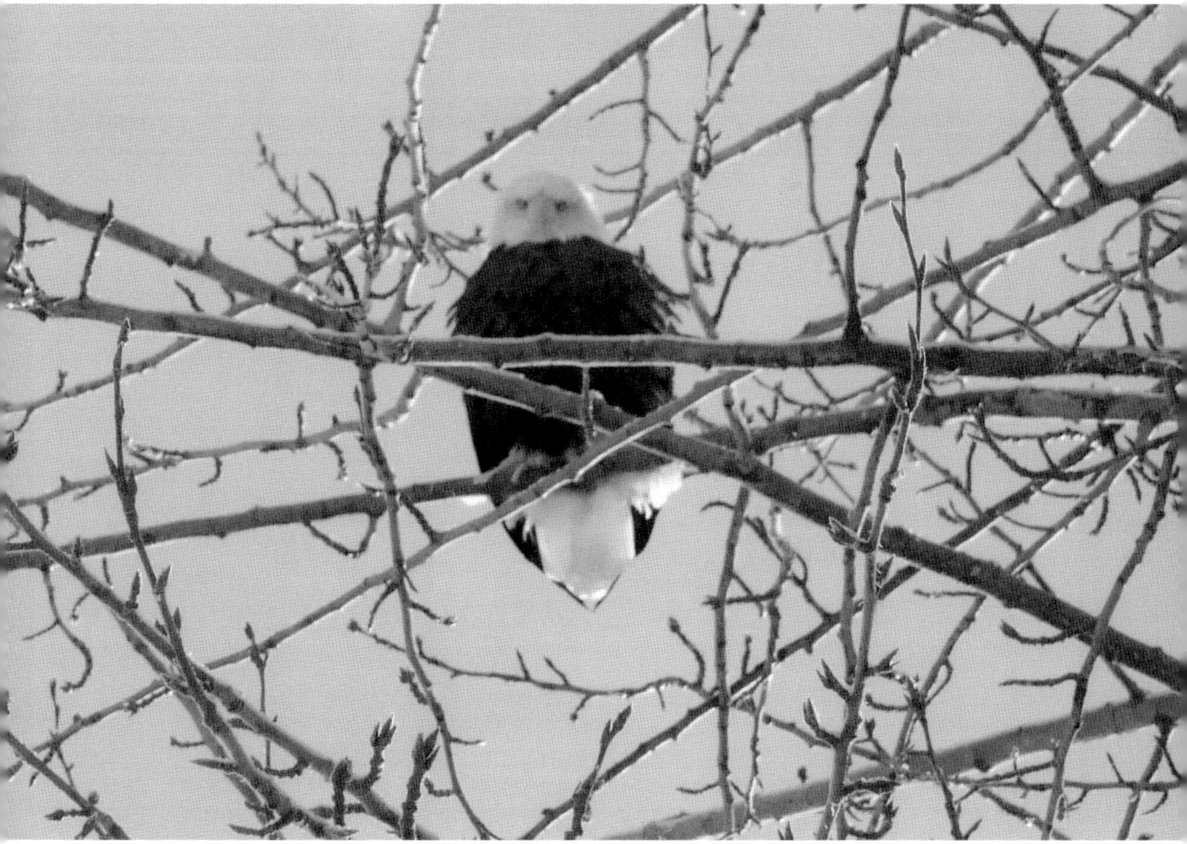

Sam Cotten

Sam Cotten's first constituents were his classmates at Chugiak High School, who elected him president of the student body for the 1964–1965 school year. After enlisting in the US Navy and doing two tours in Vietnam, Cotten, a Democrat, served Eagle River in the Alaska State House of Representatives from 1974 to 1982 and again from 1984 to 1990, with a term on the Anchorage Planning and Zoning Commission in between. He was Speaker of the House during his last term. He was elected to the state senate in 1990 but chose not to run for reelection in 1992 after a reapportionment plan placed him and political ally Rick Halford, a Republican, in the same district. Among Cotten's lasting contributions was his advocacy for bringing the Fire Lake Recreation Center (later named the Harry J. McDonald Memorial Center) to Eagle River. Cotten ran for governor in 1994 and later served on the North Pacific Fishery Management Council and as chairman of the Alaska Public Utilities Commission. (Courtesy of the Chugiak-Eagle River Historical Society.)

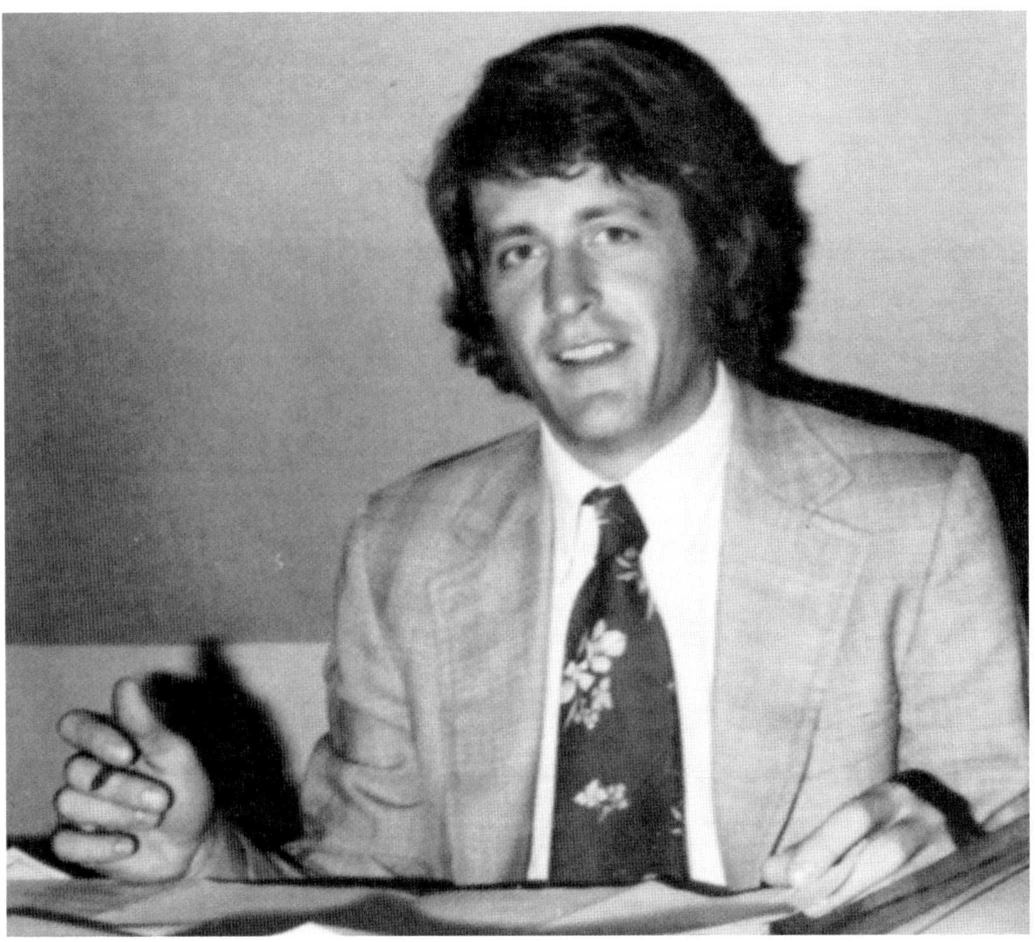

70

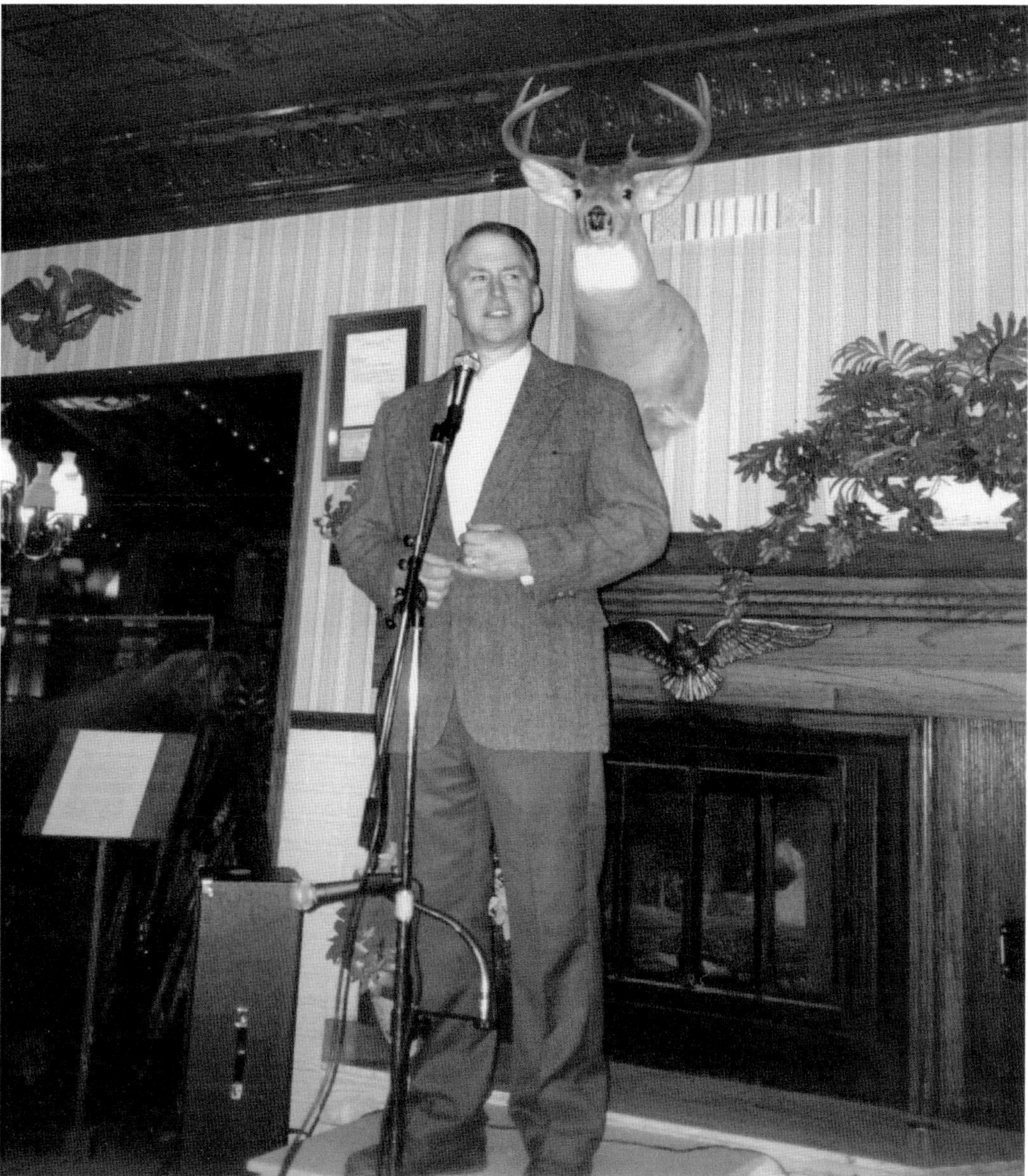

Rick Halford

Republican Rick Halford represented Chugiak-Eagle River in the Alaska State Legislature from 1978 to 2003. During the second of his two terms in the House, he took on the role of majority leader. He served five terms in the senate, two as senate president. Early on in his career, Halford helped shape the Alaska Permanent Fund and create the Permanent Fund Dividend. He was widely admired for his intellect and the respectful way he worked with fellow legislators and constituents. In 1997, Halford cohosted the first Old Timers Dinner with friend George Malekos at Malekos's North Slope Restaurant in Eagle River. Though the North Slope closed in 2007, the annual celebration remains a popular tradition. (Courtesy of the Chugiak-Eagle River Historical Society.)

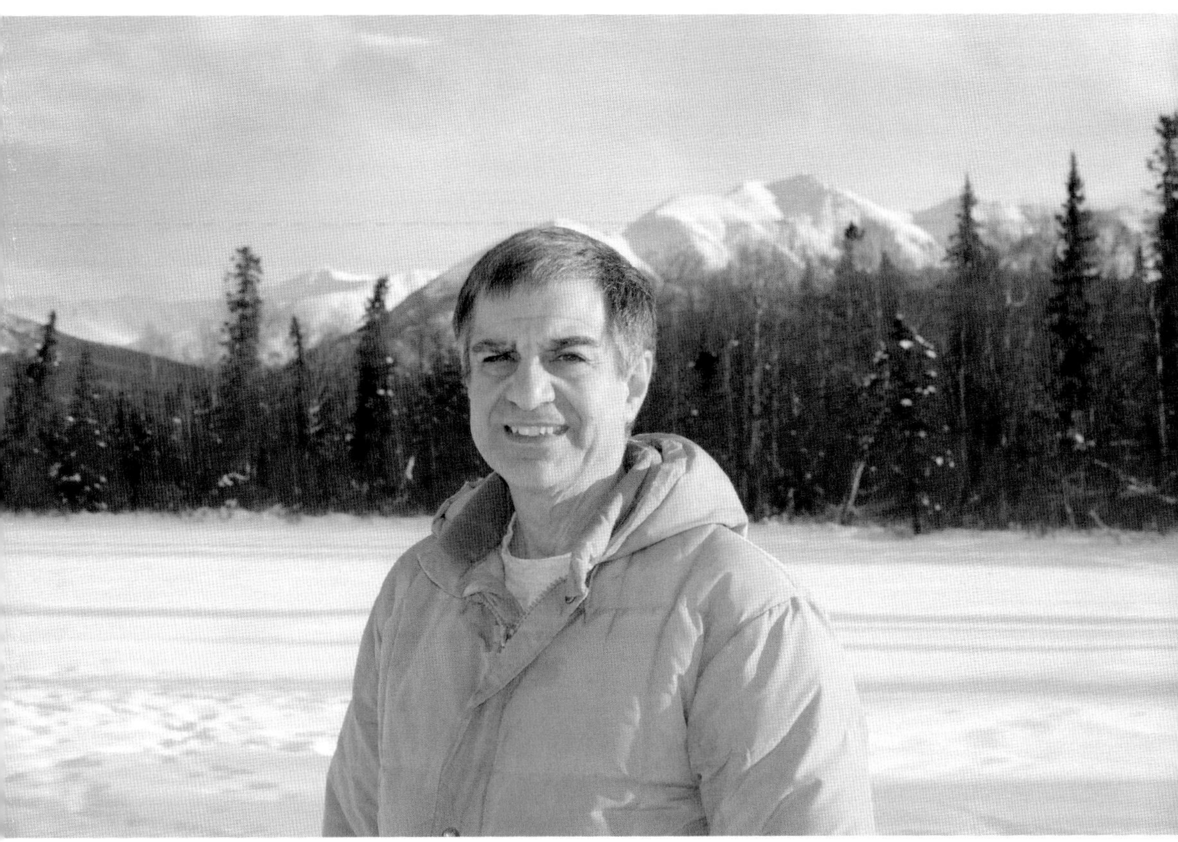

Randy Phillips

Republican Randy Phillips is among the longest-serving state lawmakers in Alaska history. Throughout his 26-year tenure, he was a staunch supporter of moving the state legislature from Juneau to Southcentral Alaska. Phillips was elected to the House in 1976, and he was in the legislature when the Permanent Fund and the ever-popular Permanent Fund Dividend program were created. During his time in the senate, from 1993 to 2003, he concentrated on education issues and helped bring the 1996 Arctic Winter Games to Chugiak-Eagle River. Phillips retired from the senate in 2003 after redistricting drastically changed the area he served. (Photograph by Anita Shepperd.)

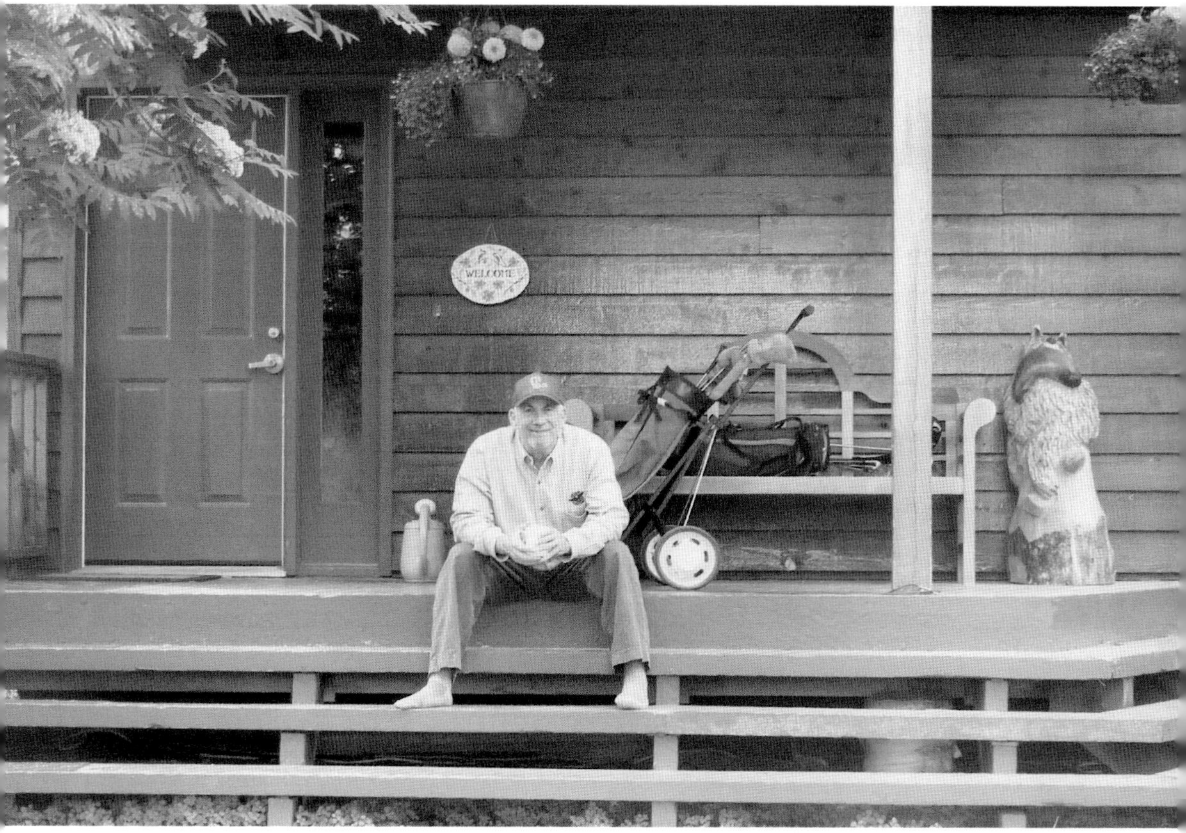

Tim Kelly

Alaska state senator Tim Kelly, a Republican representing East Anchorage and Eagle River, was a natural-born facilitator. Friends and colleagues referred to him as a "legislative mechanic" who could moderate disputes and ratchet down conflicts in order to press ahead with the senate's work. He also had a knack for distilling complicated issues and making them more readily understandable to others. Elected to the House in 1976, Kelly moved on to the senate in 1978, where he chaired Senate Rules and a number of other committees. He was in the legislature when the Permanent Fund and Permanent Fund Dividend Program were created. Kelly took on the role of senate president in 1989, stepped away from the senate in 1990 to run for lieutenant governor, and returned in 1992 and 1996. Kelly retired from the legislature in 2000 and passed away in August 2009. (Both, courtesy of Lisa Nelson.)

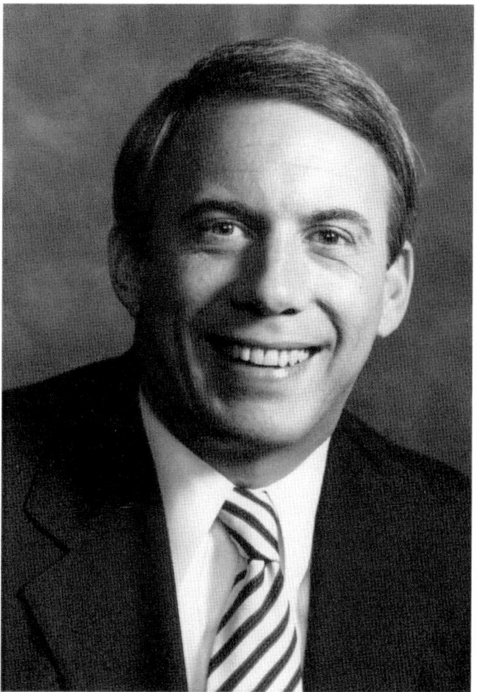

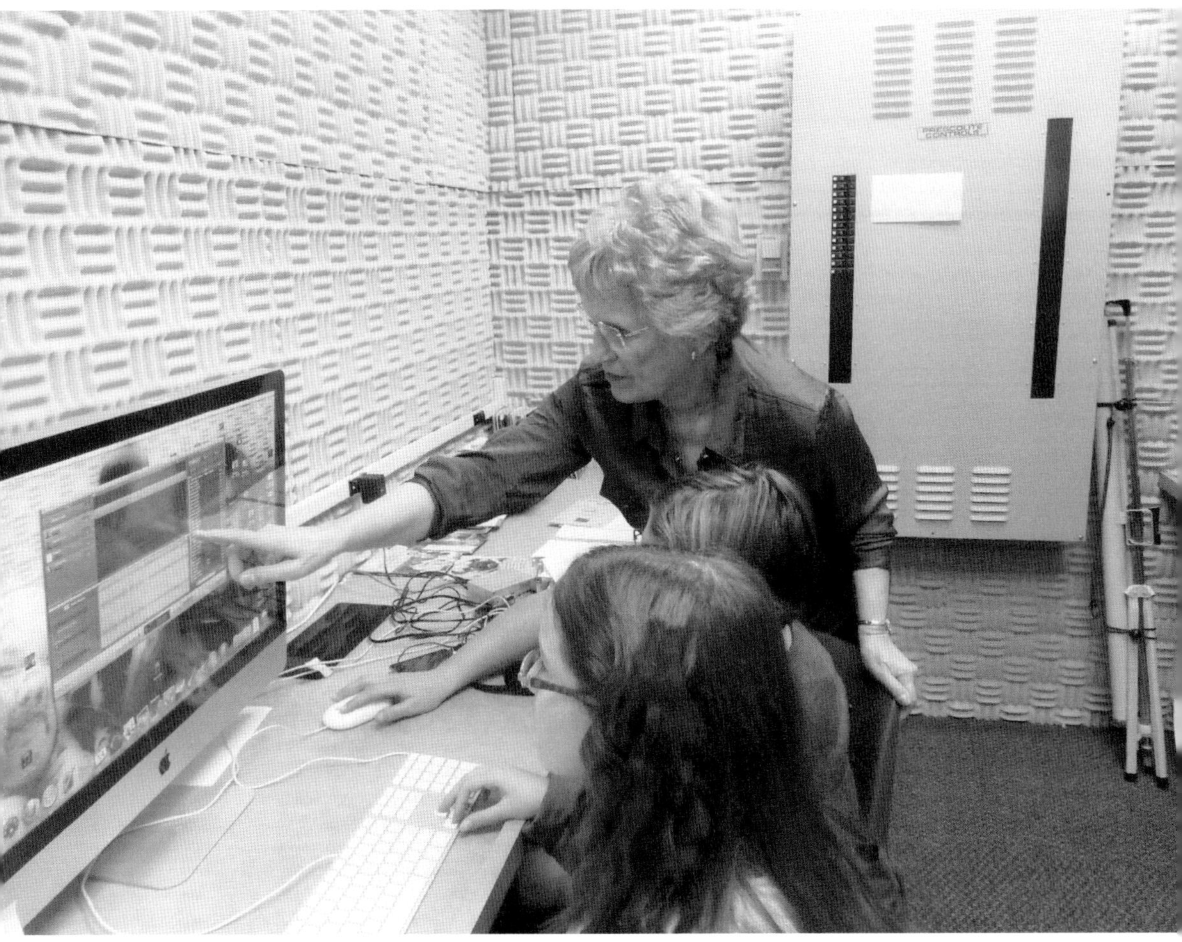

Emily Blahous

Emily Blahous has the coaching skills and wry sense of humor it takes to run a broadcasting group of seventh- and eighth-graders. The Mirror Lake Middle School Video News Team she founded in 1997 creates daily newscasts aired on closed-circuit televisions in all the classrooms. Under Blahous's guidance, a rotating group of students function as writers, editors, camera operators, producers, sound technicians, and anchors, somehow pulling together each show in the span of a 45-minute class period. They also compile a weekly informational program and broadcast it on the school's FM radio station, KAUG. (KAUG was the first FM radio station in the country licensed to a middle school. Blahous named it after the team's former mentor and Alaskan television pioneer, the late Augie Hiebert.) In addition to the practical skills she imparts to her Video News Team students, Blahous teaches piano-keyboarding/music-exploratory classes at Mirror Lake, subjects aligned with her passion for the arts. Field trips are a priority, and Blahous takes students to as many professional performances as she can. She also invites artists on tour in Anchorage to perform for the school at large. Her dedication has not gone unnoticed. Among the awards she has received are the 2005 Star Awards Educator Recognition from the Anchorage School Business Partnership, the 2006 BP Teachers of Excellence award, the 2011 Mayor's Arts Award for Youth Arts, and the 2013 Broadcaster of the Year Award from the Alaska Broadcasters Association. (Courtesy of Emily Blahous.)

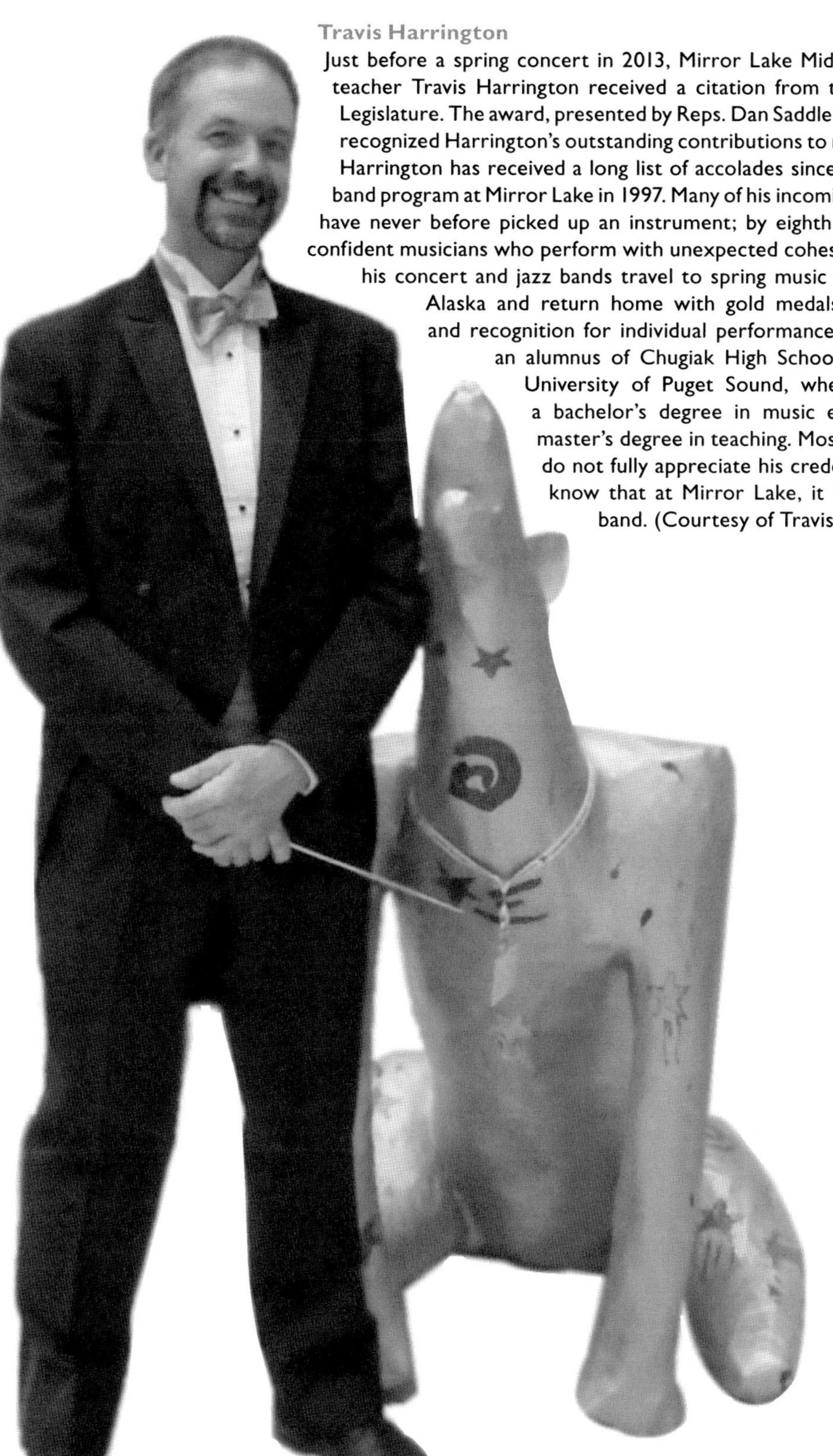

Travis Harrington

Just before a spring concert in 2013, Mirror Lake Middle School band teacher Travis Harrington received a citation from the Alaska State Legislature. The award, presented by Reps. Dan Saddler and Bill Stoltze, recognized Harrington's outstanding contributions to music education. Harrington has received a long list of accolades since he initiated the band program at Mirror Lake in 1997. Many of his incoming sixth-graders have never before picked up an instrument; by eighth grade, they are confident musicians who perform with unexpected cohesion. Most years, his concert and jazz bands travel to spring music festivals outside Alaska and return home with gold medals, spirit awards, and recognition for individual performances. Harrington is an alumnus of Chugiak High School as well as the University of Puget Sound, where he received a bachelor's degree in music education and a master's degree in teaching. Most of his students do not fully appreciate his credentials; they just know that at Mirror Lake, it is cool to be in band. (Courtesy of Travis Harrington.)

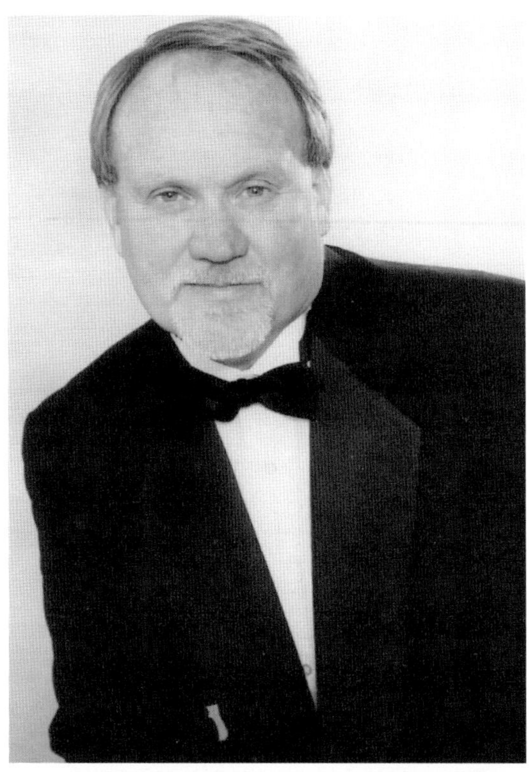

Ron Lange and the Chugiak High School Choir

Ron Lange holds his choir students at Chugiak High School to an exceptionally high standard. The proof is in the trophy case. Lange, choral director at Chugiak for nearly two decades, takes his singers to national or international competitions each year, and the groups regularly earn top honors. Nine times in the past fifteen years, the Chugiak High School Choir has taken home the Grand Champion trophy in sixteen North American and two international festivals. Lange is so effective in the classroom because he blends humor and warmth with the serious business of rehearsing. Students say he relates to them as individuals, treating them with respect and coaxing out the best in each. Onstage in the Steve Primis Auditorium, Chugiak choir performances are full-on productions, and it is not just parents buying the tickets. Exceptional music, a bit of choreography, and Lange's characteristic humor ensure that there will not be a seat left unoccupied. (Both, courtesy of Ron Lange.)

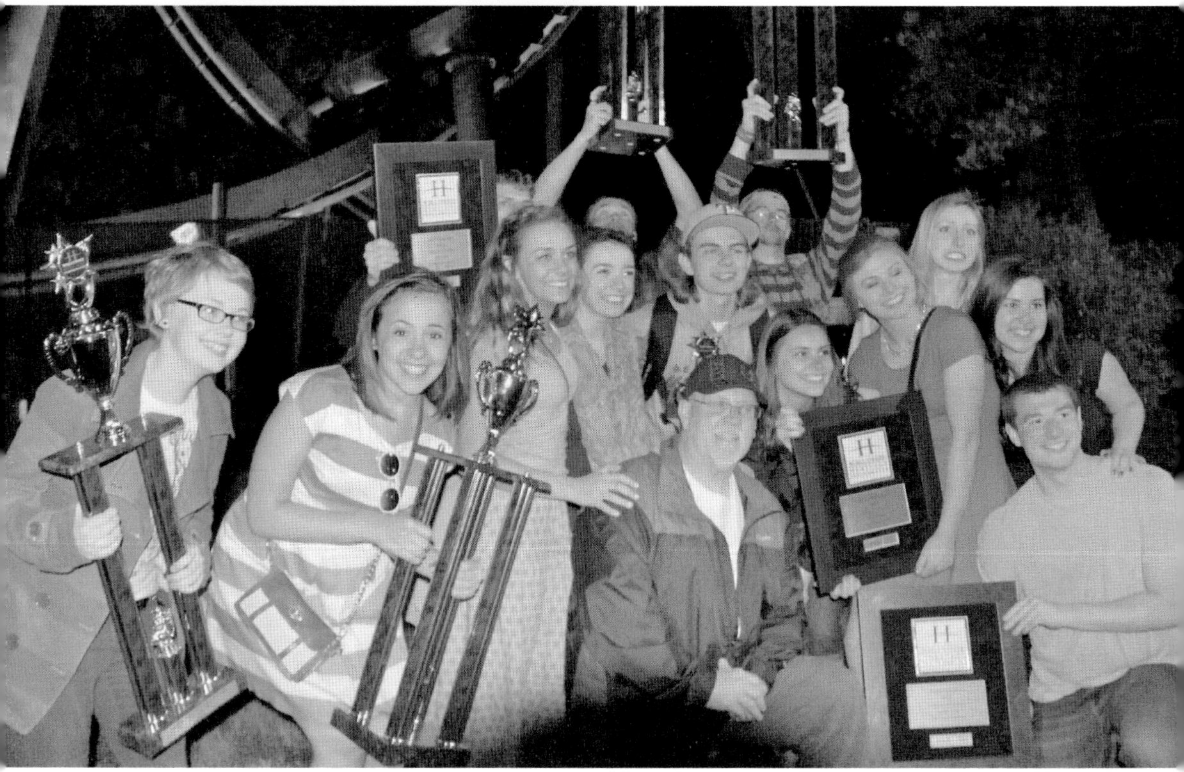

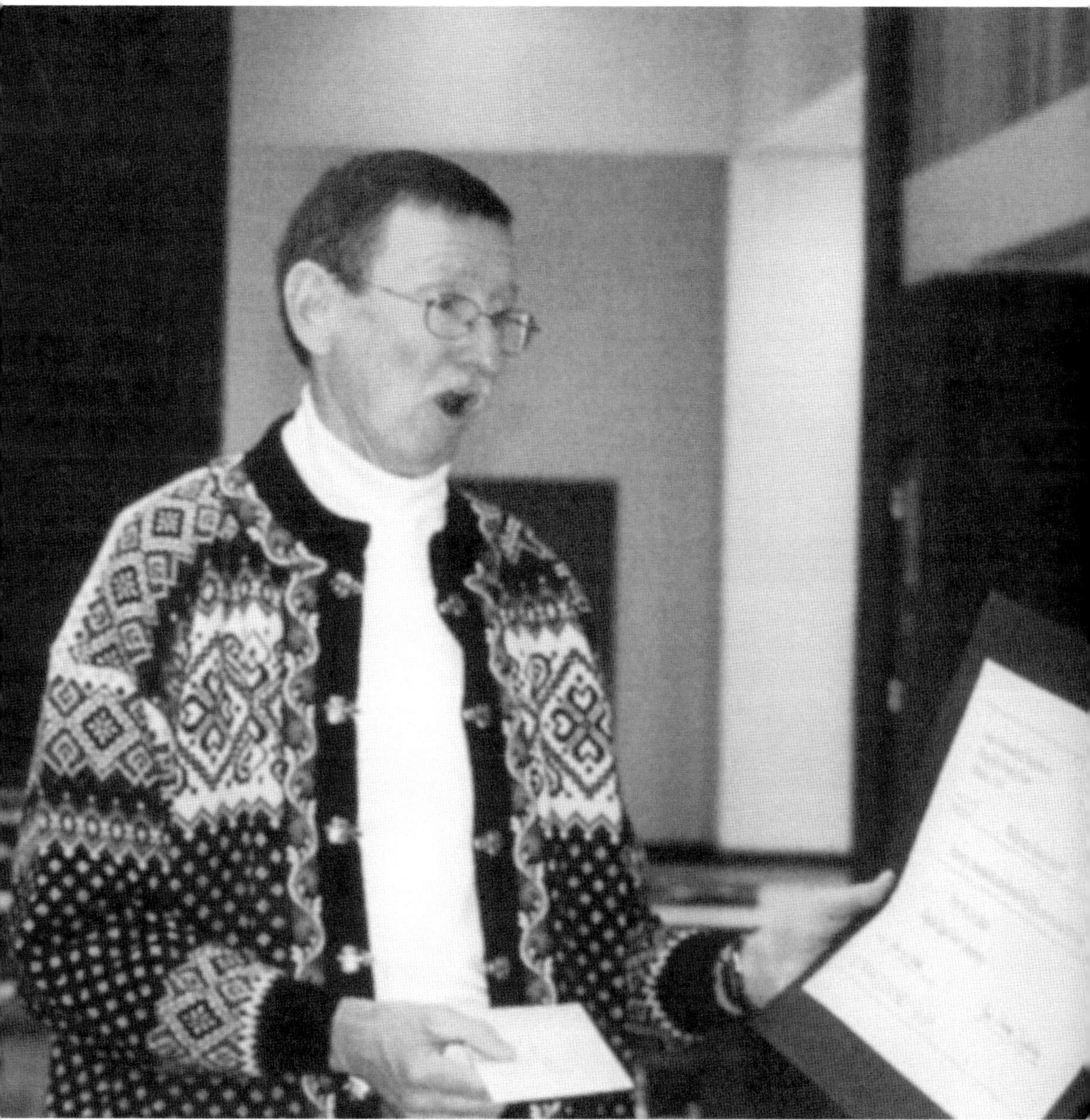

Philip Burch

Philip Burch inspired thousands of music students over the course of his career. He won the Alaska Music Educators Award for Excellence in 2006, the same year as his wife, Susan, a choir teacher at Gruening Middle School. Philip taught orchestra at Chugiak High School from 1984 to 2004 and performed with the Anchorage Symphony Orchestra. Both Burches were known for their kindness and sense of humor. After Philip was diagnosed with a rare form of stomach cancer in 2003, the Fine Arts Department at Chugiak High School held a spaghetti feed and auction that raised over $20,000 in one short evening. Philip lived another six years—long enough to celebrate 40 years of marriage—before finally succumbing in 2009. (Courtesy of Chugiak High School.)

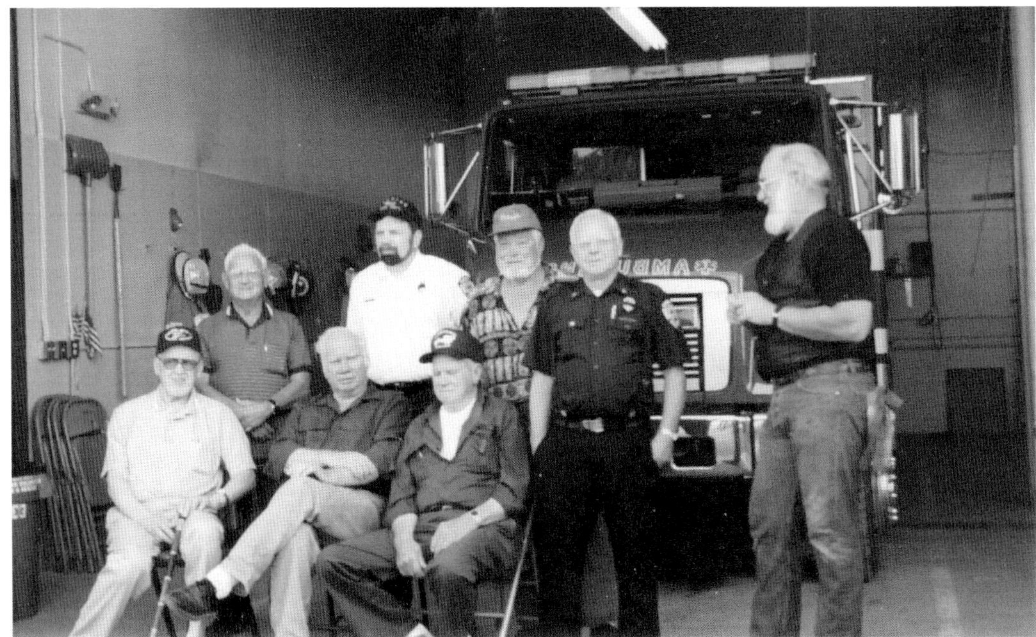

A Gathering of Chiefs
The Chugiak Volunteer Fire & Rescue Company has a long history of service and strong support within the community. Established in 1952, the company serves a population of about 14,000 in an area of 50 square miles. It has grown to include 80 volunteers and 5 separate stations: Station 31, Latimer, named after Max Latimer (the original chief); Station 32, Gilmore, named after Cliff Gilmore (chief in the late 1980s and early 1990s); Station 33, Hill, named for Linda Hill (an EMT killed on her way to a training class in the 1970s); Station 34, Wallace, named for Art and Til Wallace; and Station 35 (being reconstructed), Lowe, for Bill Lowe (the company's fire supervisor for 20 years). Pictured above is a 1999 gathering of former chiefs; below is an ambulance from the early 1970s. (Both, courtesy of the Chugiak-Eagle River Historical Society.)

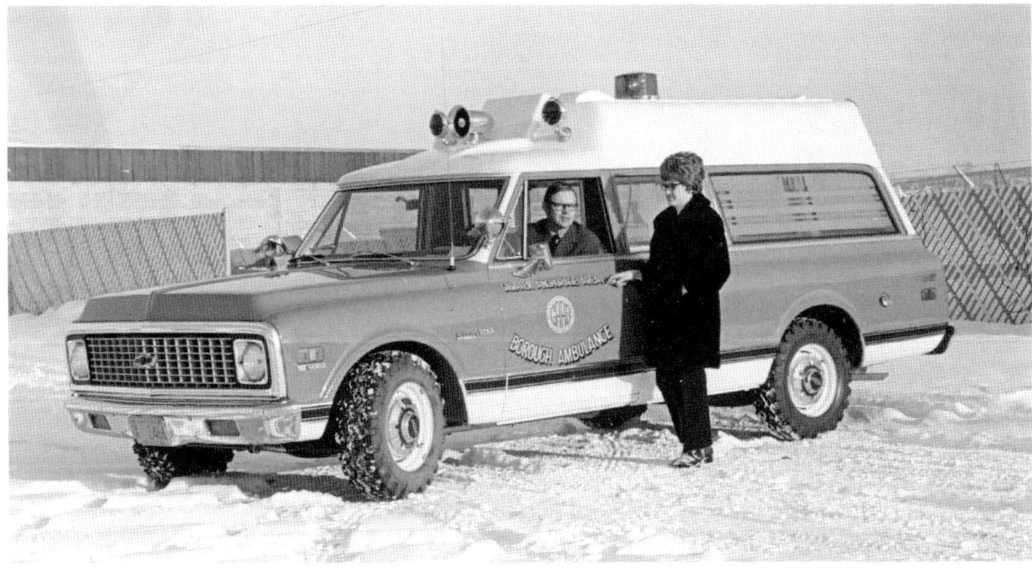

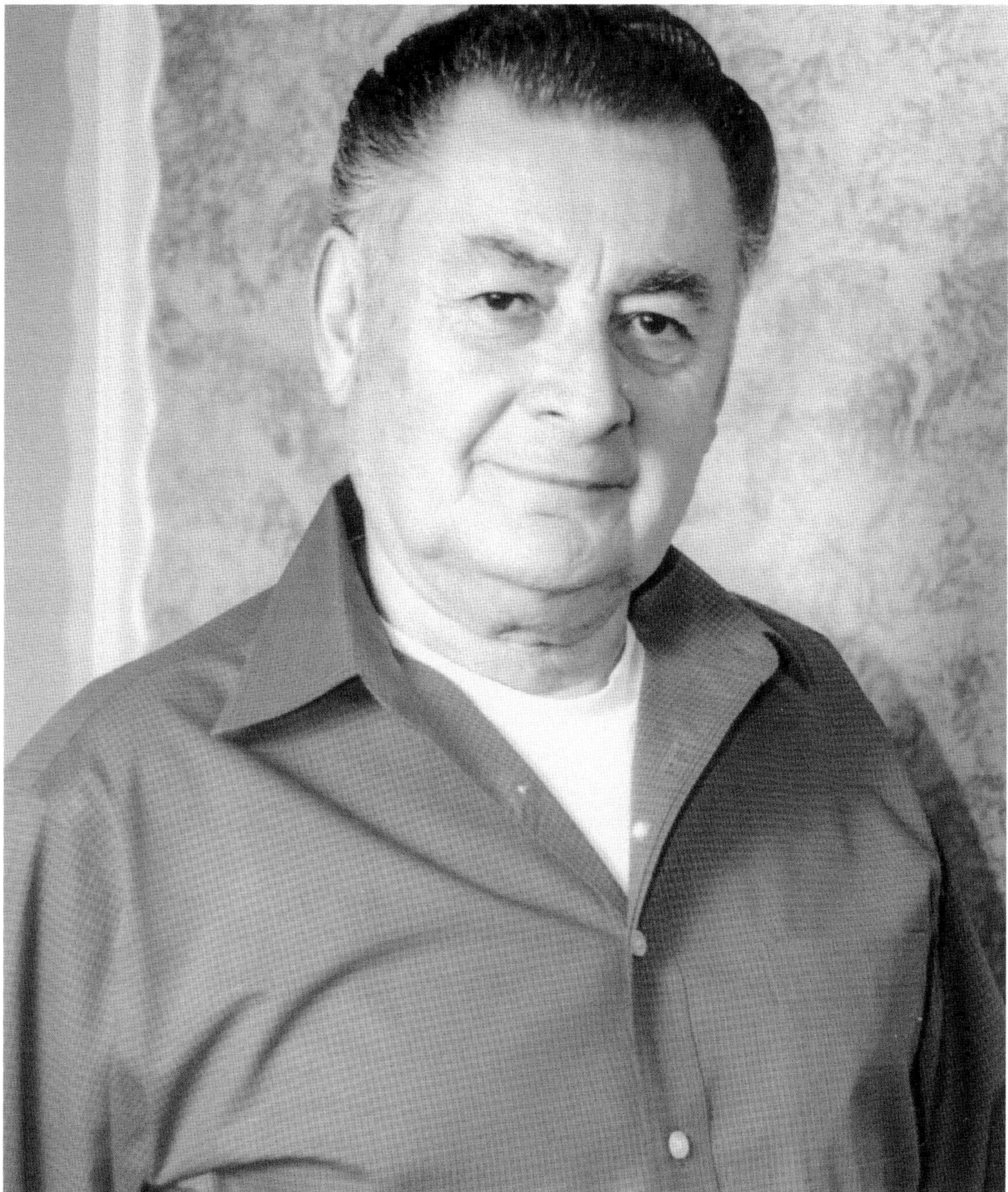

Tom Take, Longtime Eagle River Volunteer Fire Department Chief

Eagle River residents relied on the Chugiak Volunteer Fire & Rescue Company until 1959, when they started up their own volunteer force. Orrin Ivie was chief until about 1961 and was followed by the department's only other chief, Tom Take. The Eagle River Improvement Association purchased the first fire truck—a 17-year-old, 750-gallon tanker—from the Fairview Fire Department and stored it in Walter and Melva Pippels' potato barn. Eagle River's original siren system sat atop the Candle Light Inn, a high-end restaurant across the street from the potato barn. The fire department later acquired an ambulance from funds raised by the Eagle River Lions Club (with a push from Lions Club vice president Tom Slanker). The volunteer force was incorporated into the Greater Anchorage Area Borough in 1975 and was eventually absorbed by the Anchorage Fire Department. (Courtesy of Tom Take.)

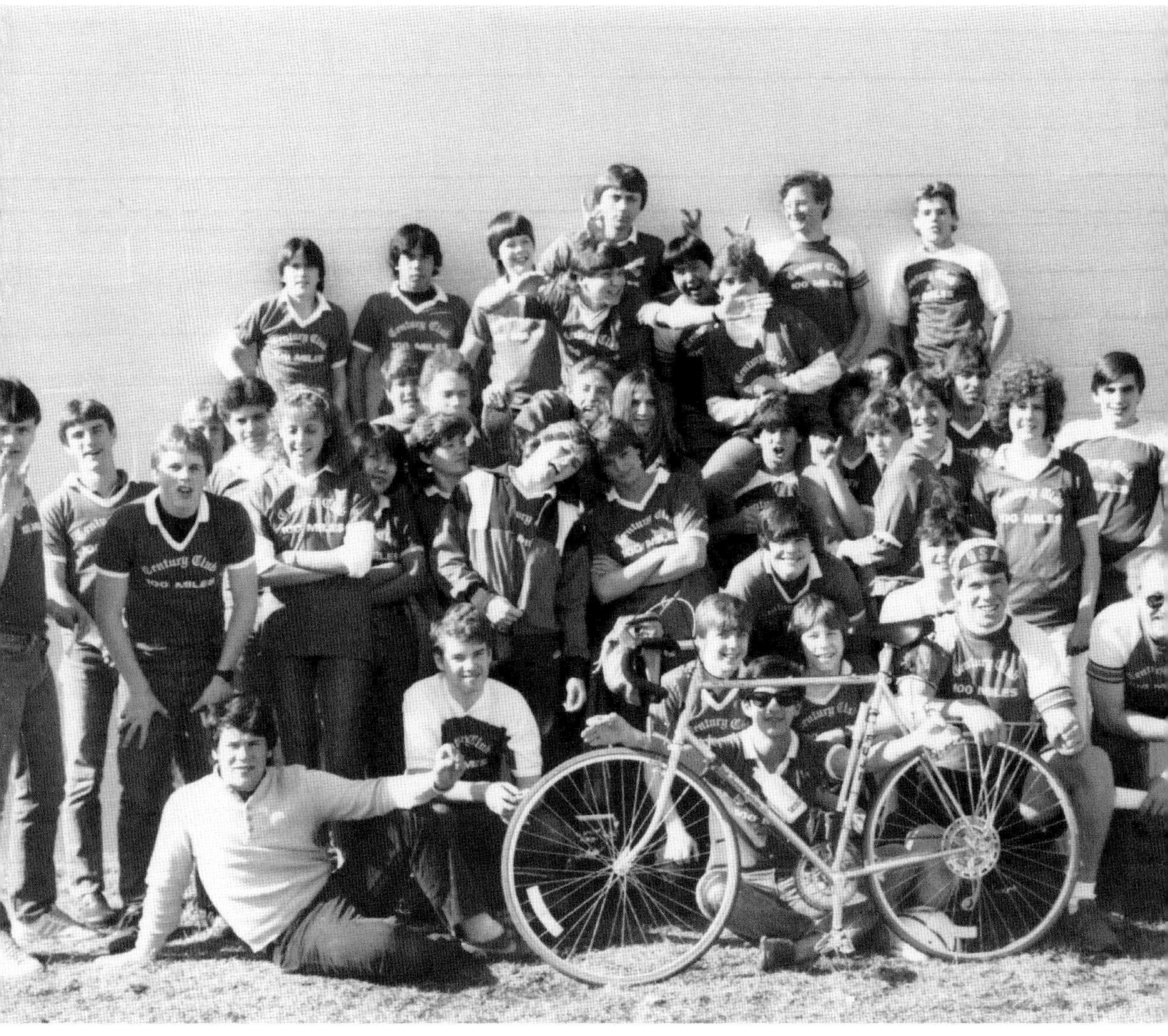

Andy Kirk

Under the direction of coach Andy Kirk (seated, far right), bicyclists who belonged to Chugiak High School's Century Club would ride hundreds of miles in a single stretch. The club—in place from 1974 to 1989—included students from all levels of the teen social strata and challenged them to push beyond their perceived limits. The goal was to complete a "century," 100 miles in 12 hours; a "double-century," 200 miles in 24 hours; or, in some cases, even a "triple-century," 300 miles in 24 hours. Kirk headed up a long-distance biking and camping trip each spring, something his former athletes still reminisce about. He coached a handful of other sports and launched the Wacko Decathlon, a student-run spirit day filled with games and races that continues at Chugiak High and other area schools to this day. Kirk retired in 1989 from a 31-year teaching career, the bulk of which was spent at Chugiak, where he infused his social studies and history lessons with the same sense of fun and adventure he displayed as a coach. He died in 1997 at age 68. (Courtesy of Jinny Kirk.)

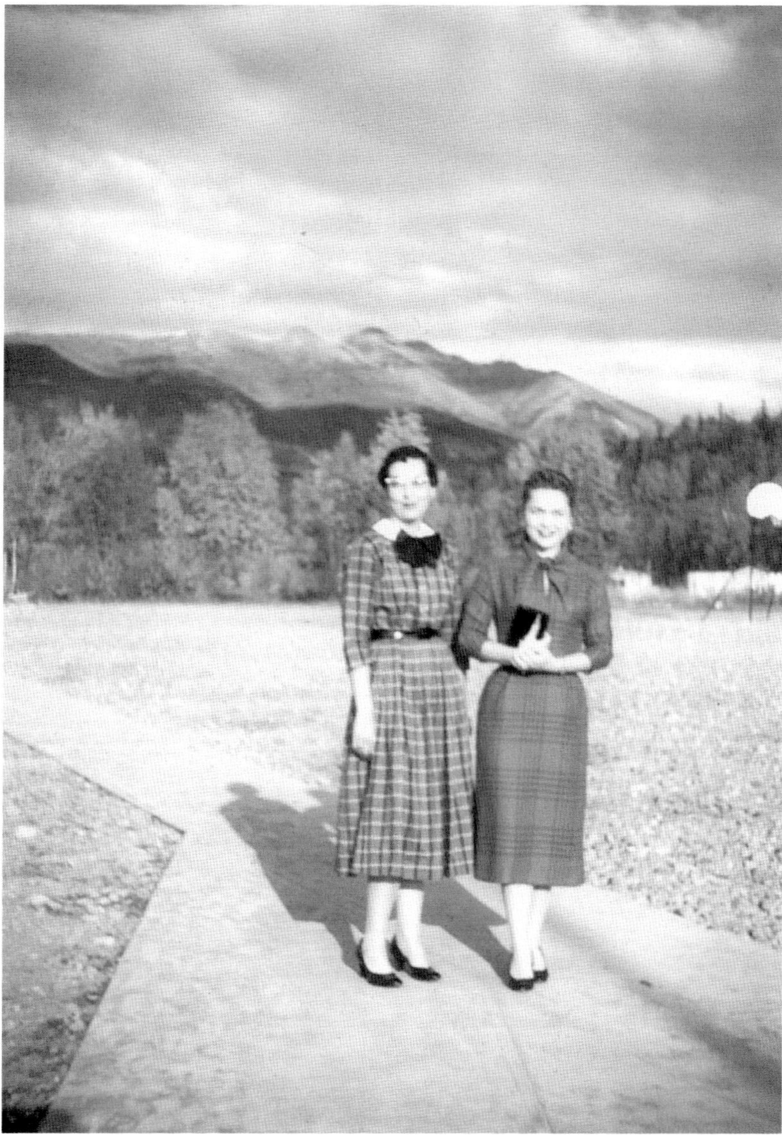

Jinny Search Kirk
It all started with a bright idea and a spare closet. In 1993, community activist Bill Lowe suggested to retired teacher Jinny Kirk that she create an organization to collect and catalog the area's historical records and treasures. Kirk agreed to take on the challenge, and the Chugiak-Eagle River Historical Society was born. Kirk recruited other longtime community members, and the 21-person charter group began meeting in the downstairs lounge of the Chugiak Children's Services Building (now the Paul Swanson Building). One closet was allotted for the original archives. As word spread, the collection multiplied. The society moved next door to the Elsie Oberg Community Center, where it still resides. Over the years, the society has presented multiple programs on the early days of Chugiak and Eagle River, bringing alive the stories housed in its file drawers and boxes. Kirk still sits on the board of directors as an emeritus member and is often the go-to person when questions arise. She is pictured (left) during her teaching days at Chugiak Territorial School with friend Zona Miles Dahlmann. (Courtesy of Jinny Kirk.)

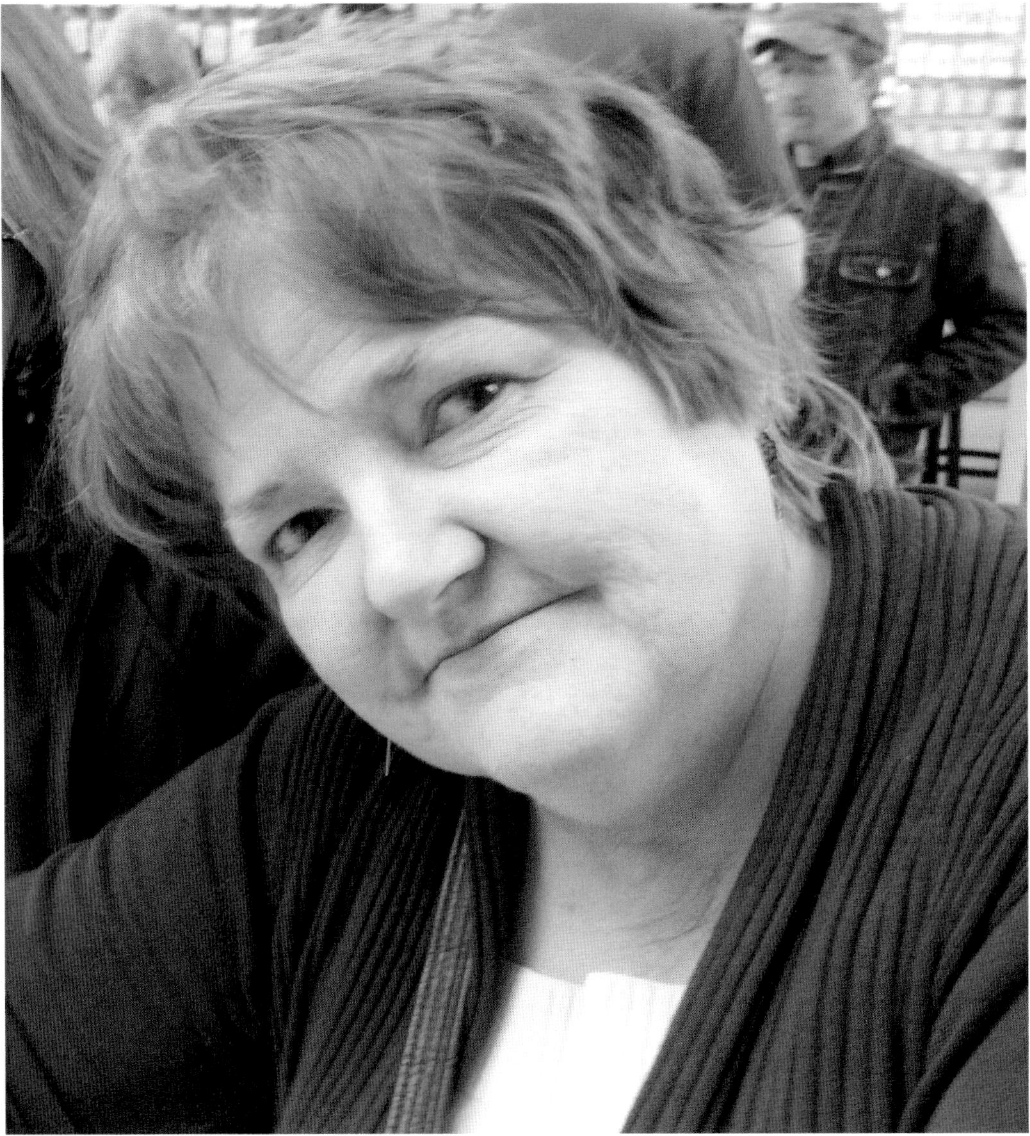

Debbie Ossiander

Debbie Ossiander's calm communication style belies the fact that she has been thrust into the middle of some contentious issues during her 20-plus years in public life. Appointed to the Anchorage School Board in the midst of a recall election in 1992, Ossiander pledged to address the school district's budget and overcrowding problems, subjects dear to her Chugiak-Eagle River constituents. She stayed on task and was elected to the board for four more terms, three of which she served as president. While on the school board, Ossiander helped inspire a grassroots effort among PTA presidents in Chugiak and Eagle River for a new high school. (She had pushed for the building of Mirror Lake Middle School and Alpenglow Elementary during her own tenure as a PTA president years before.) In 2005, shortly after she was elected to the Anchorage Assembly, Eagle River High was built. Among Ossiander's key accomplishments while serving on the assembly from 2004 to 2013 was her oversight of the rewrite of the Title 21 land-use plan. The final version, which was approved just before her term ended, included a chapter addressing the specific needs of Chugiak-Eagle River. (Courtesy of Debbie Ossiander.)

Anna Fairclough

Fiscal accountability, economic health, and job creation have been driving forces in Anna Fairclough's legislative career. In 2013, during her first session in the Alaska Senate, the Eagle River-East Anchorage Republican began chairing the Legislative Budget & Audit Committee and became vice chair of the Senate Finance Committee. She also served on Senate TAPS (Trans-Alaska Pipeline System) Throughput, Resources, Transportation, and Joint Armed Services Committees and served as an alternate on the Legislative Ethics Committee. Previously, Fairclough was an Alaska state representative from 2007 to 2012 and served as vice chair of the House Finance Committee. She represented Chugiak-Eagle River on the Anchorage Assembly from 1999 to 2006 and served as chair in 2005 and 2006. Throughout her time in public service, Fairclough has gained a reputation for being thoughtful and fair among her colleagues and accessible to her constituents. (Courtesy of Anna Fairclough.)

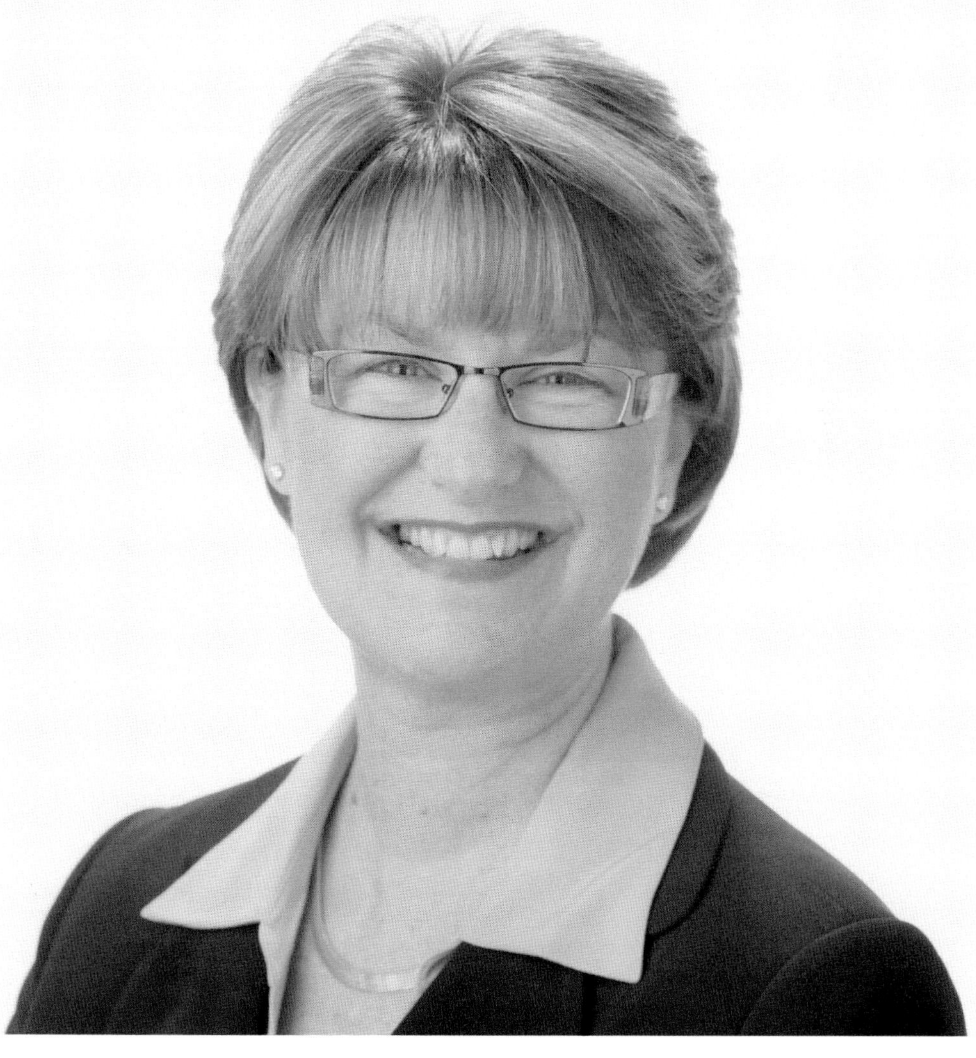

Bill Lowe

Bill Lowe received many honors for his civic activities, including the 1990 Bear Paw Service Award and the 1999 Mayor's Award for Public Service. He was the catalyst behind the Chugiak-Eagle River Historical Society, which opened in 1993, and a fixture at the now-defunct Alaska Museum of Natural History in Eagle River. Lowe kept himself and others busy on the Chugiak Benefit Association Board of Directors and spent 20 years as fire supervisor for the Chugiak Volunteer Fire & Rescue Company. After his death in a car accident in 1999, the fire department named one of its stations after him. A community-spirit award given out at the Bear Paw Festival each year also bears his name. (Courtesy of the Chugiak-Eagle River Historical Society.)

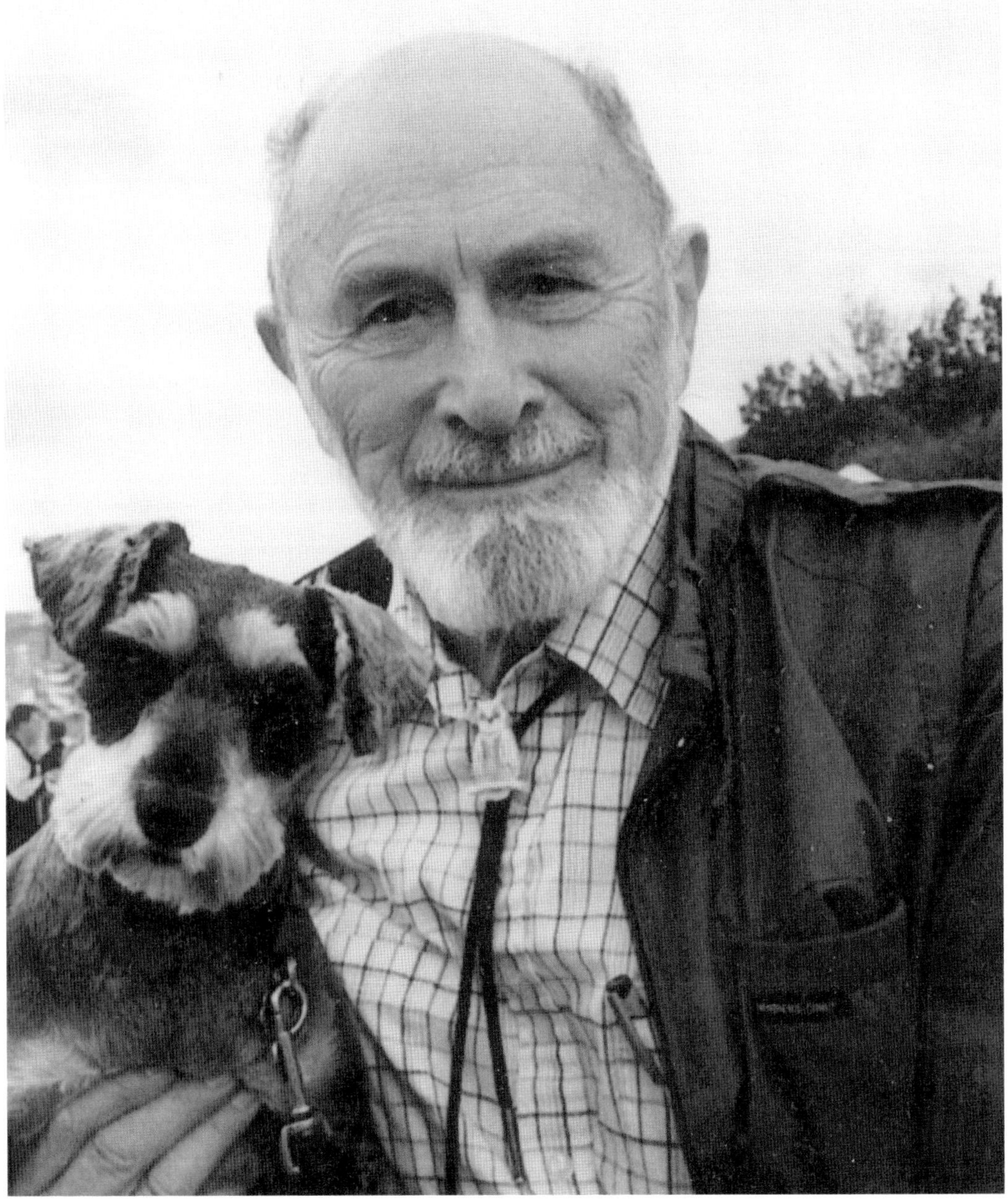

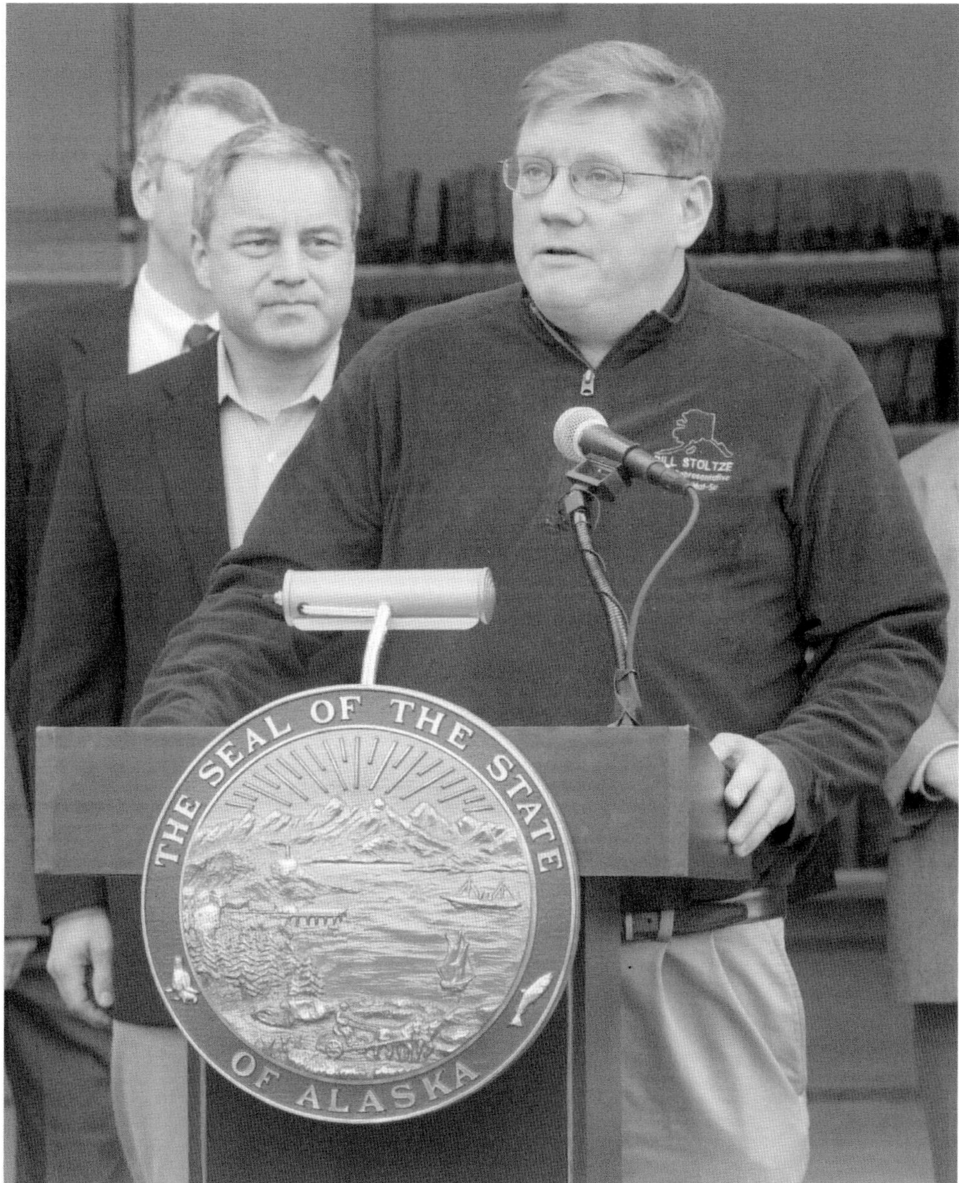

Bill Stoltze

Bill Stoltze has served Chugiak and the Mat-Su in the Alaska House of Representatives since 2002. He had previously worked for Chugiak-Eagle River legislators as a staff aid for nearly 20 years. Stoltze, a Republican, graduated from Chugiak High School and the University of Alaska Fairbanks. A member of the Finance Committee since his first term, he served as its vice chair during his second and third terms and as cochair since 2008. He also served on the Legislative Budget & Audit Committee and the Legislative Council Committee. Stoltze stays highly visible in the community and is well known through his numerous volunteer and civic activities—Elks Club, Chugiak Lions (charter member), and Chugiak-Eagle River Chinooks Booster Club (vice president). He is a life member of the Chugiak Senior Center, Inc., and was a founding board member of Denali View Housing. Stoltze received a Bear Paw Community Service Award in 2012. (Courtesy of Bill Stoltze.)

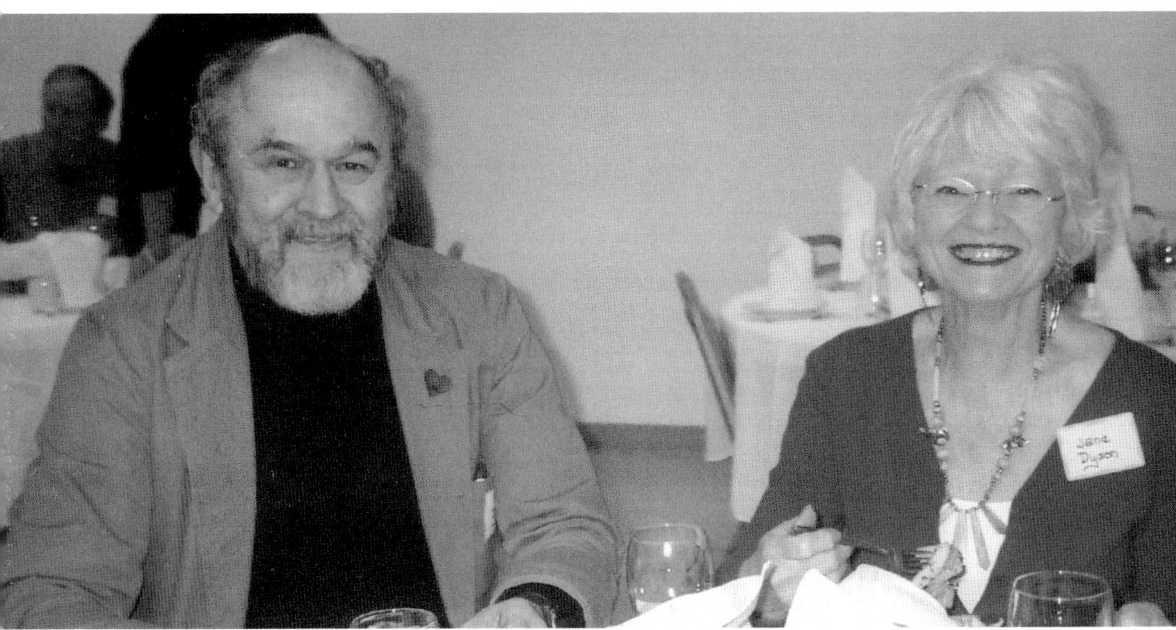

Fred and Jane Dyson

Republican Fred Dyson was first elected to the Alaska State Legislature in 1996, serving in the House until 2003 and in the senate from 2003 through the present. He represented Eagle River on the Anchorage Assembly from 1985 to 1991. He has introduced or worked on legislation on a variety of victims' rights issues—most notably child protection, domestic violence, and trafficking in persons—as well as issues of personal freedom, property rights, and conservation. Dyson and his wife, Jane, raised three daughters and a dozen foster children. (Courtesy of the Chugiak-Eagle River Historical Society.)

Joe Kapella
For most people in Eagle River from the early 1960s until the early 1990s, the name "Mr. Volunteer" would bring to mind Joe Kapella. Kapella was an assertive fundraiser who supported Eagle River's Lions and Elks clubs, Knik Little League, youth football, and Special Olympics, among other causes. His warm personality and good-natured cajoling convinced many reluctant contributors to open their wallets. Kapella had been retired from his job as a civil servant on Fort Richardson Army Base for three years when he passed away in 1993 at the age of 58. (Courtesy of Lee Jordan.)

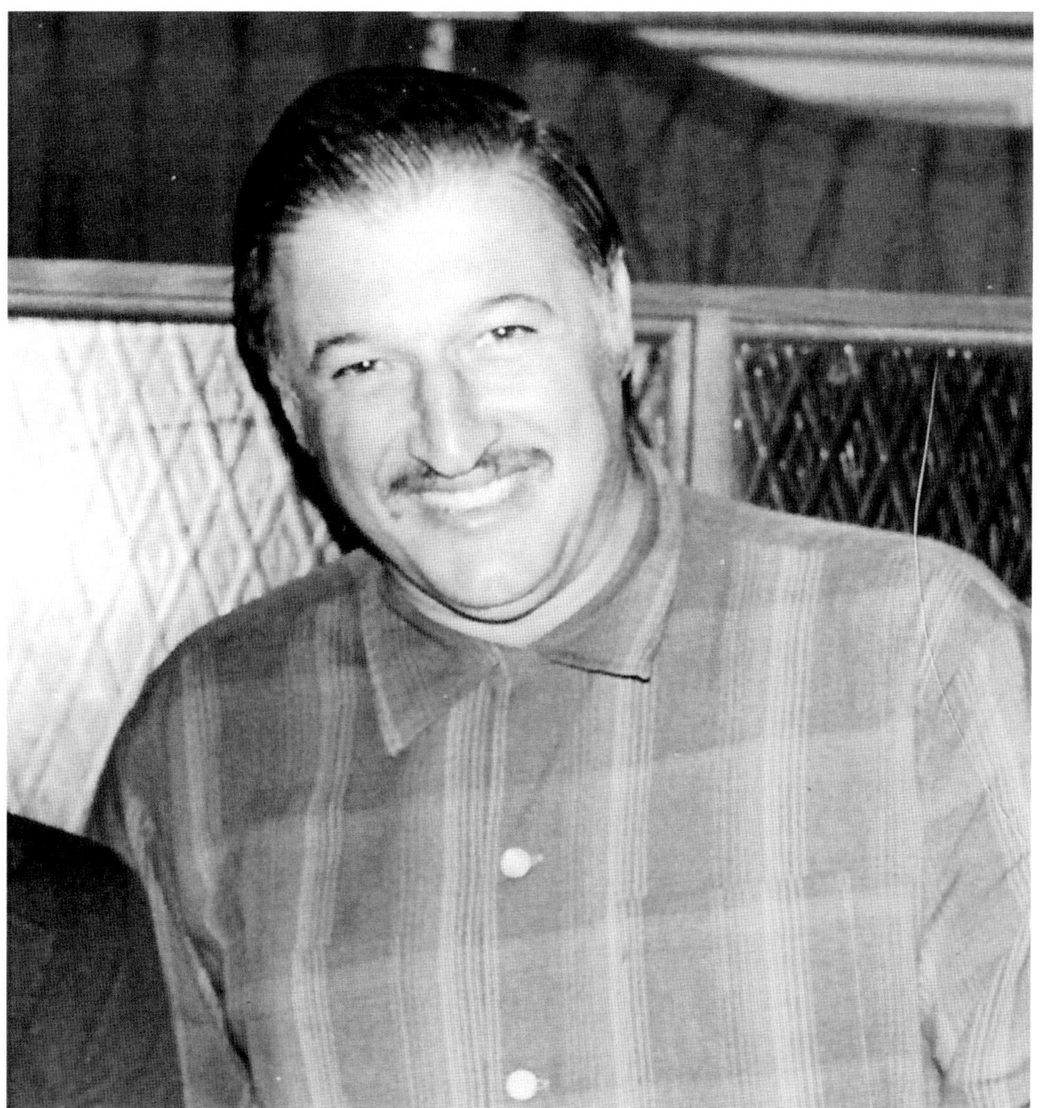

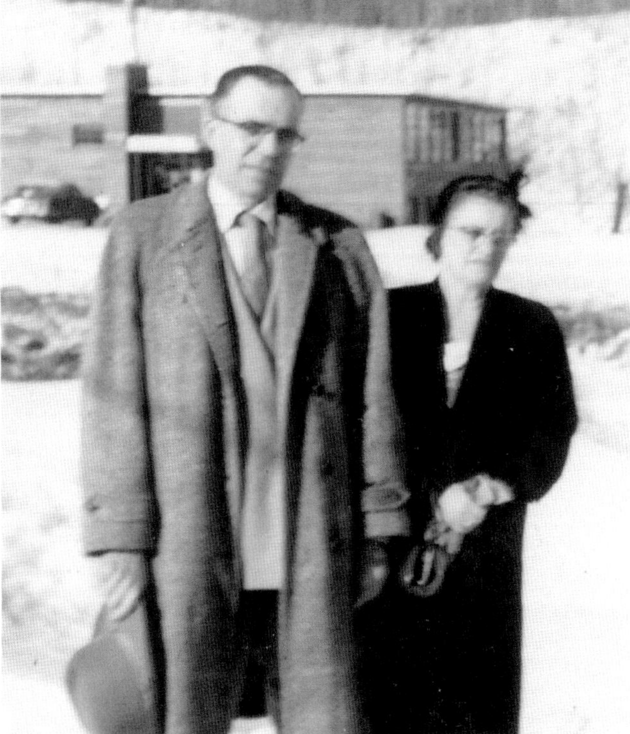

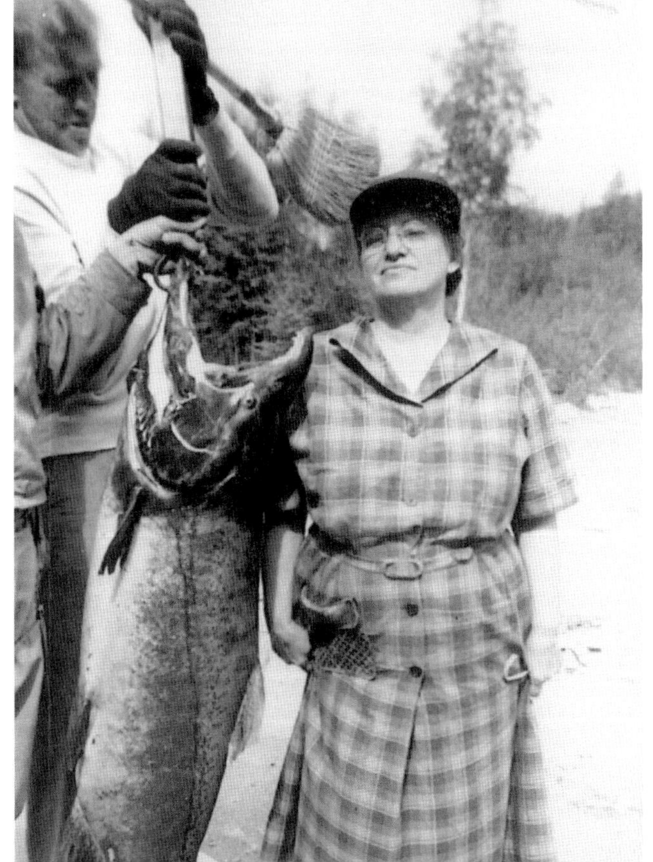

Lee and Irene Emmert
Lee and Irene Emmert (top photograph) and their teenage son Dave arrived in Chugiak in 1952, the year after the Chugiak Territorial School opened. Lee took the job of school superintendent and was, by all accounts, a kind and dedicated administrator. Irene instructed first-graders and appointed herself den mother to the young, single teachers she worked with. The couple stayed on until 1959. In the bottom photograph, Irene accepts a hand from Paul Swanson after landing a king salmon. (Both, courtesy of the Chugiak-Eagle River Historical Society.)

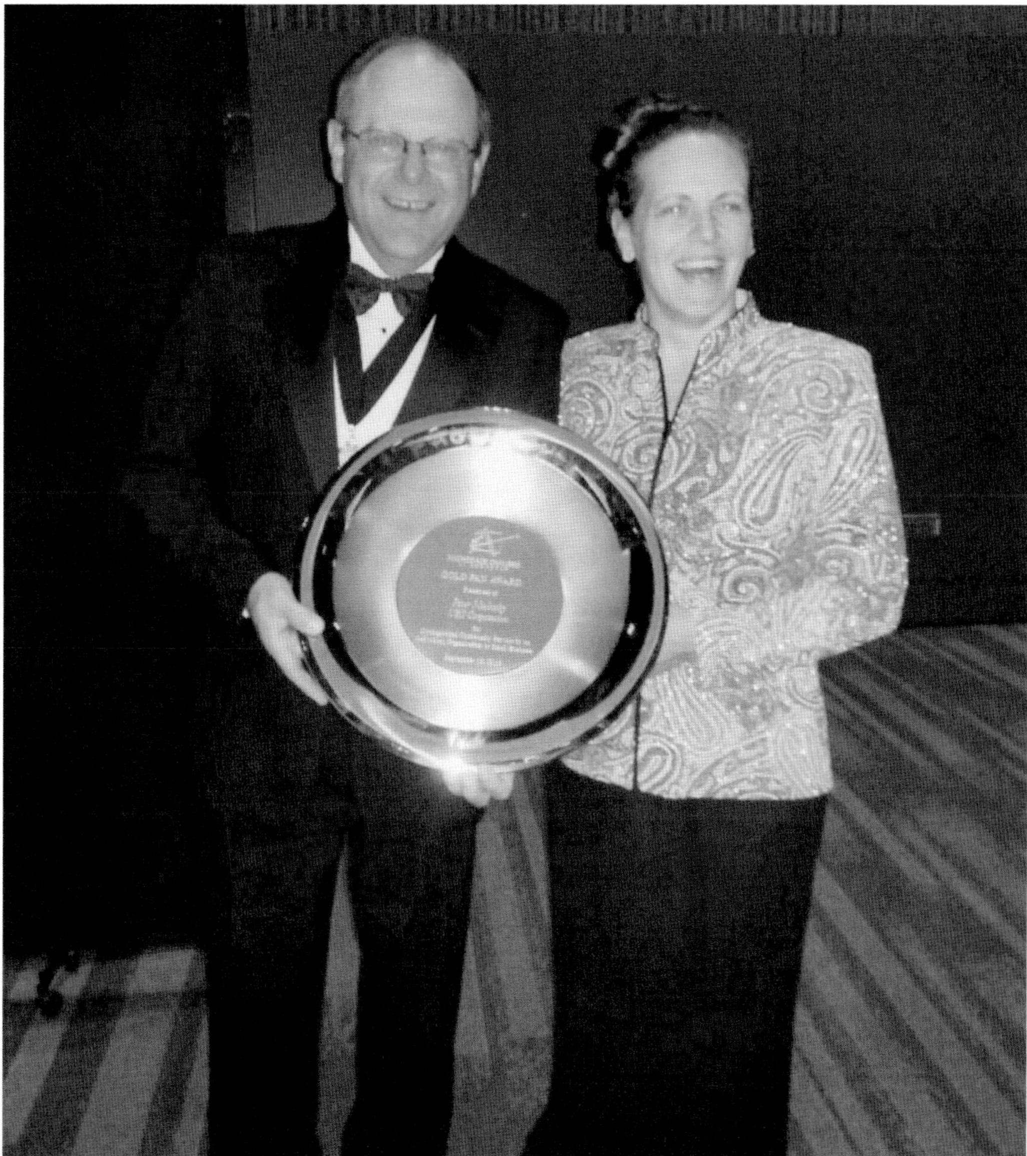

Pete Mulcahy

Retired Army colonel Pete Mulcahy has squeezed a lot of philanthropic pursuits into the 12 years or so he has lived in Chugiak. He is past president of the Eagle River Area Rotary, where he won 2010–2011 Rotarian of the Year and led a group of Rotarians to Colima, Mexico, to furnish area schools with libraries. The former Fort Richardson post commander currently works as a business-development manager for URS Corporation in Anchorage. At URS, he won the Anchorage Chamber of Commerce's Gold Pan Award for Distinguished Community Service in 2013. His volunteerism at over a dozen organizations in Anchorage and locally—including Arctic Valley Ski Area, Chugiak Volunteer Fire Department, and FOCUS, Inc. (Family Outreach for Understanding Special Needs)—led to the award. Mulcahy is president of the Chugiak-Eagle River Chamber of Commerce, which itself won an Outstanding Chamber Award from the Alaska Chamber of Commerce in 2013. He is pictured with his wife, Deb. (Courtesy of Pete Mulcahy.)

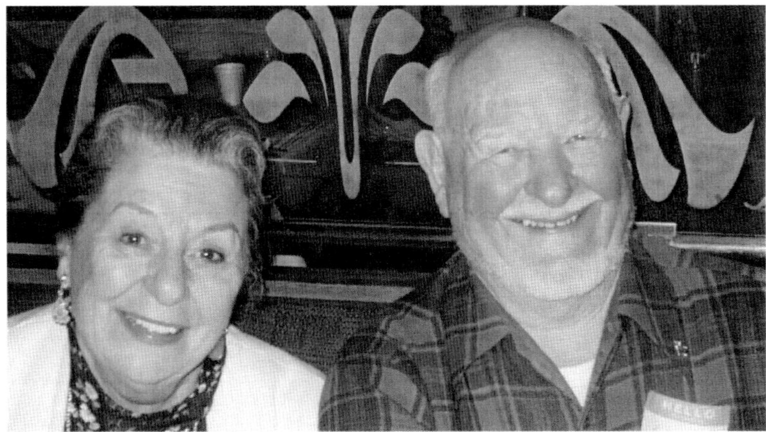

Shirl and L.B. Mauldin

Shirl Mauldin described herself as a reluctant editor when she founded the *Eagle* newspaper in 1961. Without prior experience, the stay-at-home mother of four never had any journalistic aspirations—ever. And she would not have undertaken a weekly newspaper had it not been for a visit from farmer and community leader Walt Pippel. Pippel was part of the Eagle River Improvement Association, which had just acquired a fire engine and was newly in debt. He had decided that Mauldin and the *Eagle* would lift them out. Appreciating the importance of her mission, Mauldin immersed herself in the work. The reporting was the easiest part, she has said, as people would generally phone her with news. She also took photographs; hand-lettered headlines, captions, and advertisements; drew pictures; and pasted up the 20- to 26-page paper, all on a monthly salary of $10. Her children helped mimeograph the papers and deliver them to the Market Basket grocery store and the Knik Knak Shop. Through advertisements and $25 memberships to the improvement association, the fire engine loan was paid off within two years. The association transferred ownership of the *Eagle* to Mauldin at the end of 1962. She continued producing the paper for a few more months, publishing the final edition on May 1, 1963. (Above, courtesy of the Chugiak-Eagle River Historical Society; below, photograph taken by Chris Lundgren, courtesy of *Chugiak-Eagle River Star.*)

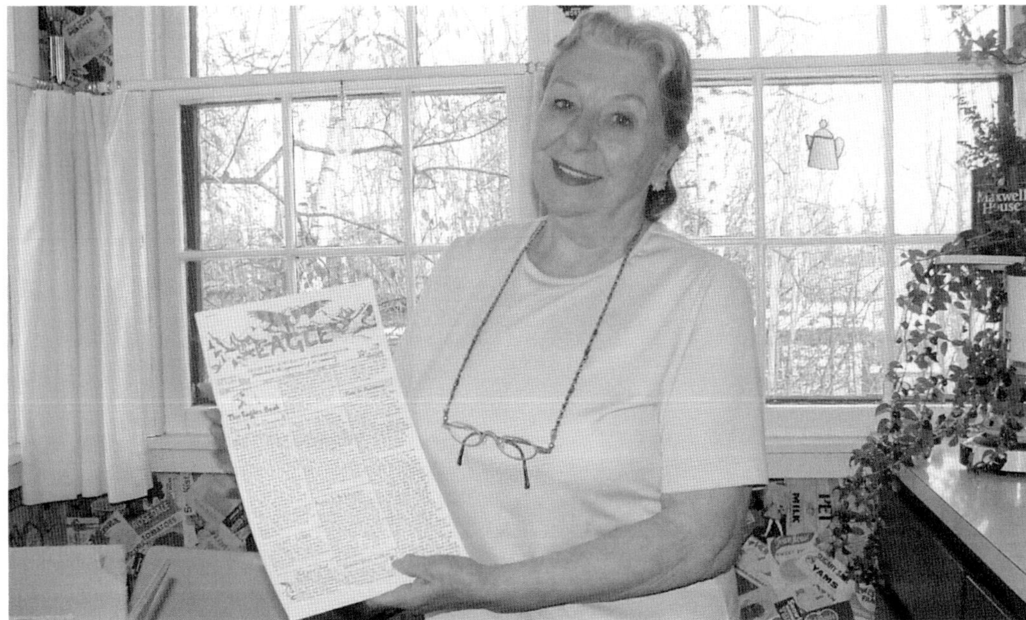

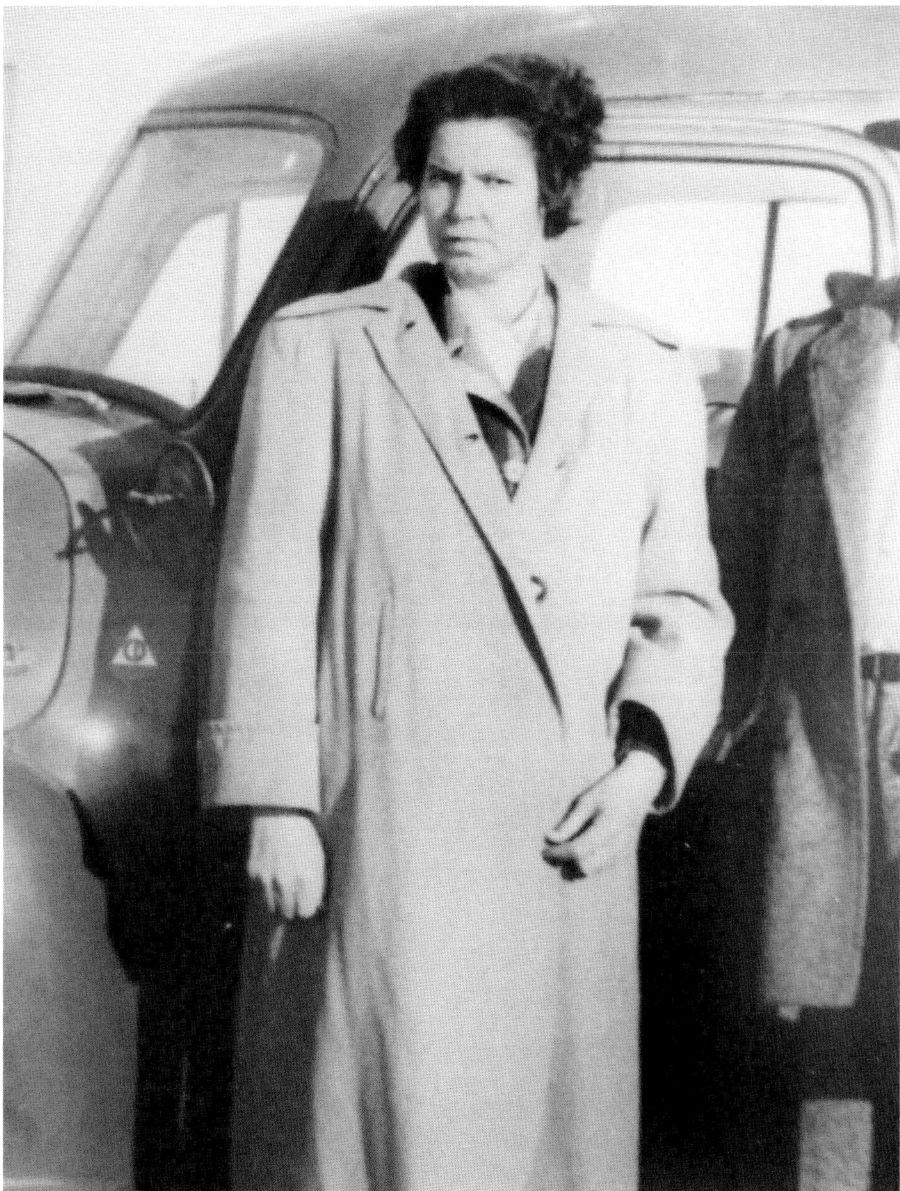

Elsie Oberg

Elsie Oberg was an educator and advocate for children. From the time she arrived on her Peters Creek homestead in 1952 until she died in 1977, Oberg served as Girl Scout leader, Little League coach, director of the Chugiak Benefit Association (which supports area charitable and educational groups), notoriously strict substitute teacher at Chugiak Elementary School, and PTA officer. She was an influential member of Operation Chugiak High School, a group that succeeded in bringing the area's first secondary school to completion in 1964. Oberg was elected to the school board of the short-lived Chugiak-Eagle River Borough, which fought to exist as a separate entity from Anchorage during the months of August 1974 to April 1975. All these things happened as she raised six children and ran a dairy farm with her husband, Russell. Today, residents know the old Chugiak Elementary School building by its official name, the Elsie Oberg Community Center. (Courtesy of the Chugiak-Eagle River Historical Society.)

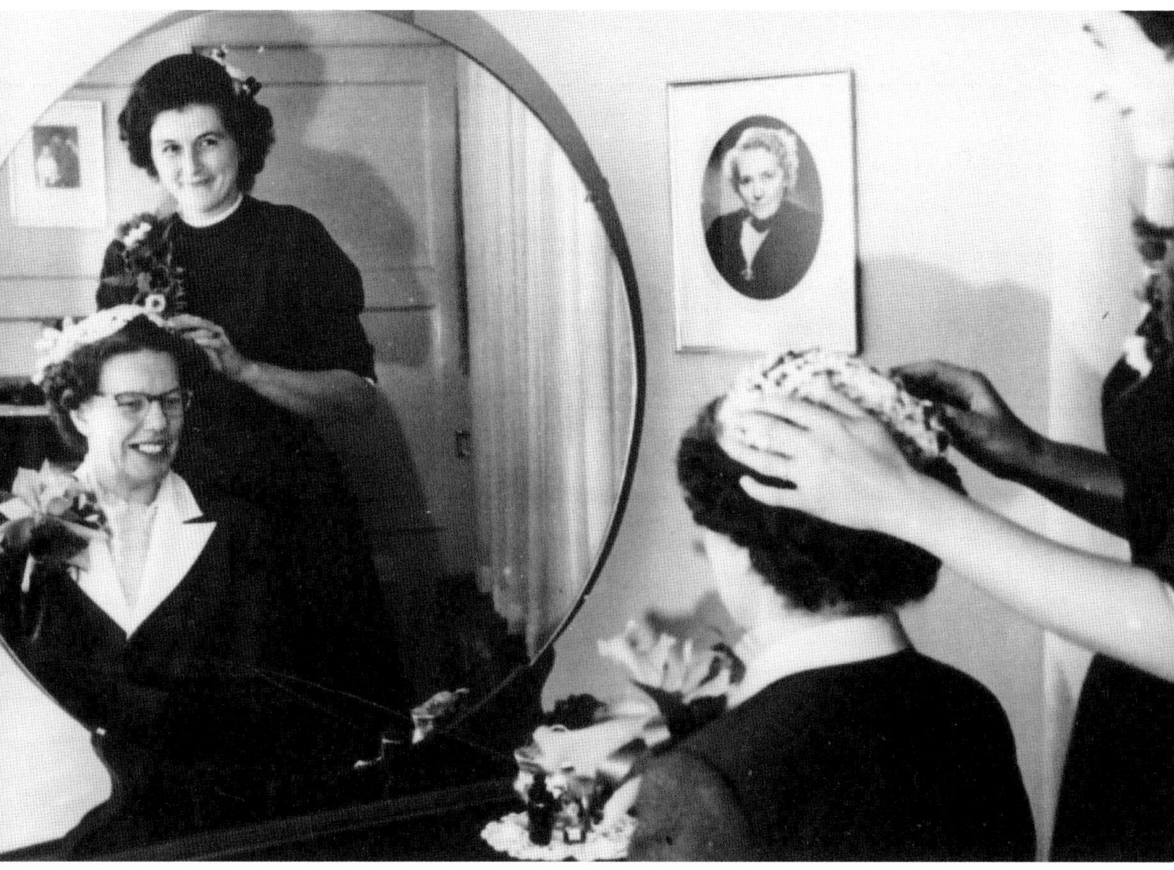

Pen Lee (ABOVE AND OPPOSITE PAGE)
Had there been elections in the early days of Chugiak, Pen Swanson Lee would have been a shoo-in for Miss Congeniality. Arriving in 1946 ahead of her brother Paul and sister-in-law Margaret Swanson, she was among Chugiak's first residents. She got to know nearly everyone in the area, communicating well despite the deafness she had experienced since childhood. Pen was popular in her civilian position on the military base. She worked in a variety of other jobs over the years, though most people remember her as Chugiak Elementary School's cook and a talented baker. Pen delighted in making cakes for weddings, birthdays, and military promotions. Airmen who earned another stripe could look forward to a chocolate cake with their name and the occasion inscribed in icing. Pen married Francis Lee in 1954. The couple loved nothing better than a good party and frequently invited friends to enjoy their basement pool. Francis died in 1972 at age 75. Pen lived on until age 91, passing away in 1998. She is pictured above with her sister-in-law, Margaret Swanson. (All, courtesy of the Chugiak-Eagle River Historical Society.)

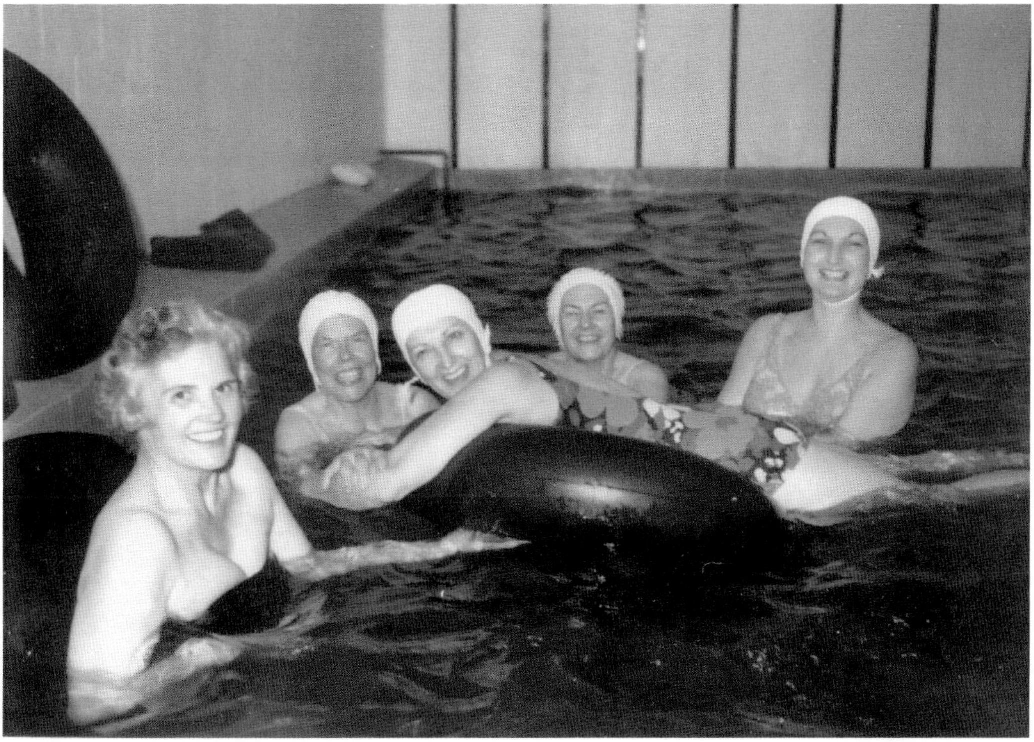

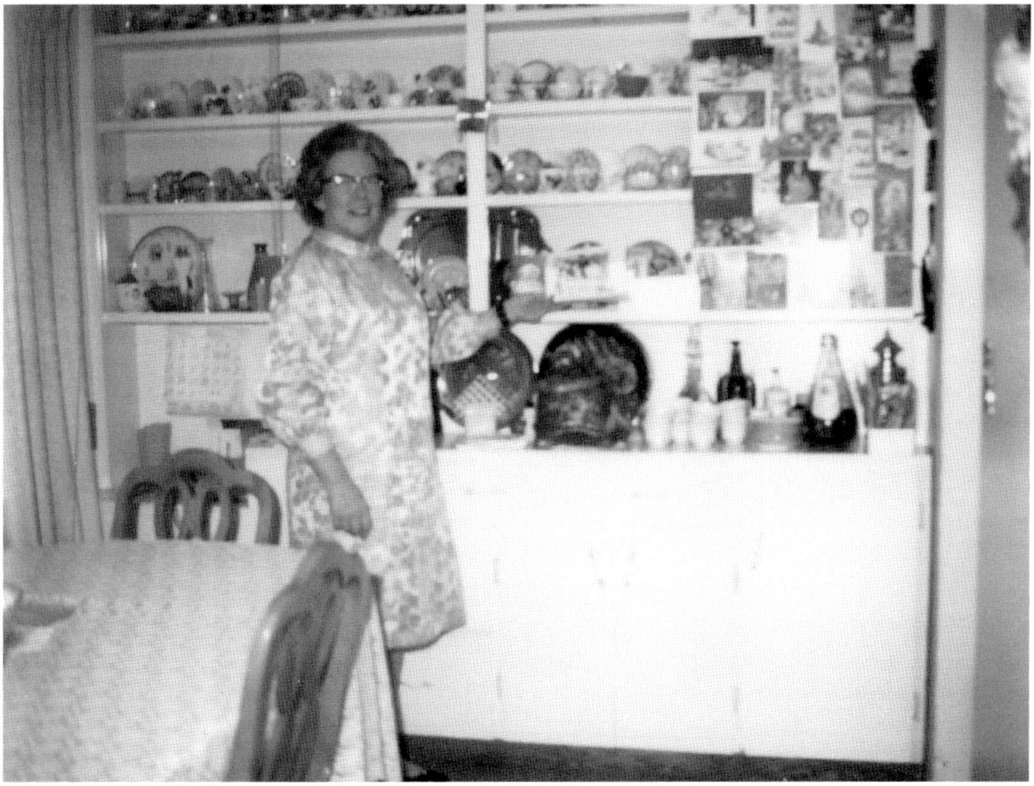

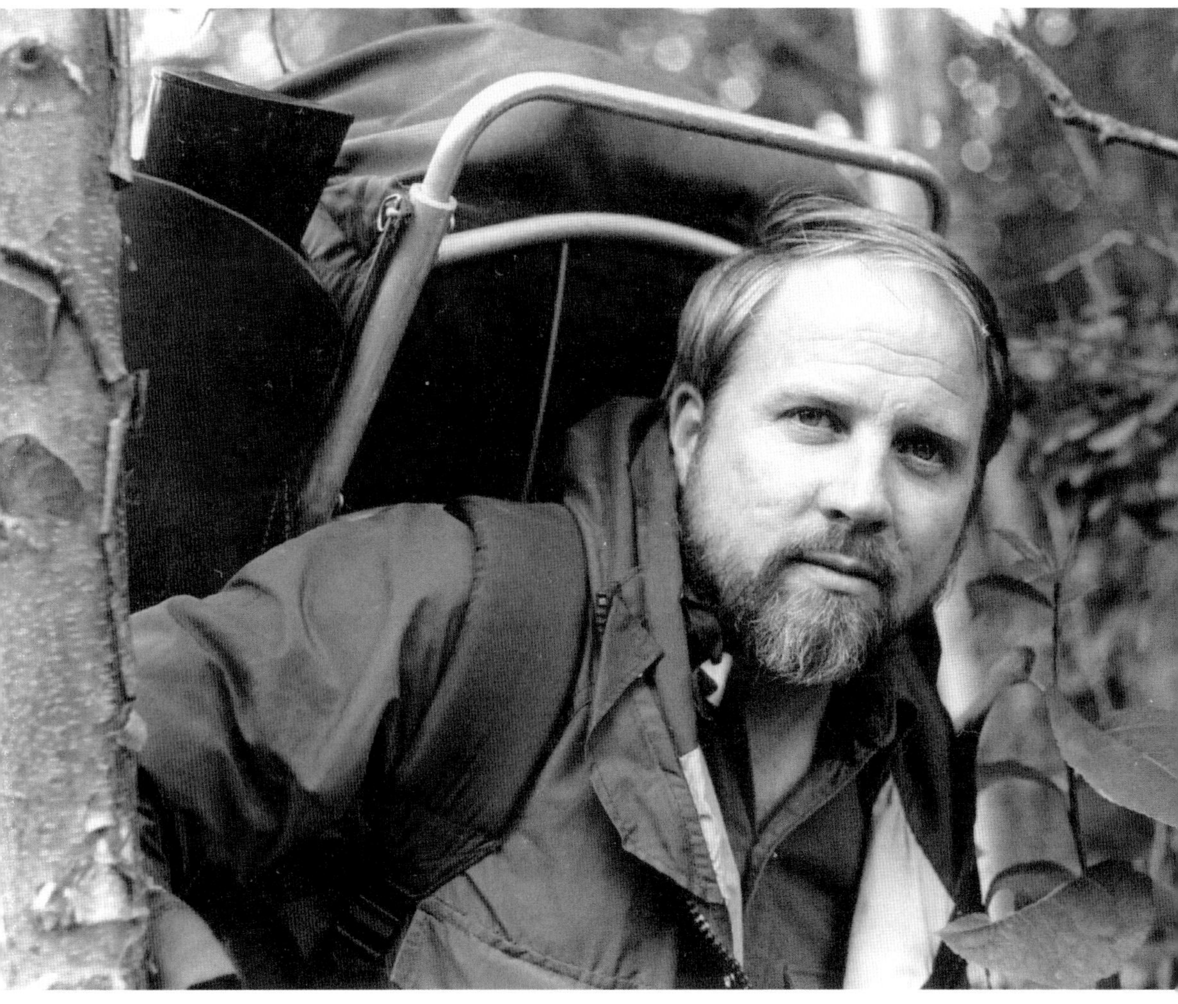

Gerry O'Connor

Gerry O'Connor represented Chugiak, Eagle River, and Mountain View on the Anchorage Assembly from 1979 to 1986, helping shape the city's growth during some of its stormiest years. He made sure his constituency reaped benefits from the oil boom, facilitating construction projects and road improvements throughout Chugiak-Eagle River. Prior to O'Connor's time on the assembly, he and wife Joyce helped bring a satellite campus of the University of Alaska Anchorage to Eagle River. O'Connor, an accountant and financial consultant by day, was an outdoorsman at heart and also owned a nonhunting guide business in the early 1970s. The O'Connors retired in Kameula, Hawaii, and Gerry passed away there in September 2005 at age 64. (Courtesy of the Chugiak-Eagle River Historical Society.)

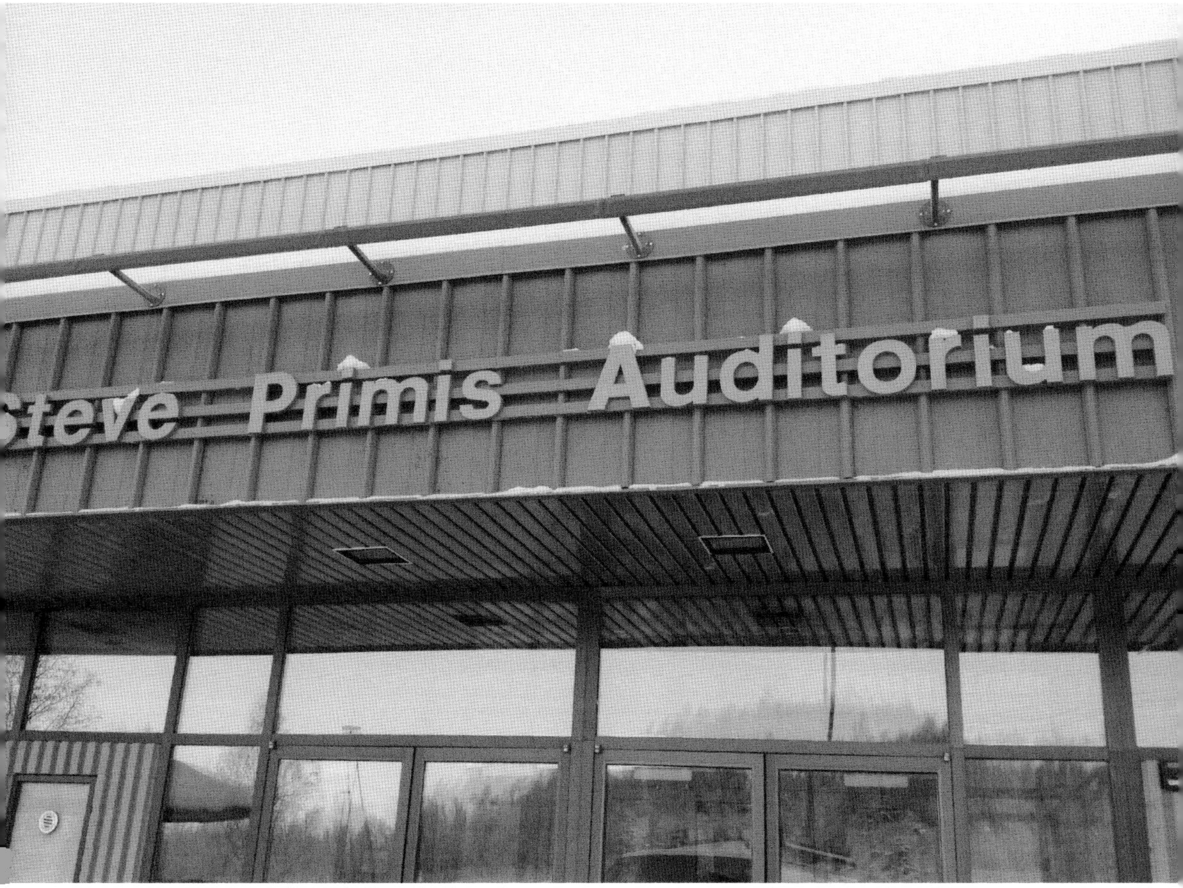

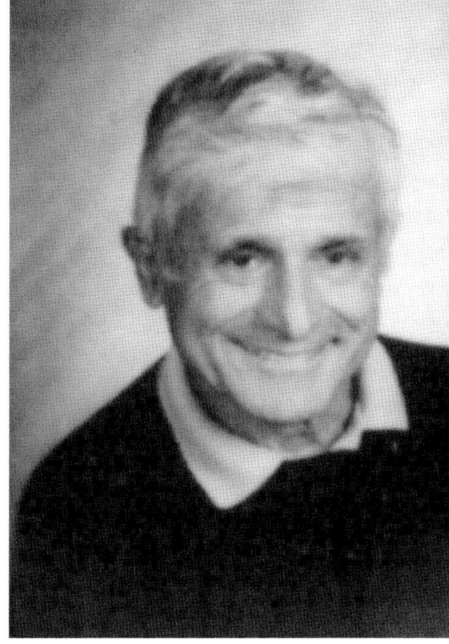

Steve Primis

Chugiak High School's auditorium bears the name of the late Steve Primis, a physical education teacher whose driving passion was dance. In young adulthood, Primis had danced professionally with the Chicago Opera Ballet, the Florentine Opera Company in Milwaukee, and on ABC-TV in Chicago. He had also performed and taught at Interlochen Arts Academy in Michigan. Primis moved to Alaska in 1971 and happily shared his talents and experience with the people of his adopted state—founding the dance department at University of Alaska Anchorage, directing the Academy of Classical Ballet in Anchorage with wife Diane, and giving life to the Primis Ballet Ensemble, an exclusive group that performed across the state. Primis also taught at the Alaska Fine Arts Camp and University of Alaska Summer Fine Arts Camp. Throughout all his dance-related activities, he continued providing a strong physical education program for his students at Chugiak. He retired from the school district in 1998 and passed away in 2001 at age 70. (Above, photograph by Chris Lundgren; right, courtesy of Chugiak High School.)

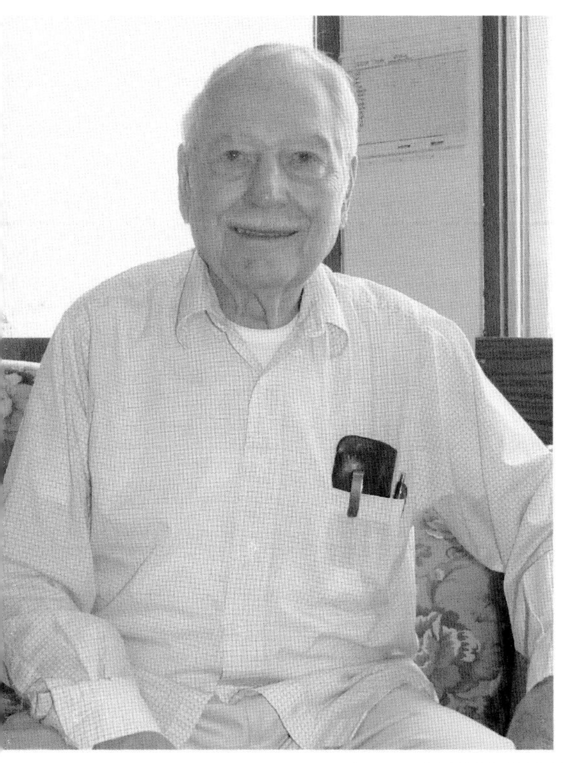

Ed Willis

Chugiak PTA president Ed Willis did not like the idea of sending local students all the way into Anchorage for high school. The 90-minute bus ride meant that all winter long, teens left home before sunrise and returned after sunset. Buses routinely skidded off glaciated roads. Students could not take part in extracurricular activities, and they had less time to study than their peers from Anchorage. So in the early 1960s, Willis and the PTA led a consortium of 26 service organizations to lobby the state legislature and prepare for a high school of their own. The group was called Operation Chugiak High School. Chairman Willis took turns with cochairman Dale Pierson flying to Juneau to seek funding for the proposed high school. They succeeded, and on September 15, 1964, Chugiak High School opened with 286 junior and senior high students. Willis went on to serve on the Alaska State Senate from 1974 to 1978 and in the House from 1992 to 1996. He and wife Joyce had five children. (Left, photograph by Chris Lundgren; below, courtesy of the Chugiak-Eagle River Historical Society.)

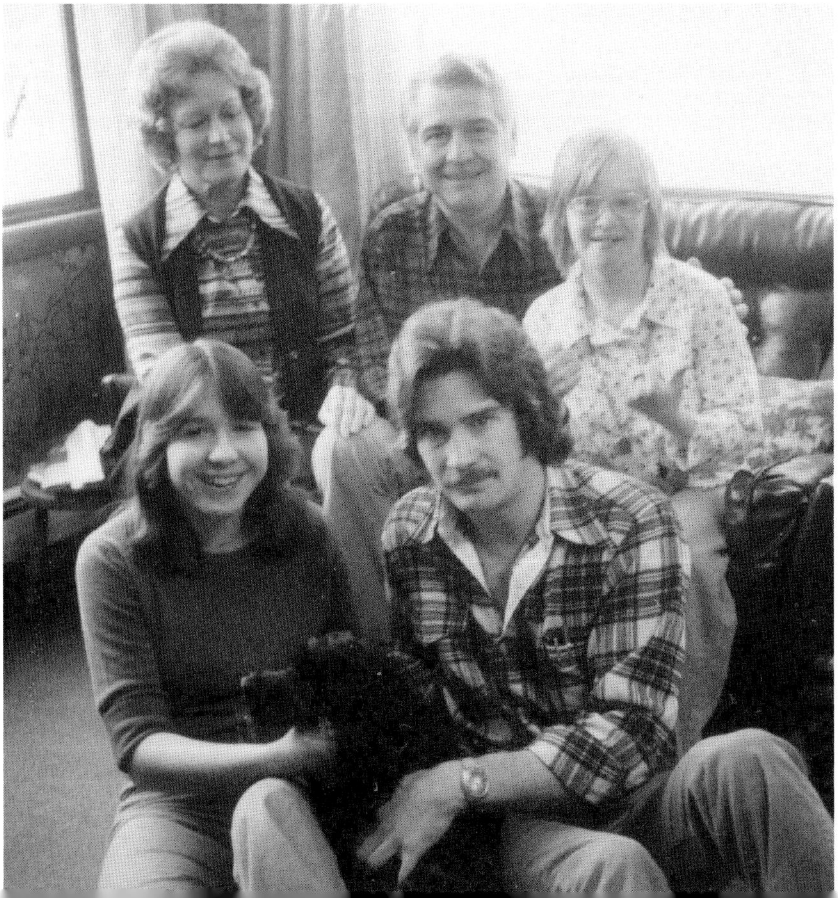

CHAPTER FOUR

Athletes, Coaches, and Supporters

For a young community, Chugiak-Eagle River has a sports legacy that runs deep. Quintessentially Alaskan sports such as Nordic skiing and dog mushing are often front-page news. The Eagle River Nordic Ski Club runs well-attended programs for adults and children both, and the Chugiak Dog Mushers Association has held races since it was founded more than 60 years ago. Team sports are popular, too. Chugiak-Eagle River athletes play hockey, soccer, baseball, hockey, football, basketball, hockey, volleyball, and hockey. Occasionally, someone is heard boasting about the area's two recent Olympic medalists—a trap shooter and, naturally, a hockey player—as well as the community's current WNBA player. Baseball is big, too, as Alaska's long summer evenings lend themselves to the sport. In fact, Knik Little League turned 50 years old in 2013. New on the scene is the Alaska Baseball League team the Chugiak-Eagle River Chinooks, which held its inaugural game in 2012 and has enticed hundreds of spectators to its games at Loretta French Sports Complex ever since. With so much enthusiasm, the sports scene in Chugiak-Eagle River can only get bigger and better.

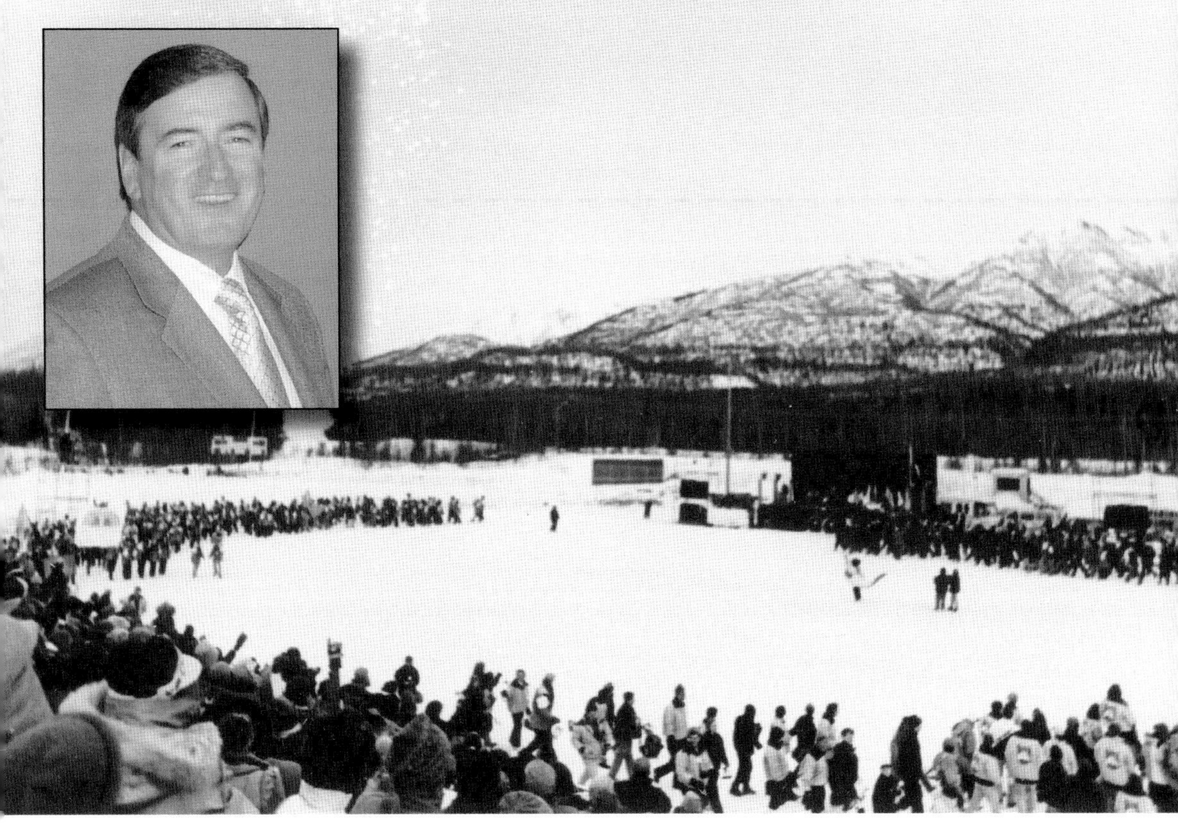

The Arctic Winter Games

Athletes from the world's northern regions came together in Eagle River, Chugiak, and occasionally Anchorage to compete in a medley of 19 sports during the Arctic Winter Games held March 2–8, 1996. In addition to Team Alaska's 325 athletes, representatives from Greenland, the Northwest Territories, Alberta, Yukon Territory, and Tyumen and Magadan of the Russian Federation took part, bringing the total number of competitors to 1,525. Cheap ticket prices drew thousands of spectators to a quirky selection of sports: one day's schedule listed wrestling, snowshoe biathlon, indoor soccer, speed skating, and table tennis. Fans bought official Arctic Winter Games merchandise galore, and profits from the event helped fund the Chugiak-Eagle River Foundation, which awards scholarships and grants to local students and nonprofits. Current Anchorage mayor Dan Sullivan (inset) served as executive director of the 1996 Arctic Winter Games. (Above, courtesy of the Chugiak-Eagle River Historical Society; inset, courtesy of the mayor's office, Municipality of Anchorage.)

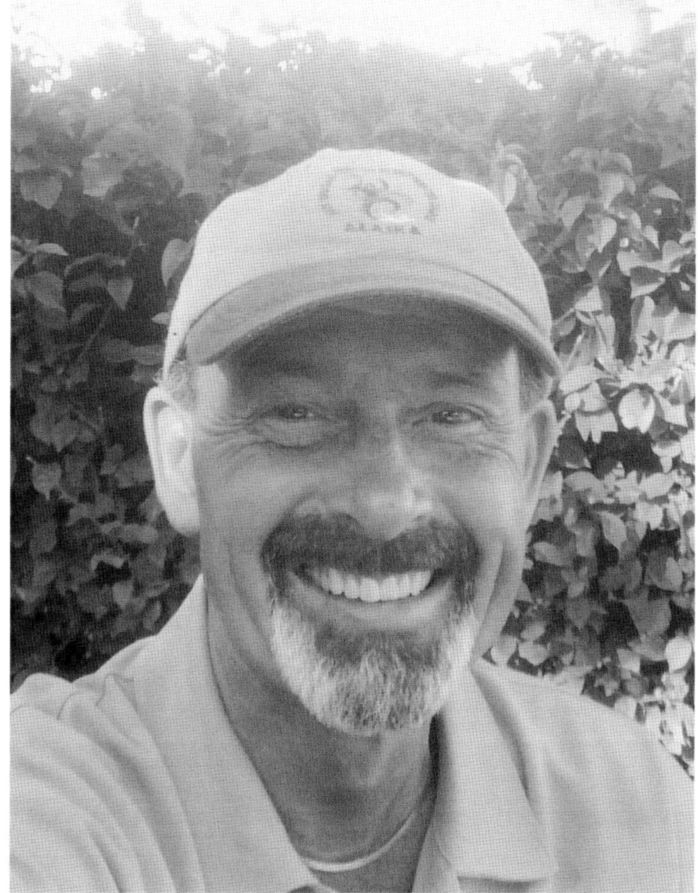

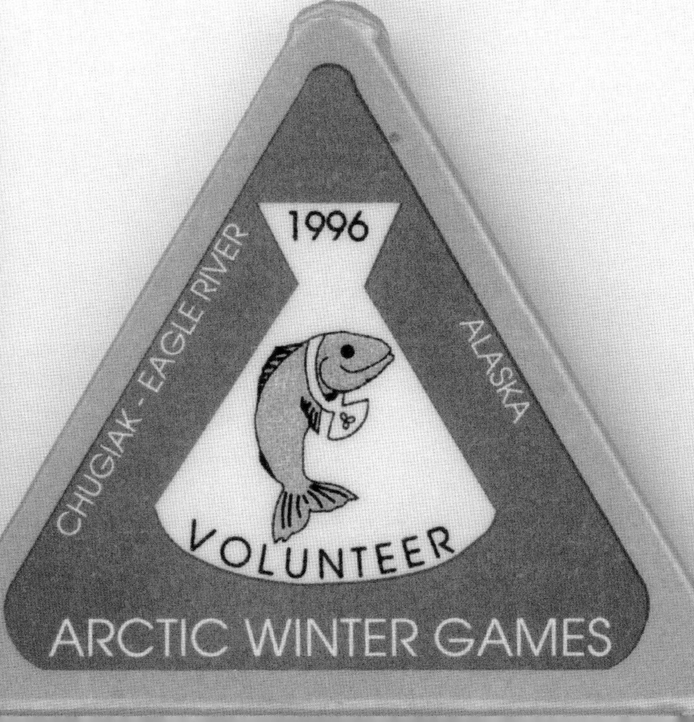

John Rodda

Sometimes when locals open their mouths to say, "Parks and Rec," the name "John Rodda" comes out instead. To many, the two terms are synonymous. Rodda has been the driving force behind Chugiak-Eagle River's recreational facilities and community development since 1997. He has held the director's position for Parks and Recreation both in Eagle River and Anchorage since 2002. His collaboration with the Chugiak-Eagle River community has led to the development of and improvements to many public facilities, including the Oberg Soccer Fields, Eagle River Commons and Town Square Parks, Loretta French Park Ball Fields, and Eagle River Town Center. Previously, he was involved in the development, construction, and management of the Fire Lake Recreation Center (now the Harry J. McDonald Memorial Center) in Eagle River.

Rodda and Susie Gorski, executive director of the Chugiak-Eagle River Chamber of Commerce, wrote the bid for Chugiak-Eagle River to host the 1996 Arctic Winter Games, and Rodda served from 1993 to 1996 as host-society president for the games. He is also a longtime director on the Arctic Winter Games International Committee, representing the state of Alaska and areas south of the Alaska Range. (Top, courtesy of John Rodda; bottom, courtesy of the Chugiak-Eagle River Historical Society.)

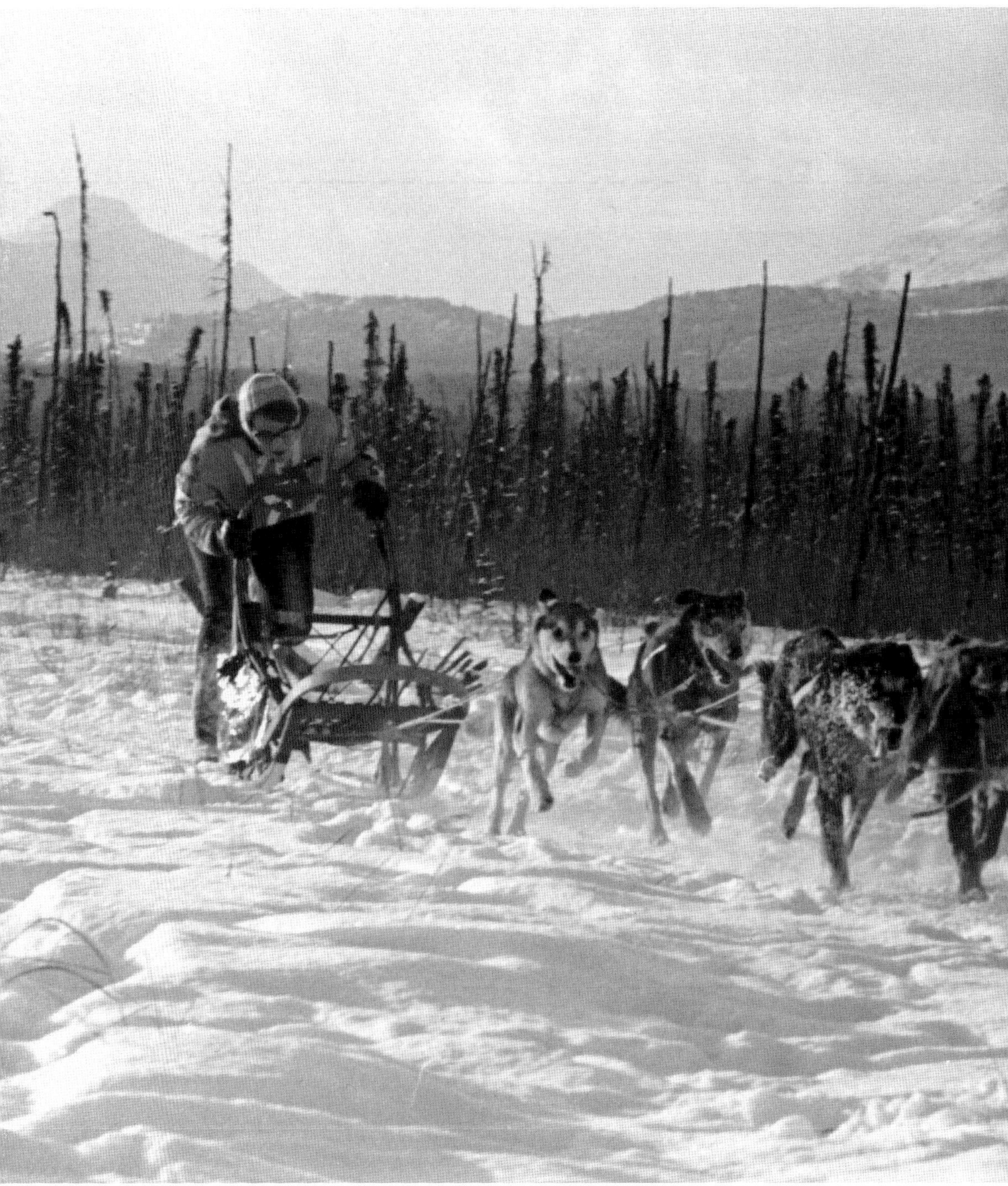

Shirley Gavin

Eagle River's Shirley Gavin earned a place in the international spotlight in 1966, 1969, and 1970 by winning the Women's World Championship Sled Dog Races held in Anchorage. Her record-breaking lead dog was an Irish setter named Blaze who doubled as the family pet. Gavin started mushing in 1961 at the behest of her husband, Myron, who was her chief supporter. According to Shirley, Myron built

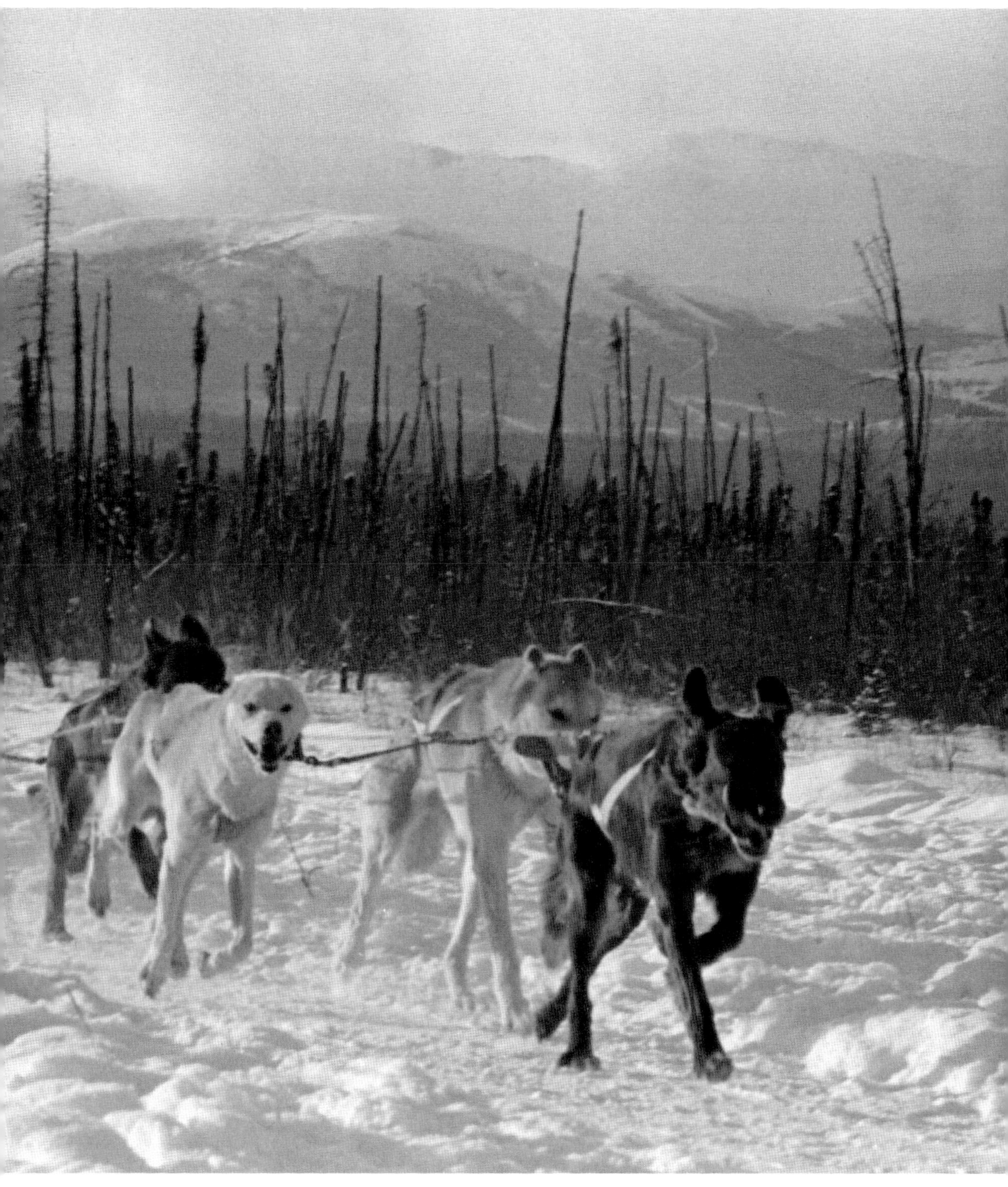

her sleds, fashioned harnesses for the dogs, and did all the repair work. Myron and others founded the Chugiak Dog Mushers Association in 1950. He also owned a successful breeding and training operation called Tuffluk Kennels. Myron passed away in 2003 at age 74. Shirley still lives in Eagle River, though she cares for a pair of little Westies now instead of a kennel of sled dogs. (Courtesy of Shirley Gavin.)

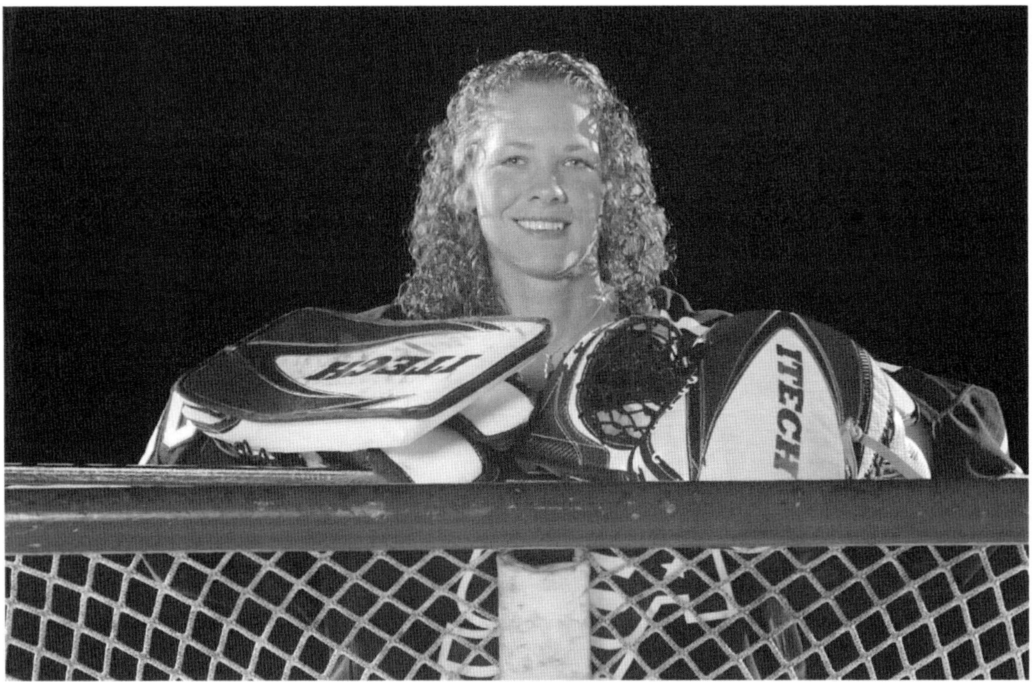

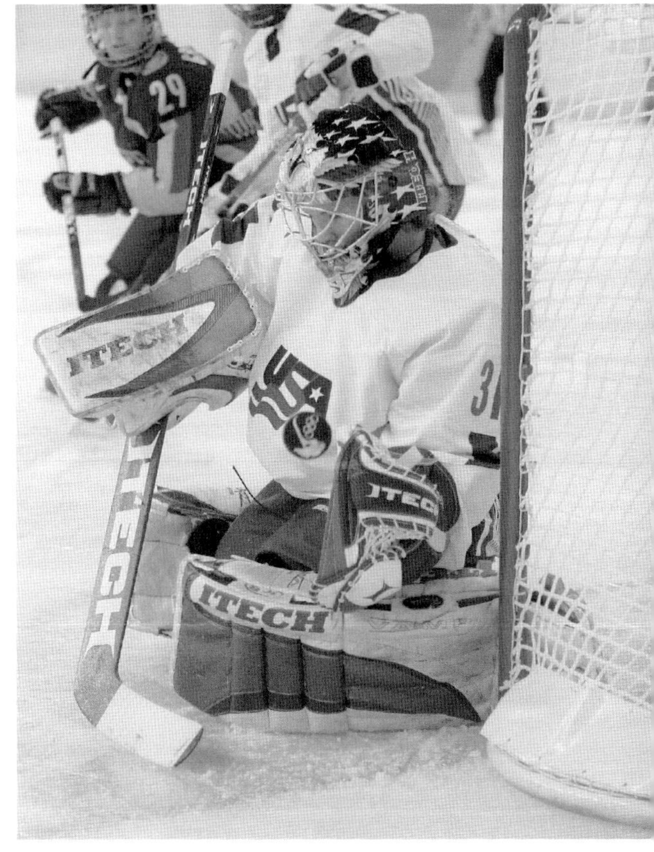

Pam Dreyer
Pam Dreyer was a starting goalie for the Chugiak Mustangs and team MVP as a senior in 1999. She led her Brown University team to the 2002 Eastern College Athletic Conference Championship and a berth in the national championship game. She tore her rotator cuff in 2004 and endured two surgeries and months of rehabilitation at the Olympic Training Center in Lake Placid, New York. Despite the huge setback, Dreyer rallied; in 2006, at age 24, she was part of the US women's hockey team that won a bronze in the Olympics at Turin, Italy. She played 60 minutes and had 10 saves. Nowadays, Dreyer lives in Eagle River and works as a health and safety advisor for BP out of the company's Anchorage office. (Courtesy of USA Hockey.)

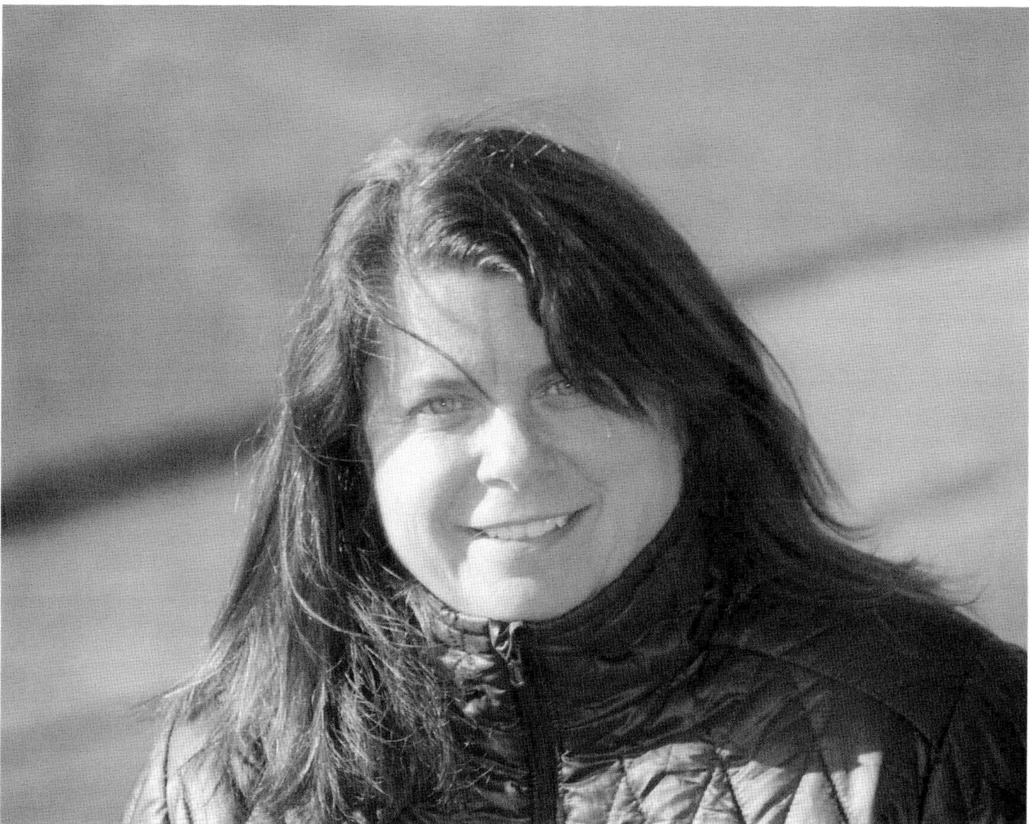

Holly Odegard

Holly Odegard wants children to develop a lifelong love of sports and recreation. In fact, it is her mission. Odegard has cast a wide net over athletics in Alaska. As one of the founders of the Chugiak Youth Sports Association, she ran the group's original soccer and basketball programs in the 1990s. She has taught physical education at Gruening Middle School in Eagle River for 15 years and has coached middle school soccer, volleyball, basketball, and track as well as high school soccer and cross-country running. She heads up the Adventure Program after school at Gruening to introduce students (mostly from military families) to new activities. Odegard's 20-year involvement with Arctic Winter Games began in 1994 when she coordinated the soccer venue for the 1996 games in Chugiak-Eagle River. Many roles followed, including *chef de mission* (team leader), assistant chef, mission staff, and Team Alaska Board of Directors member. Most recently, she was sport manager for the 2014 games in Fairbanks and oversaw all 20 of the tournament's sports. (Courtesy of Holly Odegard.)

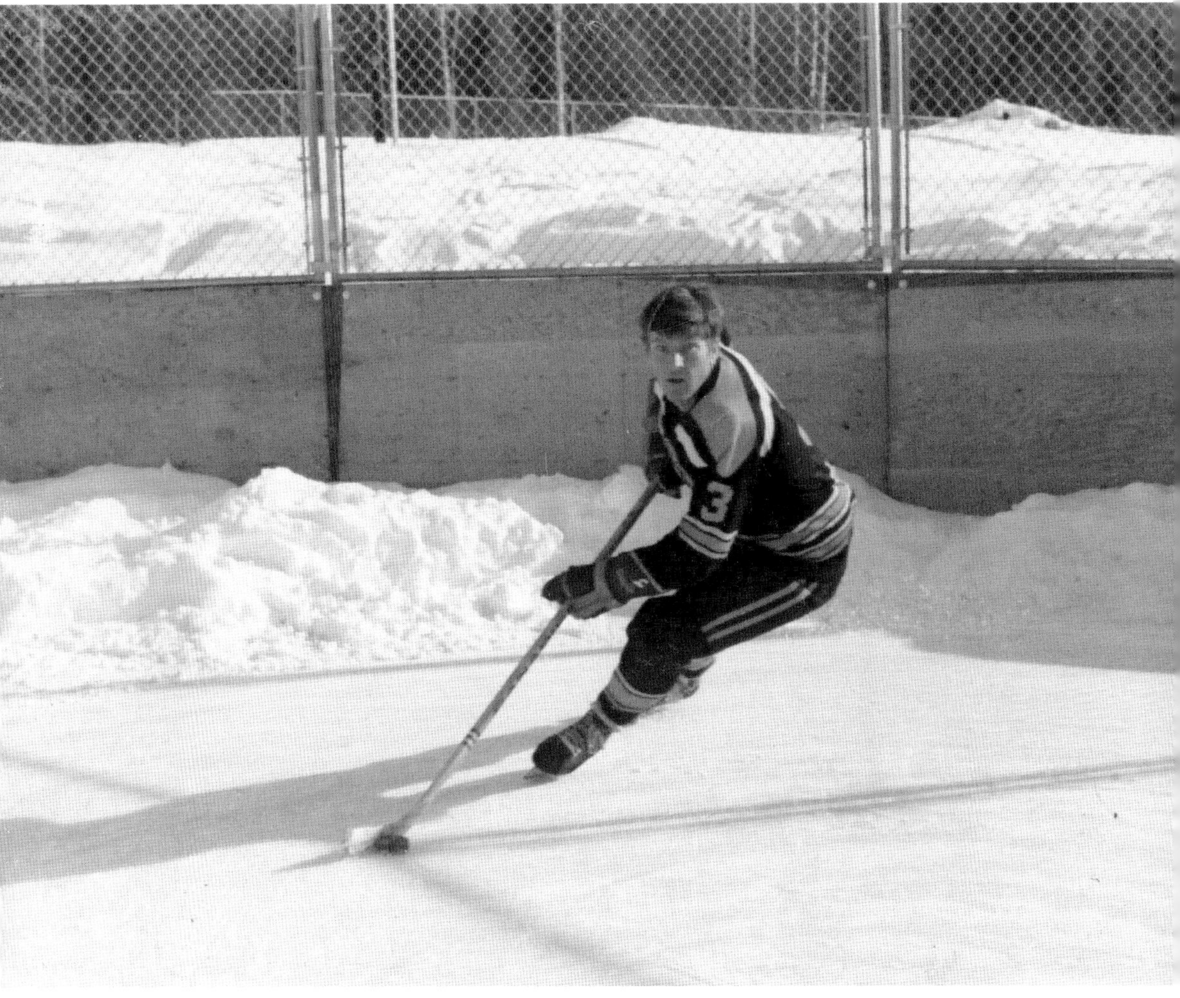

Harry McDonald

Harry J. McDonald, affectionately known to thousands of athletes as "Coach Mac," is considered the father of hockey in Chugiak-Eagle River. McDonald served as a teacher and coach at Chugiak High School for 27 years. In the early 1980s, he helped establish the Mustang Hockey Association for kids and was instrumental in the building of the Fire Lake Recreation Center, whose Olympic-sized rink kept players from having to travel to Anchorage for practices and games. Soon after Coach Mac's death in

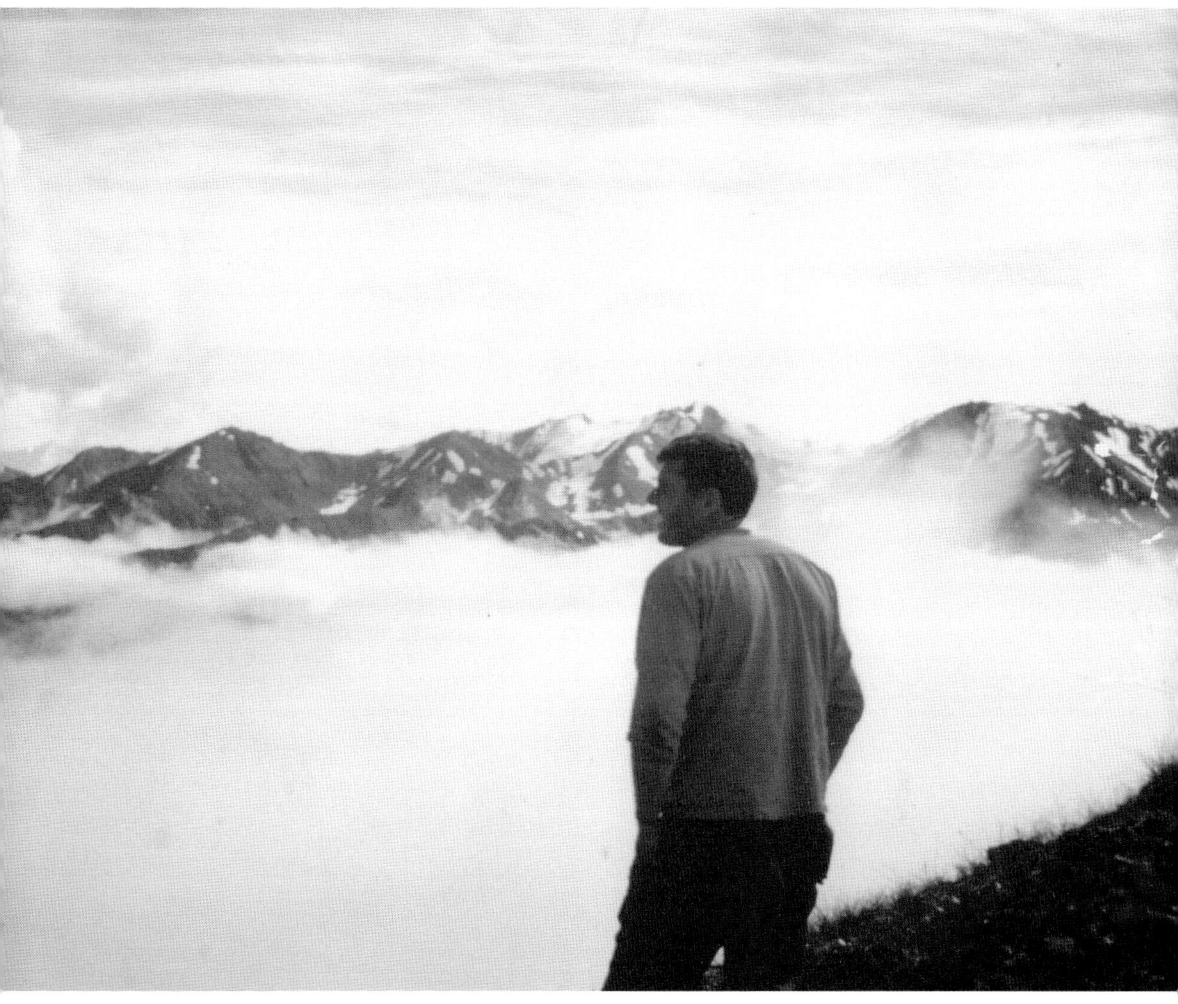

a small plane crash in 1994, the community rechristened the facility the Harry J. McDonald Memorial Center. Both Mustang Hockey and the memorial center have burgeoned, and the center now includes a multiuse indoor turf field. Coach Mac's legacy lives on in other ways. Son Reid McDonald has been general manager of the center since 1997, and all eight of Harry's grandchildren play or have played hockey. Coach Mac posthumously received the 2012 Walter Yaciuk Award from USA Hockey for his outstanding contribution to coaching. (Both, courtesy of Carole McDonald.)

Tom Huffer Sr. and Tom Huffer Jr.

"Huffer" is a well-known name among Chugiak High School sports fans. After all, their stadium is named after Tom Huffer Sr., the school's first football coach, whose career began in 1969 and spanned nearly two decades. Huffer's teams gained traction in the late 1970s, and from 1979 until 1989, he led them to three Cook Inlet Conference Championships, two state titles, and three second-place finishes. He also helped develop wrestling in the state, having coached the sport and served as head of the Anchorage Wrestling Officials Association from 1982 to 1995. Son Tom Huffer Jr. earned 10 letters in football, wrestling, and track in his four years of high school in the 1980s. He was part of the powerhouse football team that his father coached, playing tight end, linebacker, and placekicker and earning a spot on the all-state football team in all three positions in 1983 and 1984. As a kicker, Huffer Jr. was 17-of-25 for his career. Huffer Jr. has coached track and serves as Chugiak's head wrestling coach. He helped lead Mustang wrestlers to four of five region titles and one state title in 2002. The Huffers were inducted into the Alaska High School Hall of Fame in 2006 (Huffer Sr.) and 2011 (Huffer Jr.), the first father-son duo to gain the distinction. (Photograph by Stella Huffer.)

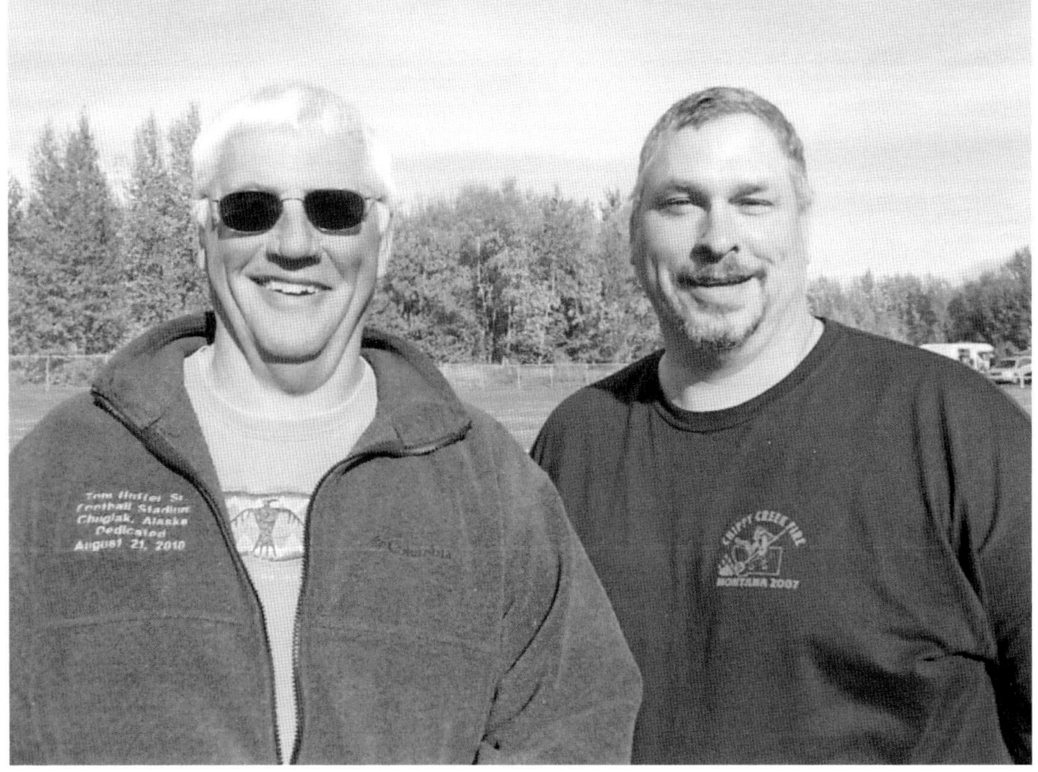

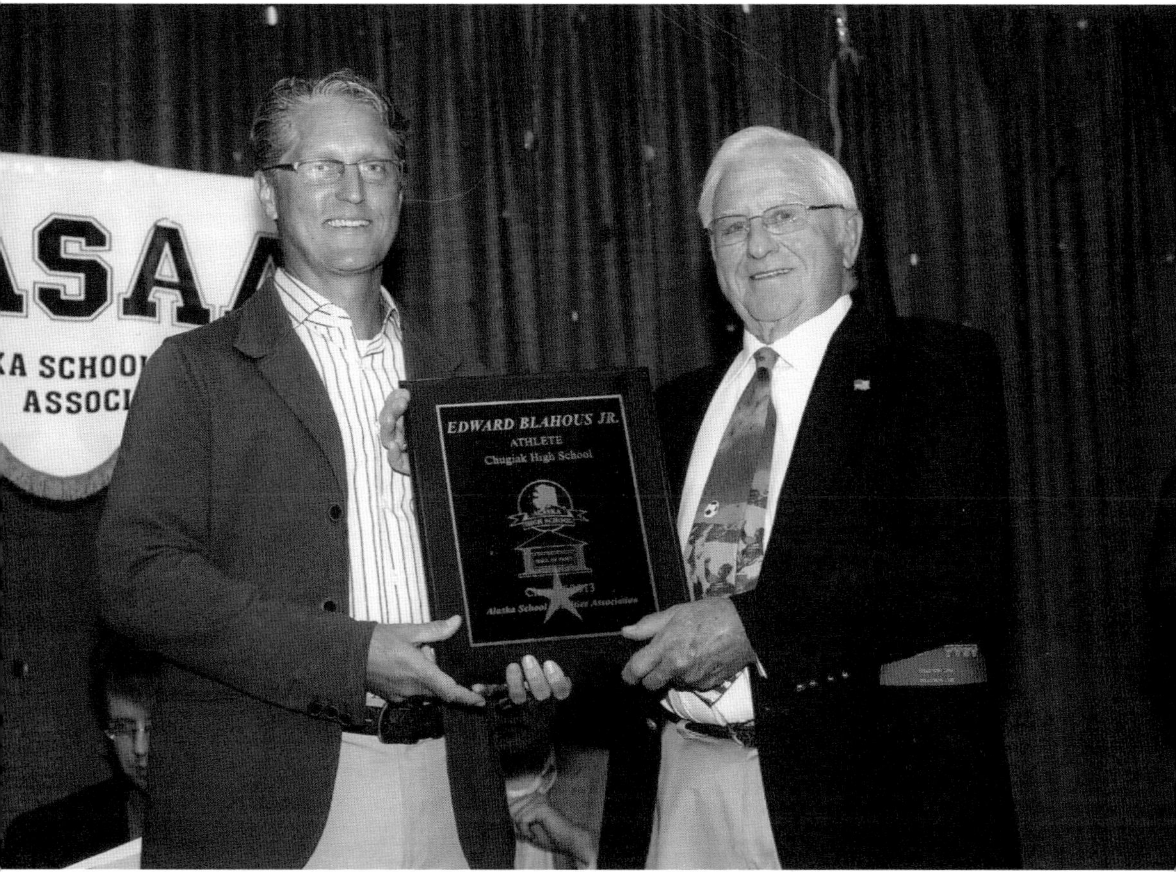

Edward Blahous Sr. and Edward Blahous Jr.

Ed Blahous and Edward Blahous Jr. were inducted into the Alaska High School Hall of Fame in 2012 and 2013. The elder Blahous coached varsity soccer at Chugiak from 1983 to 2002, leading his teams to win eight state titles. Known as a motivator, teacher, and even a father figure to his players, Blahous also received an Anchorage Father of the Year award in the 1980s. Son Edward Jr. ("Eddie") was among Blahous's standouts and also lettered in basketball and football. He was named to the All-Region Boys Soccer Team from 1983 to 1985 and went on to play at Seattle Pacific University (SPU) and was a member of the NCAA D-II National Championship team. Eddie graduated cum laude from SPU and magna cum laude from California College of Podiatric Medicine, his love of sports accompanying him all the way. He is now the chief podiatrist at the Seattle Sports Medicine Clinic in Washington. Ed's wife and Eddie's mother is fellow legendary local Emily Blahous. (Courtesy of the Blahous family.)

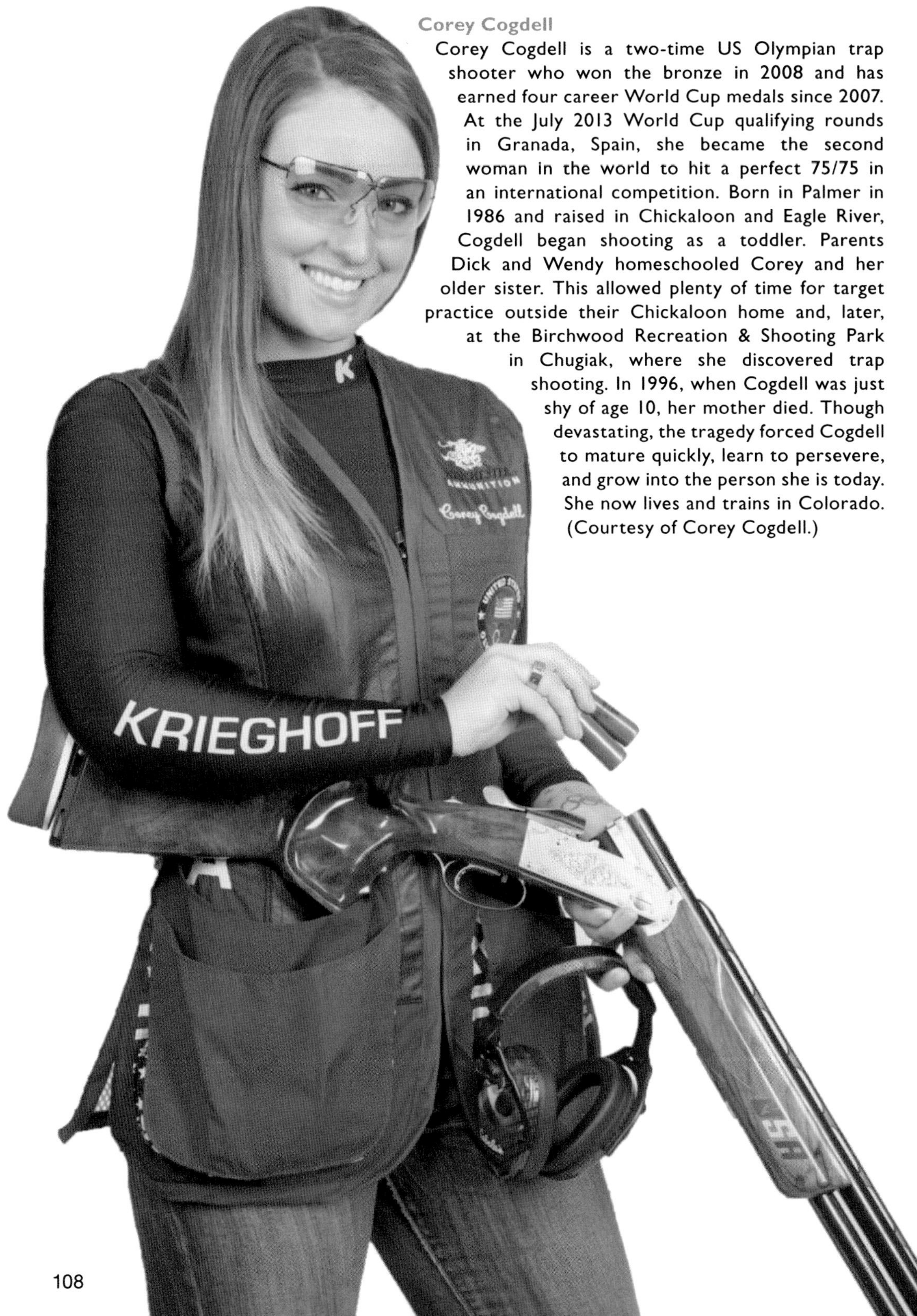

Corey Cogdell

Corey Cogdell is a two-time US Olympian trap shooter who won the bronze in 2008 and has earned four career World Cup medals since 2007. At the July 2013 World Cup qualifying rounds in Granada, Spain, she became the second woman in the world to hit a perfect 75/75 in an international competition. Born in Palmer in 1986 and raised in Chickaloon and Eagle River, Cogdell began shooting as a toddler. Parents Dick and Wendy homeschooled Corey and her older sister. This allowed plenty of time for target practice outside their Chickaloon home and, later, at the Birchwood Recreation & Shooting Park in Chugiak, where she discovered trap shooting. In 1996, when Cogdell was just shy of age 10, her mother died. Though devastating, the tragedy forced Cogdell to mature quickly, learn to persevere, and grow into the person she is today. She now lives and trains in Colorado. (Courtesy of Corey Cogdell.)

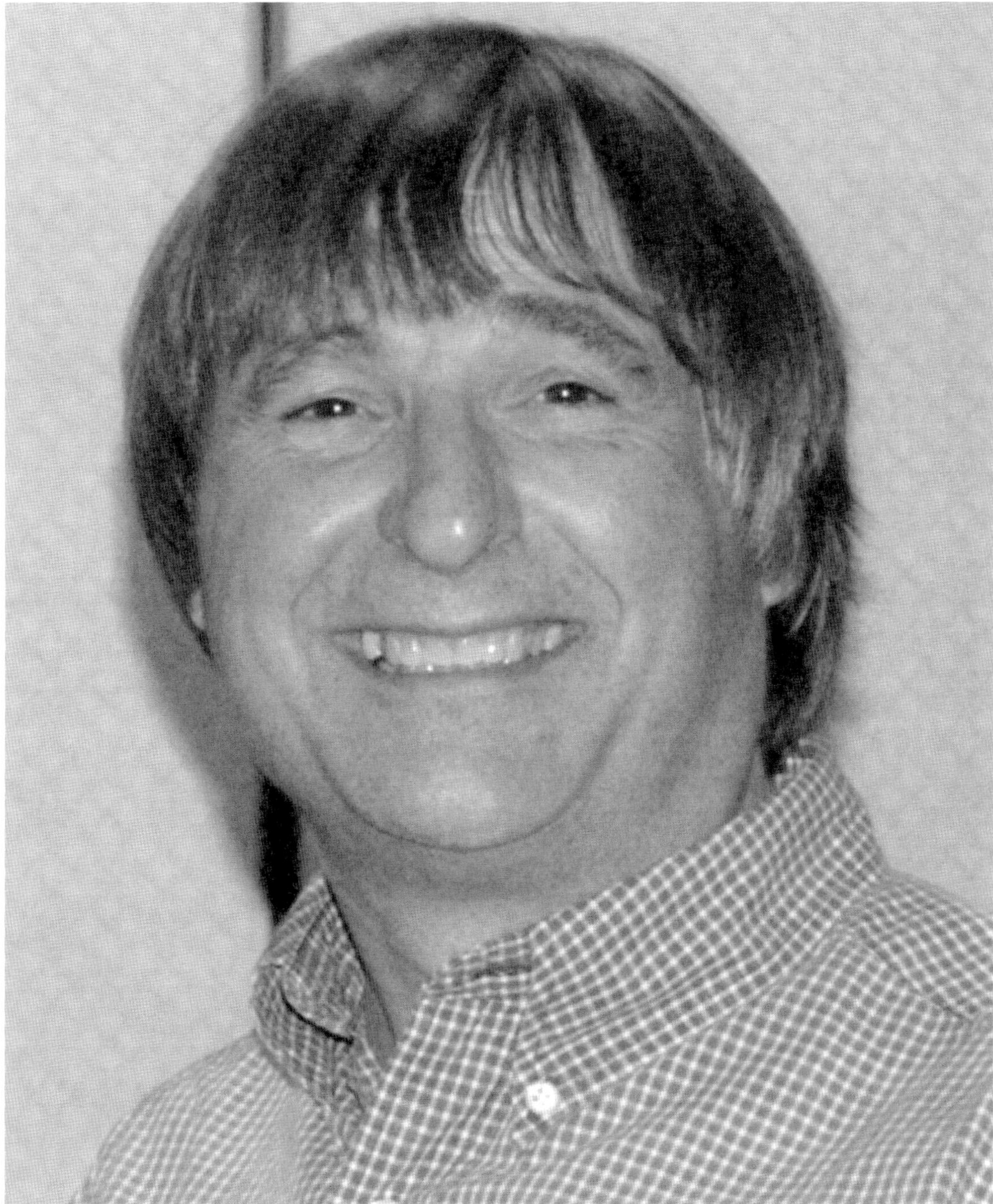

Paul Brauneis

Extreme coaching success landed Chugiak alum Paul Brauneis in the Alaska High School Hall of Fame in 2012. As head of his alma mater's varsity hockey program from 1984 to 1994, Brauneis transformed the team from a 37-229 record to a 149-100 record and was named State Coach of the Year three times over. The Mustangs collected three state titles and one conference championship during his tenure. Brauneis was also assistant varsity football coach at Chugiak from 1981 to 1988, and teams under him won state championships in 1984 and 1988. Brauneis teaches math at Chugiak and serves as the school's athletic director, Anchorage School District hockey program coordinator, and tournament director for Alaska State Activities Association hockey and football. (Courtesy of Brauneis family.)

Mark Hufford

Mark Hufford's image is etched in the collective memory of Chugiak-Eagle River: a hand cyclist who apparently knew only one speed—fast—rocketing around town, black curls flying out from under his helmet. The 1989 Chugiak High graduate suffered an accident while bear hunting in 1995, leaving him paraplegic and later requiring the amputation of his legs. Despite his challenges, Hufford earned a bachelor's degree in human services from University of Alaska Anchorage in 2000. He worked as a

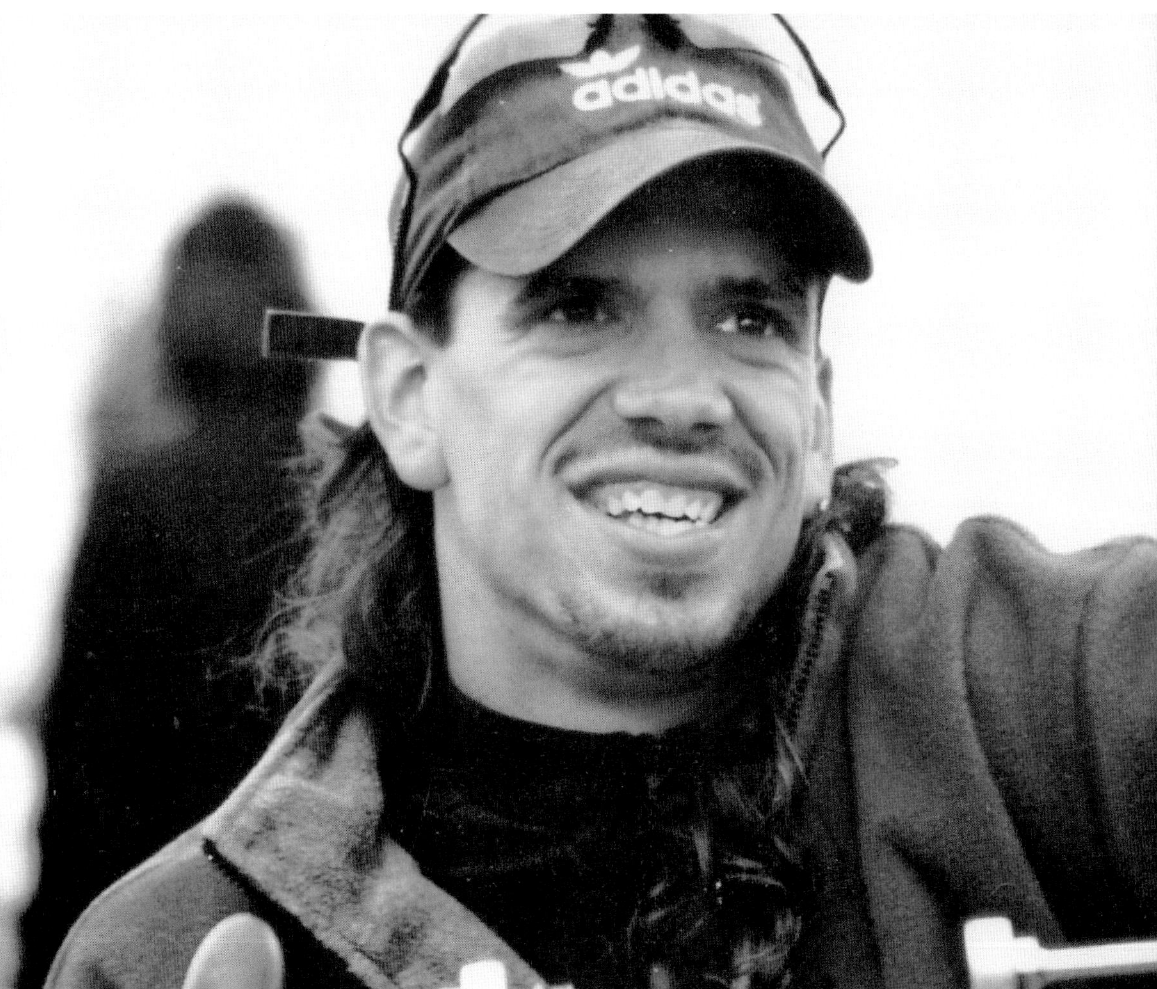

counselor with the Alaska Division of Vocational Rehabilitation from 2004 to 2011, helping others with disabilities find and maintain work. His clients there were inspired by his participation in the Sadler's Alaska Challenge, a weeklong, 267-mile race between Fairbanks and Anchorage. Hufford participated seven times between 1999 and 2007 and twice won the race's Speedy Sourdough Award for being the fastest Alaskan. He died at age 40 in January 2011. The Mark Hufford Trail along Eagle River Loop Road was established in April that same year to commemorate him. (Both, courtesy of the Hufford family.)

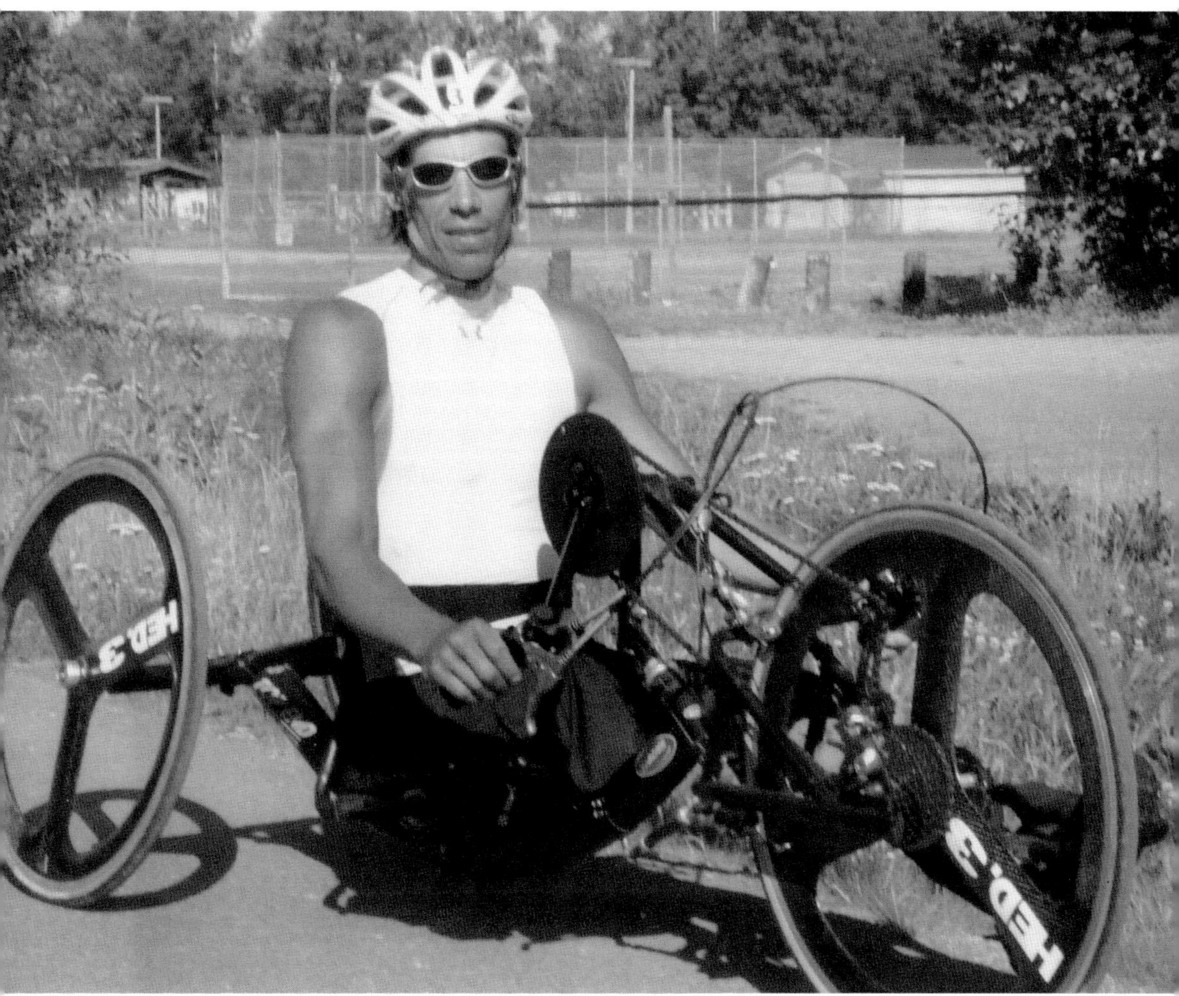

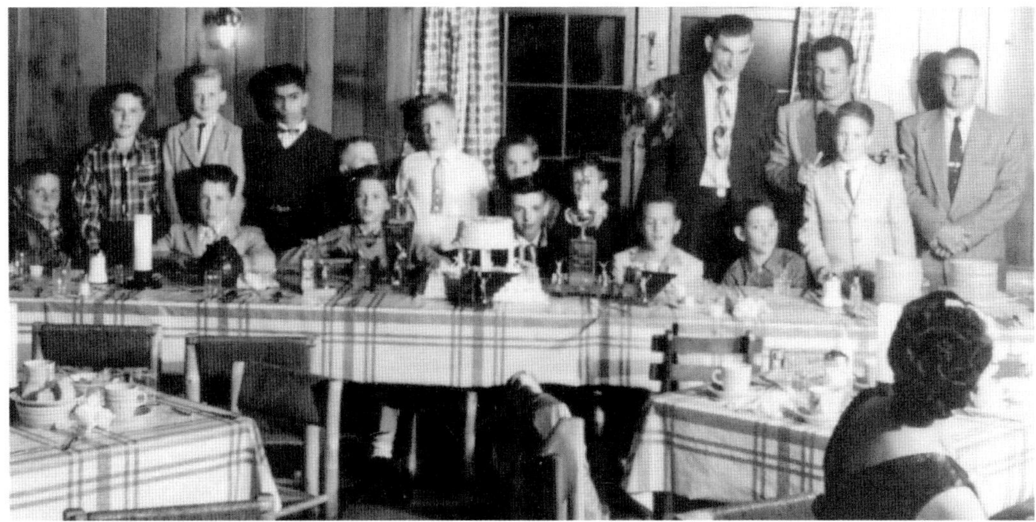

Knik Little League

Knik Little League celebrated half a century of baseball in 2013. Del Spellman and Lee Jordan were president and vice president of the league back in 1963 when there were only four teams. Over time, the league mushroomed to 43 teams, and it now boasts nearly 500 players. The name "Knik" of course represents the Knik Arm of the Cook Inlet, but it also represents a compromise between Chugiak and Eagle River about which place the league would be named after. The original Knik ballpark stood where the Chugiak-Eagle River Senior Center is now, though players used the fields at Chugiak and Eagle River Elementary Schools as well. Former Anchorage Assembly member Dan Kendall has been the league president since 2008. Above is the first Knik Little League banquet, in 1963. Below, from left to right, are coaches Bud Fillmore, Tom Slanker, and Rodger Jonrowe. (Both, courtesy of Chugiak-Eagle River Historical Society.)

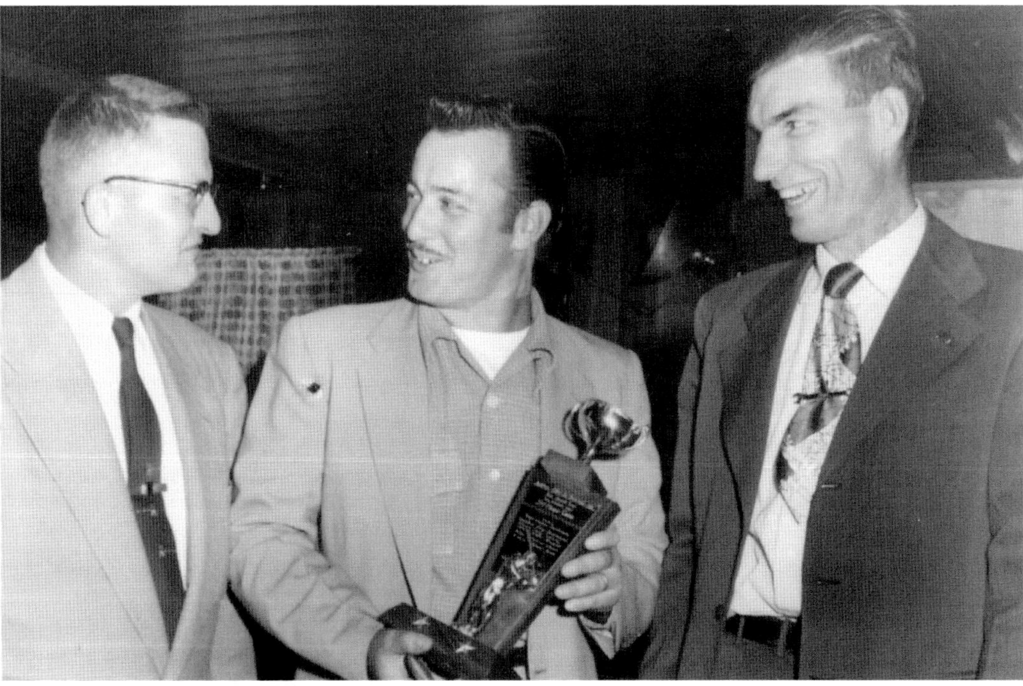

Chugiak-Eagle River Chinooks

Although the Chugiak-Eagle River Chinooks only recently arrived in the area, the Alaska Baseball League team has left an indelible mark on local sports. The Chinooks played their inaugural game against the Anchorage Glacier Pilots in June 2012 and have continued to pack the stands at Loretta French Sports Complex ever since. The team is made up of NCAA players from around the country. Players raise their own funds to defray the team's travel costs, while the Chugiak-Eagle River Chinooks Booster Club, headed by Lee Jordan, fills in the gaps and whips up fan support. Pictured below is the 2013 Military Appreciation Day. (Courtesy of Lee Jordan.)

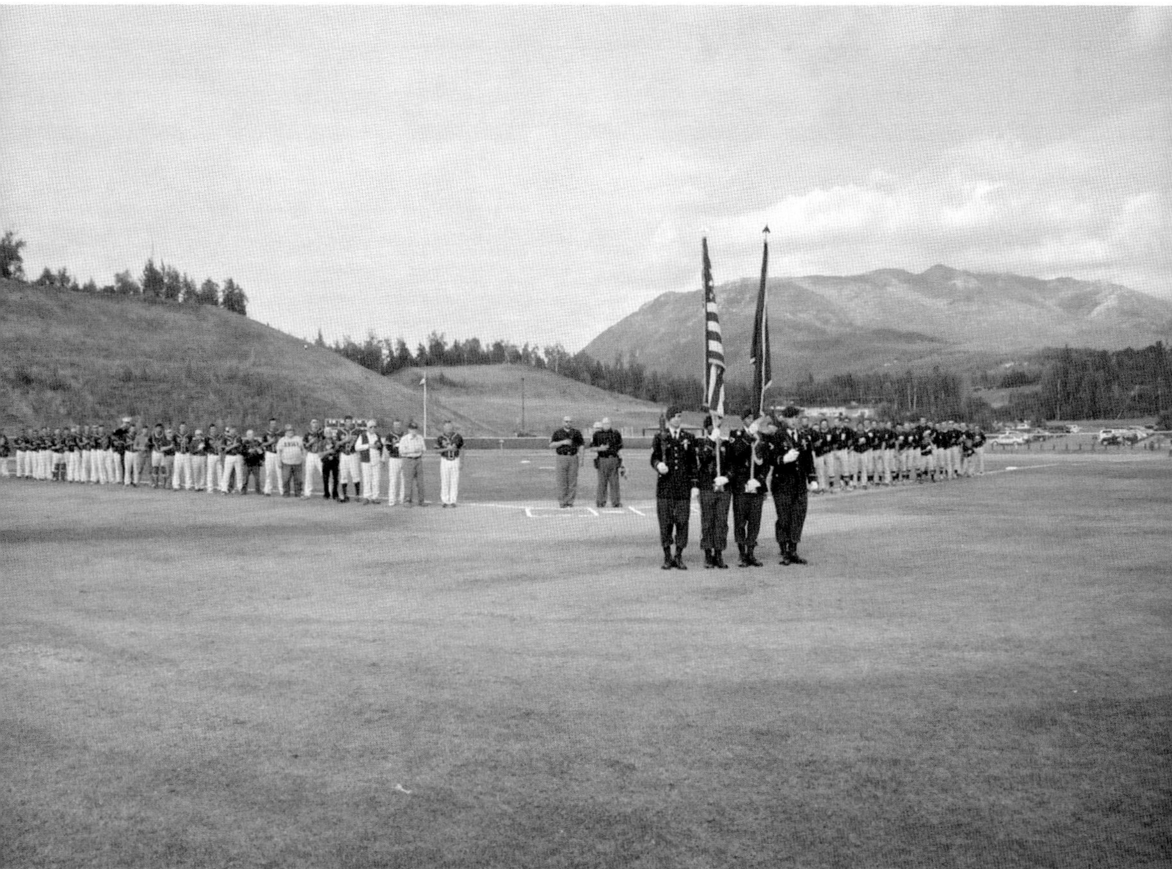

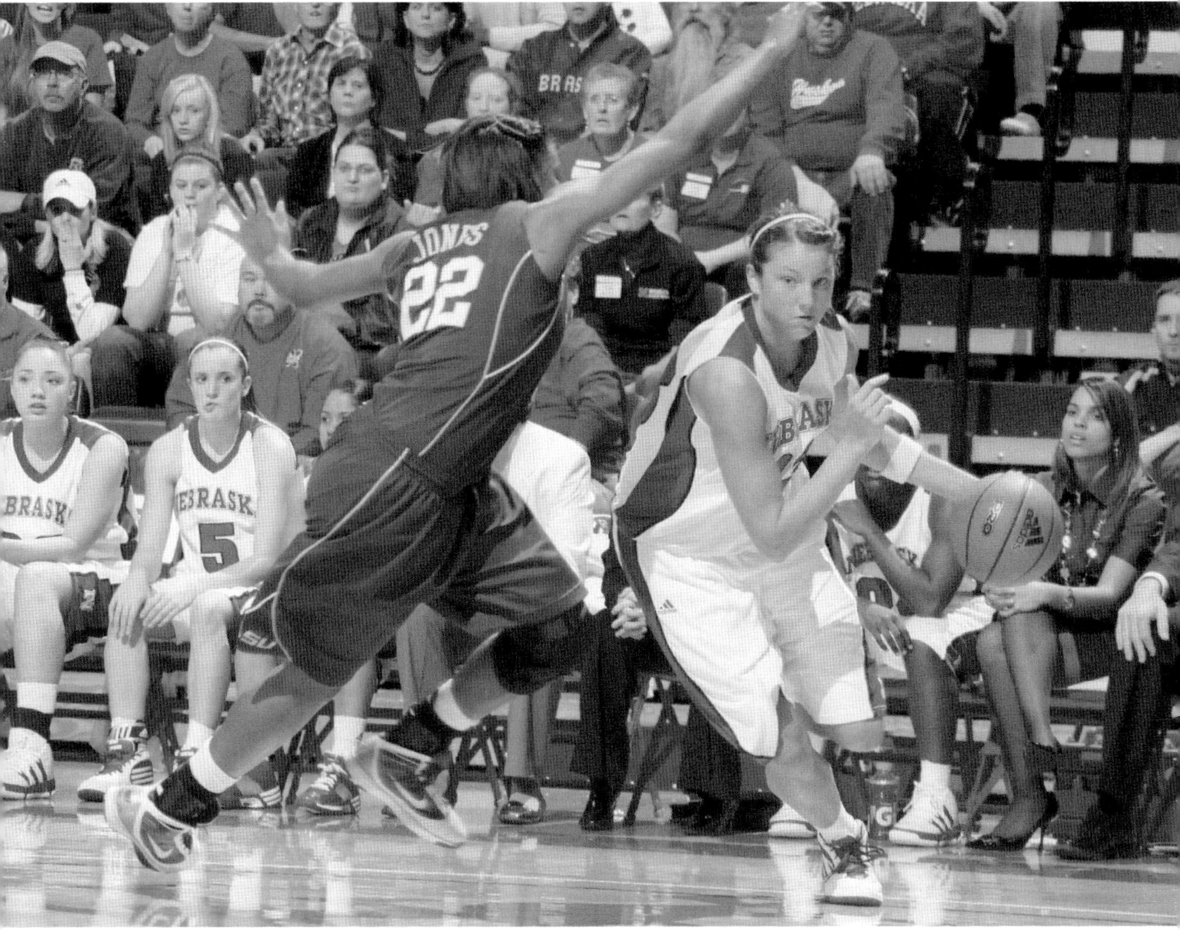

Kelsey Griffin

Kelsey Griffin is a Women's National Basketball Association player who was the number-three pick in the 2010 WNBA draft. She has been on the Connecticut Sun roster ever since, landing in the power forward position in 2013. Griffin also plays on the Australian Women's National Basketball League (WNBL) team Bendigo Spirit, which she helped lead to a 2013 WNBL championship (winning an MVP award along the way). The 2005 Chugiak High graduate spent her college career with the Nebraska Cornhuskers, where she received more than a dozen awards and honors and was named to several all-America teams. She is one of a very few Alaskans to earn the distinction of being an NCAA Division I First Team all-American athlete. (Courtesy of Kelsey Griffin.)

CHAPTER FIVE

Musicians, Artists, and Entertainers

It is no wonder so many creative people choose to live in Chugiak-Eagle River; they need only step outside and glance around for inspiration. Musicians, artists, and entertainers have been part of the community since the beginning. Among the most notable were Eagle River homesteaders Art and Eleanor Braendel, founding members of the Anchorage Symphony Orchestra and originators of the Alaska Fine Arts Academy. The academy was both a life's dream and a gift to the community, and it has provided a starting point for hundreds of budding artists and performers. Others, such as singer-songwriter Chelsea Berry and guitarist Kyle Harrington, got their starts independently. Pianist Kevin Barnett moved to Alaska from Outside but has made Eagle River his home. His first CD, *Alpenglow*, pays tribute to the local scenery in winter. Margaret Mielke, Alaska's first poet laureate, gathered her inspiration in Chugiak, as does internationally renowned artist Jon Van Zyle.

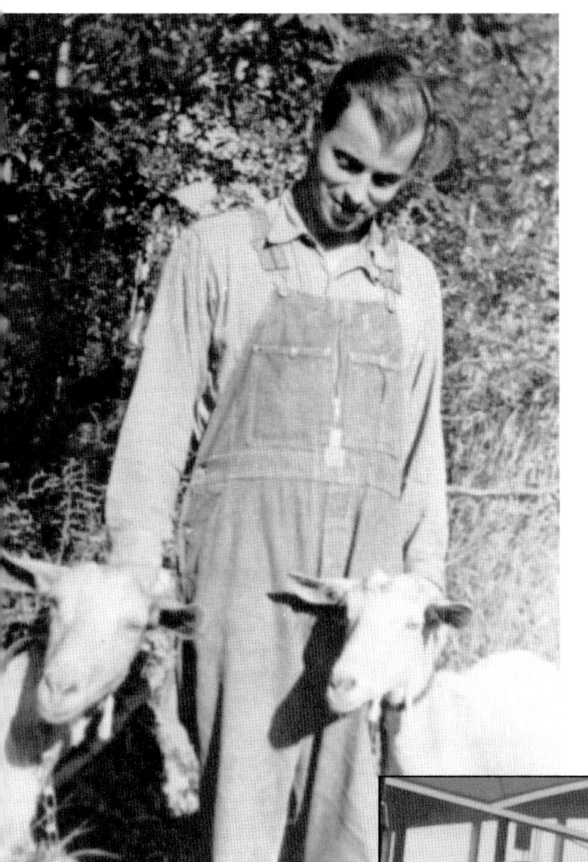

Arthur and Eleanor Braendel

Upon meeting Arthur and Eleanor Braendel on their Eagle River homestead in the late 1940s, one might not have believed they were accomplished musicians and founding members of the Anchorage Symphony Orchestra. The couple was just beginning a 60-year stretch with the symphony that lasted until their retirement in 2006. They rarely missed a rehearsal or performance in all that time, despite primitive roads and unpredictable weather. The Braendels elevated the music scene in Eagle River as well. Eleanor taught lessons to local children—including her own four—on the family's grand piano, which served as the centerpiece of their tiny cabin. She also taught violin and viola. In 1984, the Braendels founded the nonprofit Eagle River Fine Arts Academy, which still operates today as the Alaska Fine Arts Academy, a place where visual arts, music, and theater are taught and performed. The couple was awarded the Anchorage Mayor's Lifetime Achievement Award in 2004, Bear Paw Community Service Award in 2008, and the Governor's Lifetime Achievement in the Arts in 2008. (Both, courtesy Arthur Braendel Jr.)

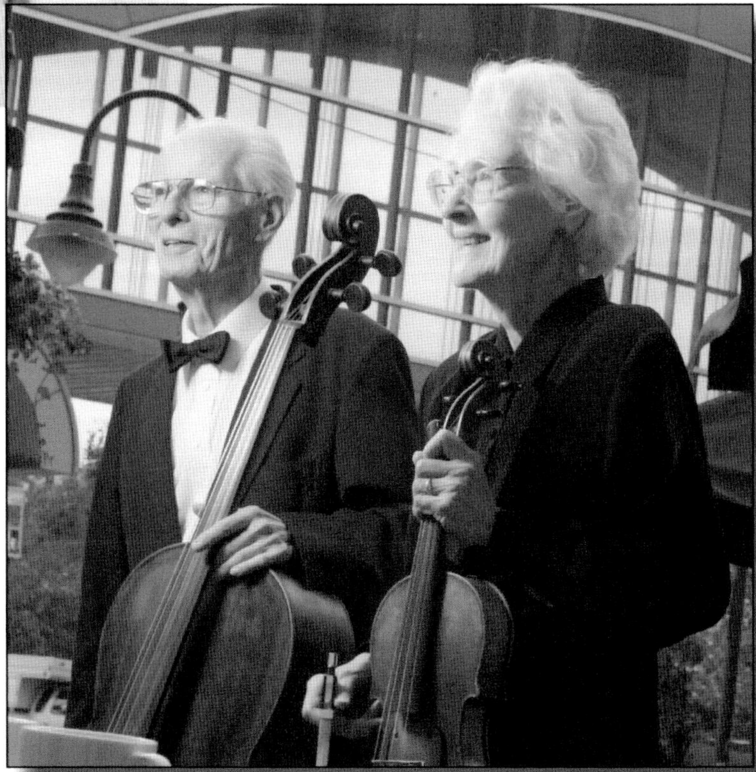

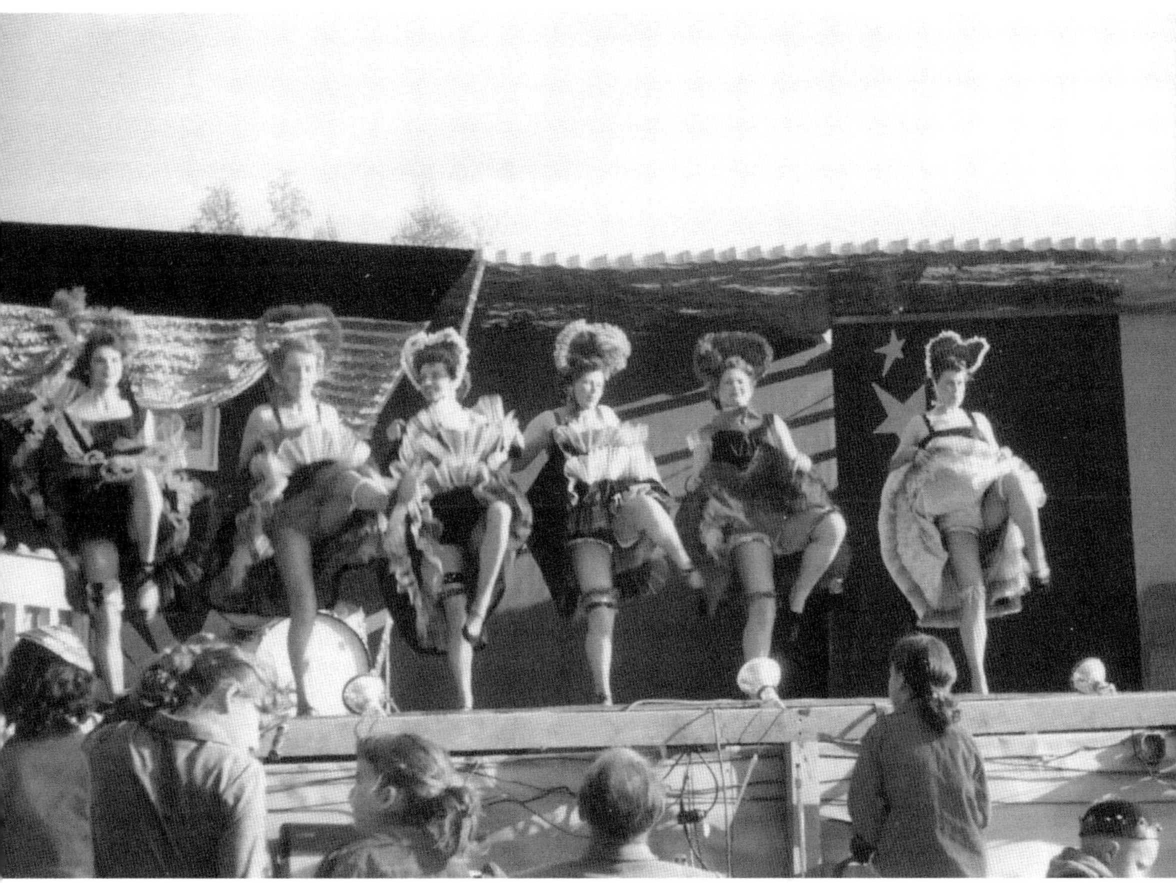

Chugiak Belles

Dubbed "Chugiak's Dancing Housewives" by the *Anchorage Times*, the Chugiak Belles proved one of the most popular attractions at the community's second annual Spring Carnival in 1955. The carnival's purpose was to raise funds for the Chugiak Volunteer Fire Department and other desperately needed services. The Belles tailored their handmade costumes to the numbers they were performing: a frock with petticoats for the cancan, a flapper dress for the Charleston, and a shoulder-to-ankle bathing suit for the old-time song "By the Sea." The group became so popular, they even danced for Anchorage audiences. The shows continued through the last Spring Carnival in 1959. Pictured are Lois Riddell, Rusty Bellringer, Katie Phillips, Virginia Parks, Mary Lou Briggs, and Ruth Alice Briggs. Not pictured are Liz Harriman, Jan Briggs, Maxine Hendricks, Jerry Jahr, Bonnie Flint, Dee Steeby, Virginia Lewis, Laura Jean Van Duren, Joe Anne Vanover, and Christa Burg. (Courtesy of the Chugiak-Eagle River Historical Society.)

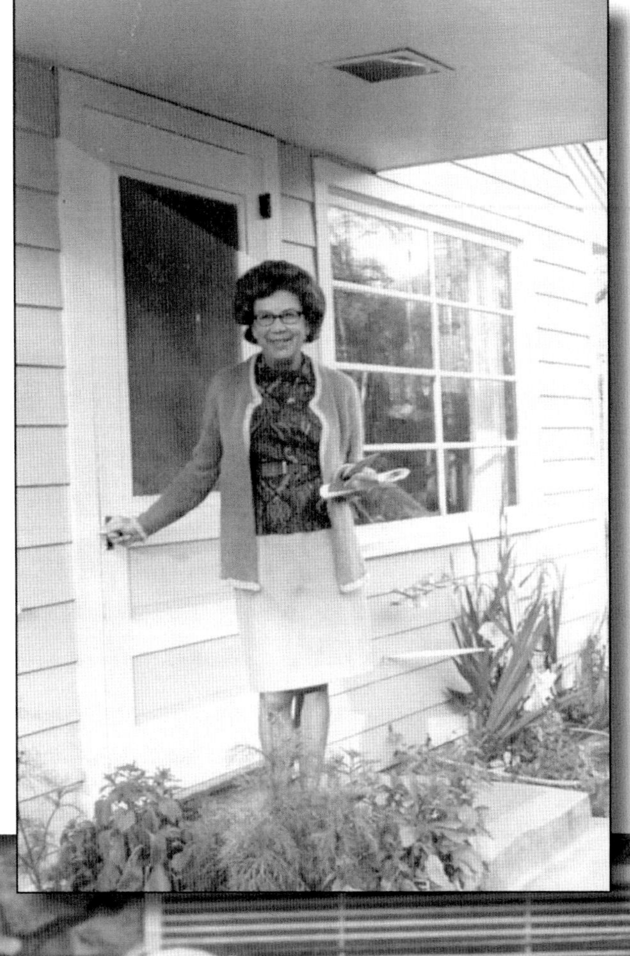

Margaret Mielke
Margaret Mielke was named the state's first poet laureate in 1963. Already a published poet in the states, she had moved to the Alaska Territory with her husband, John, in 1940. The Mielkes started building a home in Chugiak in 1955, and they moved there in 1962 when John retired from the civil service on Elmendorf Air Force Base. Eventually becoming a mother of six, Margaret continued to write, and her work appeared in newspapers, national magazines, and anthologies. She compiled and edited the *Anthology of Contemporary Alaskan Poetry* and worked as the poetry editor for the *Alaska Times*. Mielke died in 1980 at age 68. (Courtesy of Mielke family.)

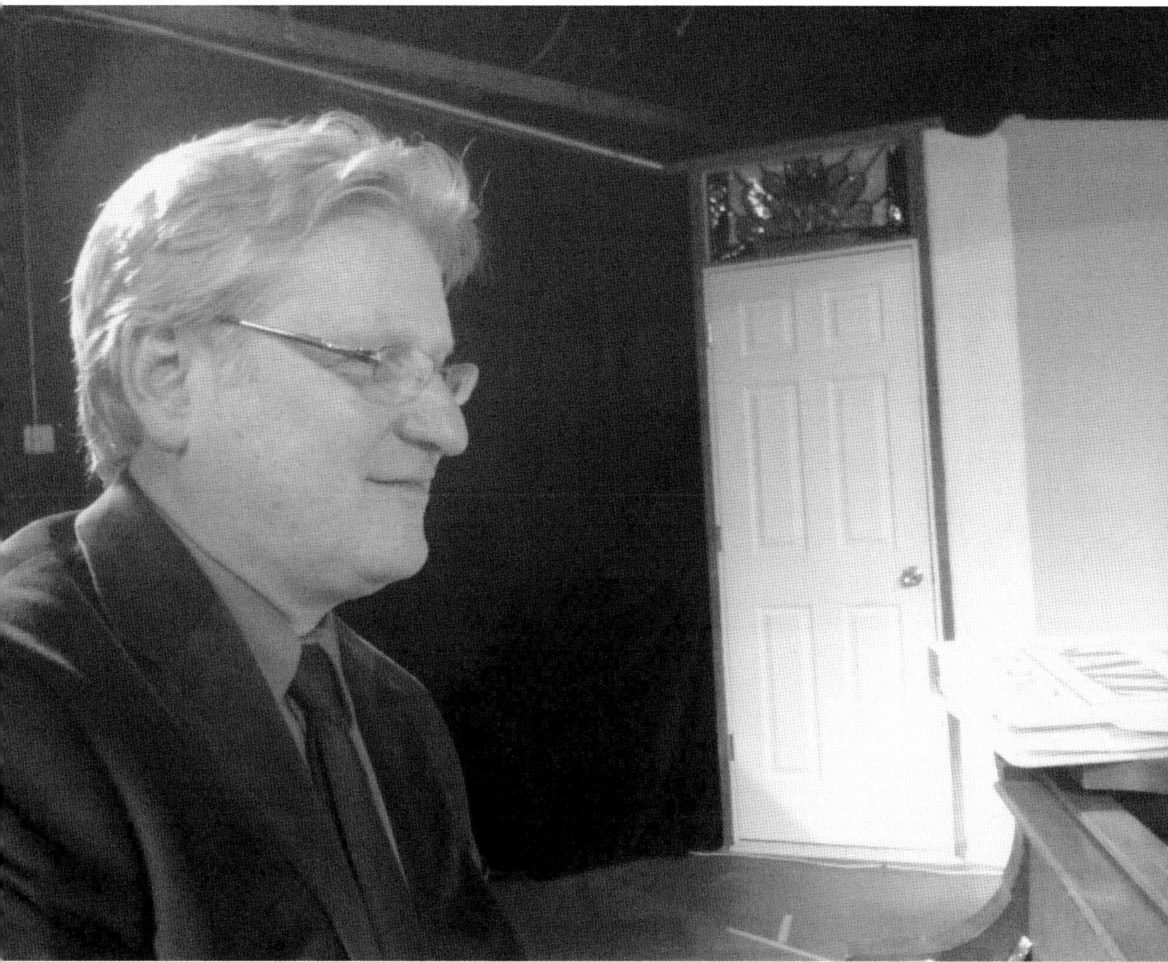

Composer and Pianist Kevin Barnett
Alaska Public Radio's weekly call-in show, *Hometown Alaska,* features a cut from Kevin Barnett's 2010 CD, *Alpenglow.* Barnett is a composer, pianist, keyboardist, recording engineer, and producer. He completed *Alpenglow* at his home studio, Lovin'Dog Music in Eagle River. Nowadays, Barnett is also the engineer and composer for Mirror Studios of Anchorage, Los Angeles, and Washington, DC. His playing and compositions accompany many locally produced commercials and documentaries. He performs around Anchorage with the Kevin Barnett Quartet; his jazz group, Lovin'Dog Kennel Club; Lee Pulliam's AKSAXO Jazz; the rock group Chill Factor; and other artists. Barnett and his wife, Regina, an elementary school teacher, actor, and singer, share their home with a husky mix named Kaya. Barnett has two more CDs on the way. (Courtesy of Gina Barnett.)

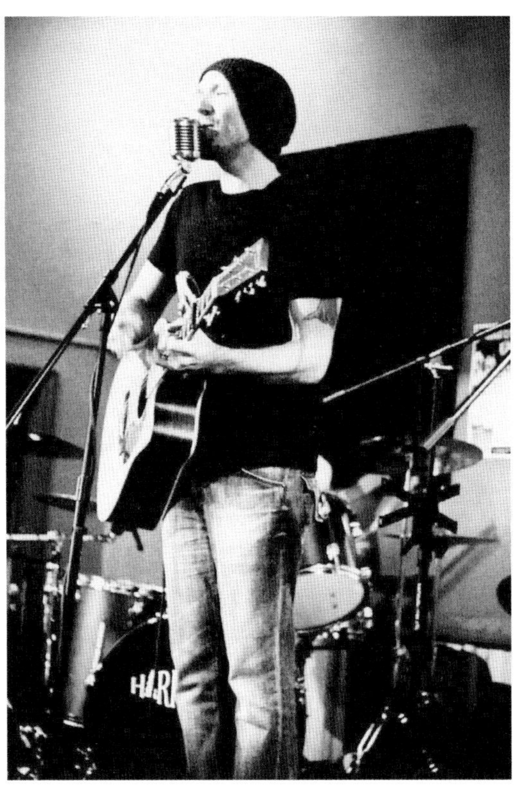

Kyle Harrington

Kyle Harrington did not wait until high school graduation to launch his three-pronged career as a guitar teacher, songwriter, and performer. He joined his first band as a sophomore, around the same time he started offering lessons to friends and neighborhood kids out of his parents' house. As his talents and abilities grew, so did his reputation as a musician and easygoing instructor who could inspire the most reluctant kid to practice. Harrington began teaching in the studios at Mike's Music in Eagle River in 2005 and quickly gained a waiting list of would-be students. With two CDs on the market and a third in the works (with his band, Jolly Good Fellow), he draws capacity crowds at local venues. Harrington's brother is Mirror Lake Middle School teacher Travis Harrington. (Both photographs courtesy of Kyle Harrington, taken by Blaine Shillington.)

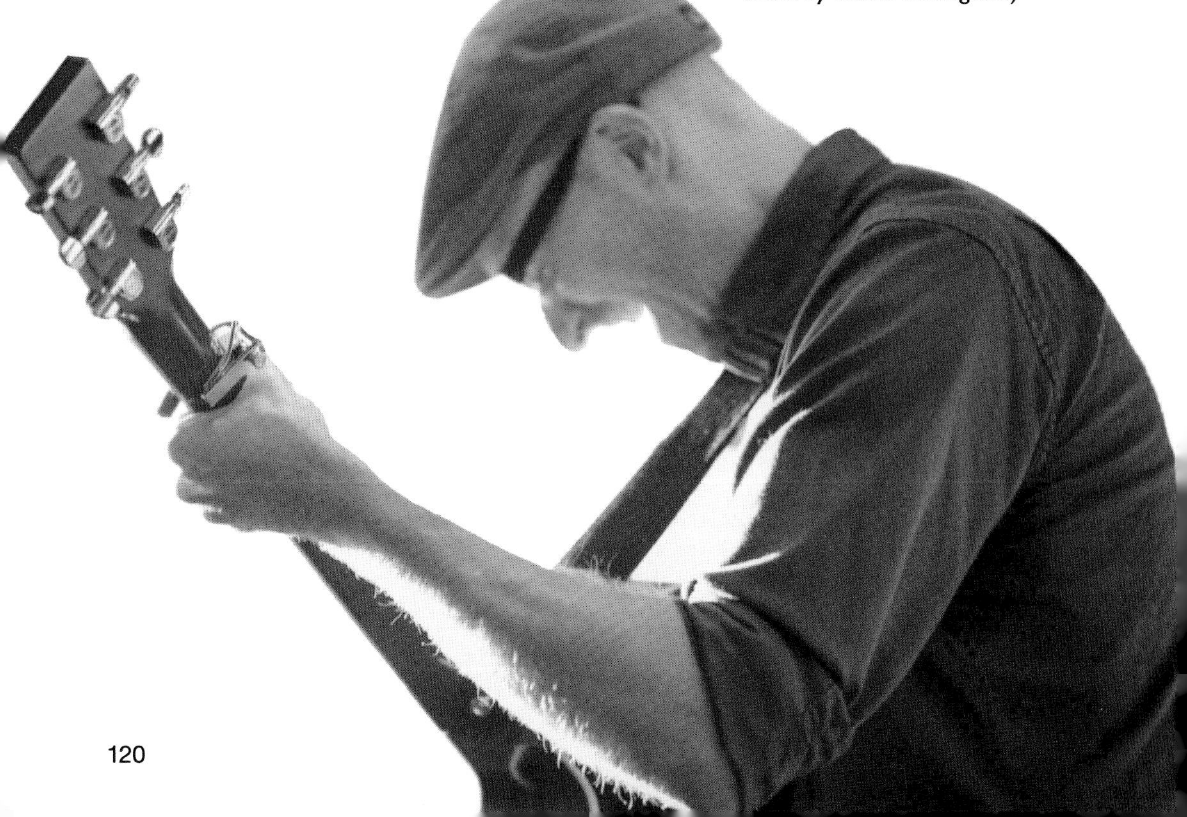

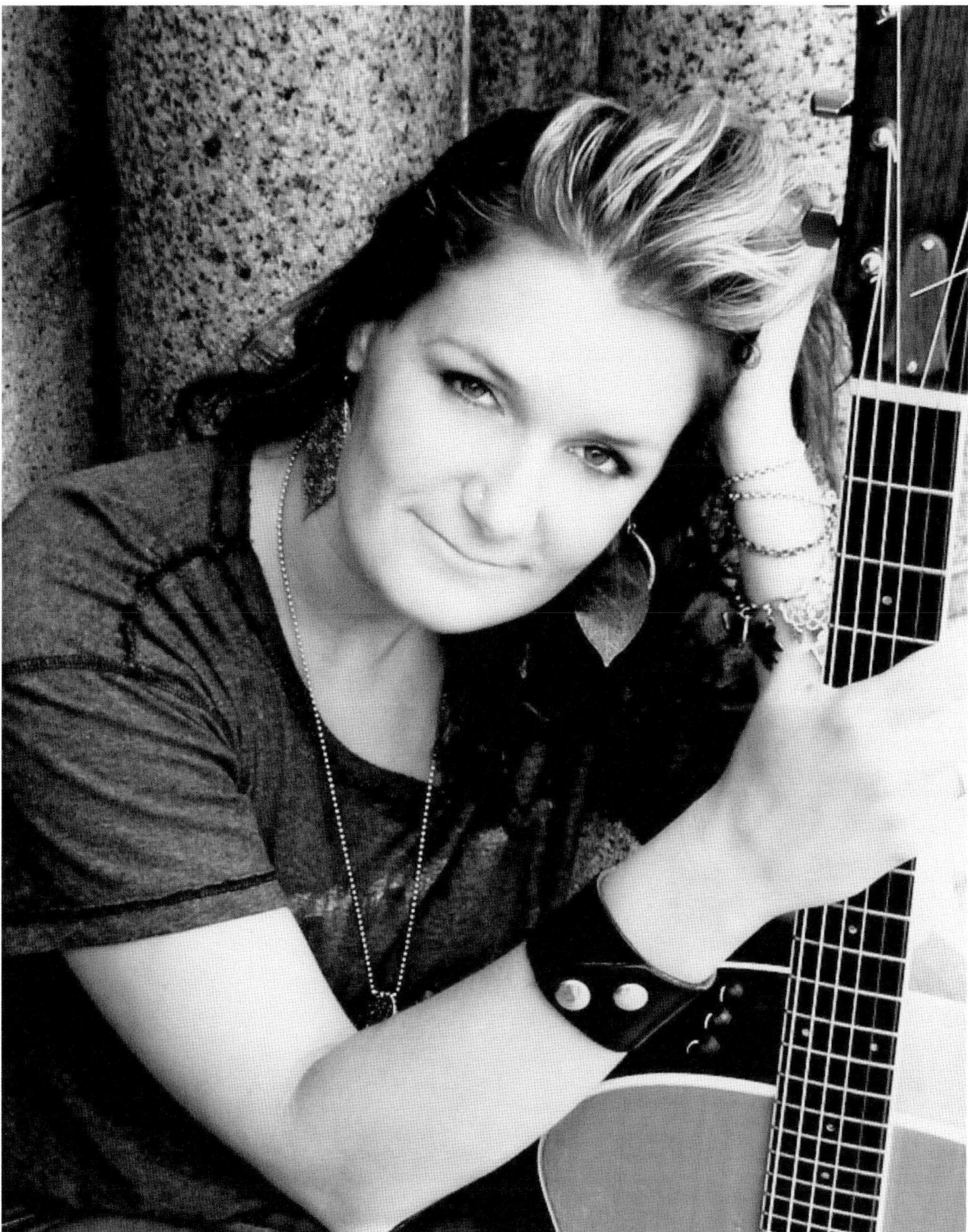

Chelsea Berry

Chelsea Berry's first break was at age 14 when she sang and played guitar at Jitters Coffeehouse in Eagle River for an audience of family and friends. The 2001 Chugiak High graduate has since performed at hundreds of locales across the United States and became part of the Boston music scene a few years ago as she worked on a bachelor's degree in songwriting from the Berklee College of Music. Berry's rich voice has begun filling larger and larger venues in recent years, and she has a loyal following in the Boston area. (Courtesy of Chelsea Berry.)

Robin Hopper

Robin Hopper is no ordinary music teacher. The native of Potsdam, New York, has taught for over three decades, a majority of that time at Homestead Elementary in Eagle River. A well-received folk singer and guitarist, Hopper plays in festivals and concerts around the country and has recorded five CDs to date. She shares her songwriting talents with her Homestead students and has created many pieces for the choirs to perform. Hopper enjoys the interplay among the various aspects of her career. Keeping students engaged, she says, is a lot like keeping a concert audience engaged. With such dedication to her students and her craft, Hopper has received recognition from a variety of places. She was commissioned to write the theme song for the 1996 Arctic Winter Games in Chugiak, which she performed at the opening and closing ceremonies and many times in between. In 2000, the Anchorage Education Association named Hopper Outstanding Educator of the Year, and she won Alaska Public Radio Network's 2003 Song of the Year. She received a nomination in 2013 for a new Grammy award, the Music Educator of the Year. Up against 30,000 other teachers from across the country, Hopper made it as far as the quarterfinals—with just 217 on the list. Although another teacher ultimately received the Grammy, Hopper continues to embody the ideals of the award, making a lasting contribution in the field of music education. She plans to continue writing, performing, and teaching for the foreseeable future. (Courtesy of Robin Hopper.)

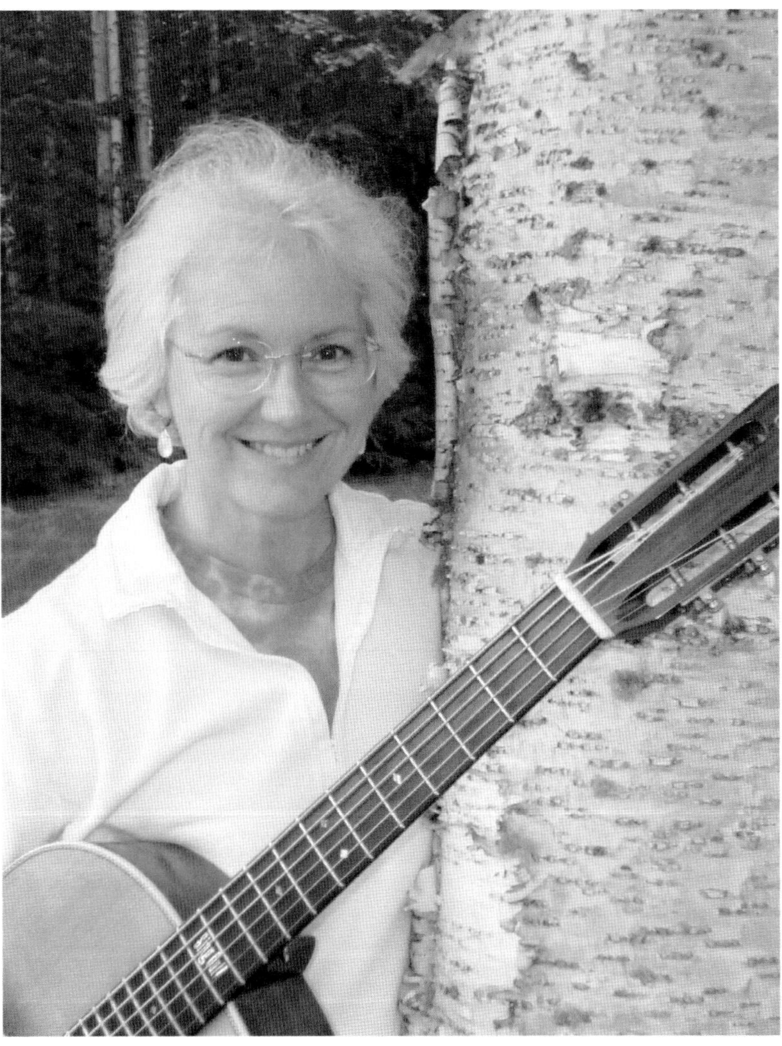

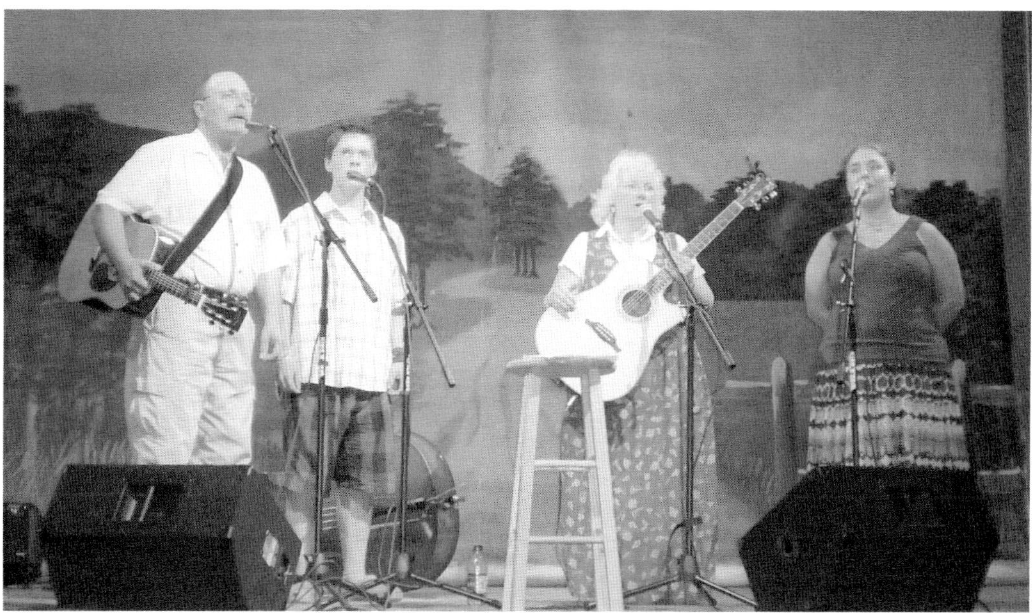

Hopper Family Band

Robin Hopper could not help but infuse her family with a love of music. She and husband Bruce, daughter Caiti, and son Grady spent much of their time singing together at home and in the car throughout the children's early lives. Both siblings studied piano and evolved into accomplished musicians. When Caiti was six, she started mixing harmony into her vocals, and an idea took root in Robin's mind. She allowed the Hopper Family Band to evolve naturally. They began performing about 12 years later, with Bruce and Robin on guitar, Grady playing string bass, and Caiti as lead vocalist. The band plays the Anchorage Folk Festival each January as well as Music in the Park in the summers. (Both, courtesy of Robin Hopper.)

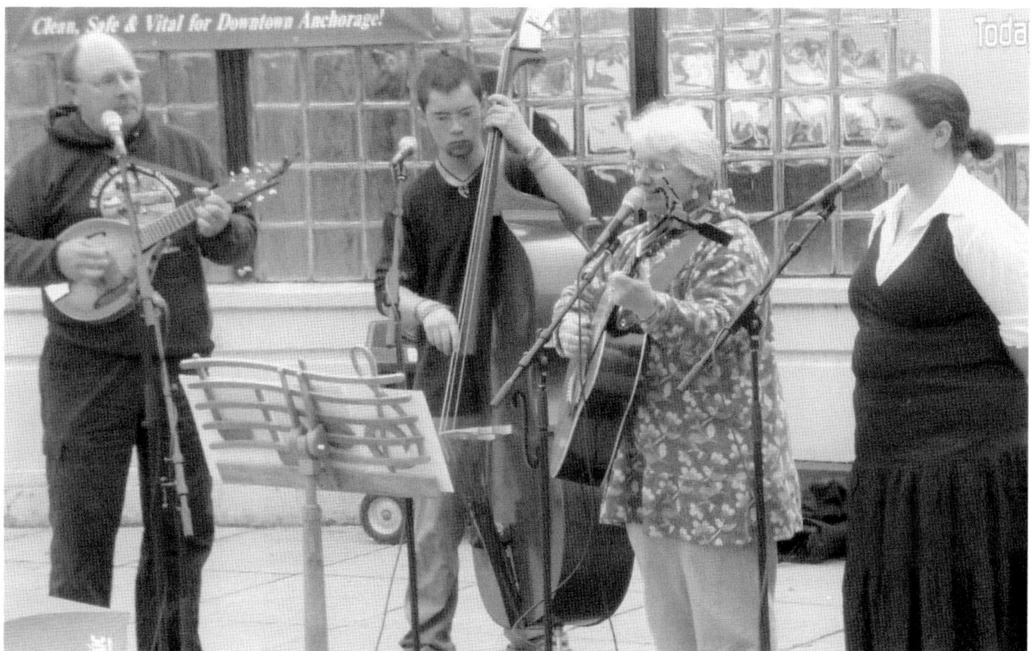

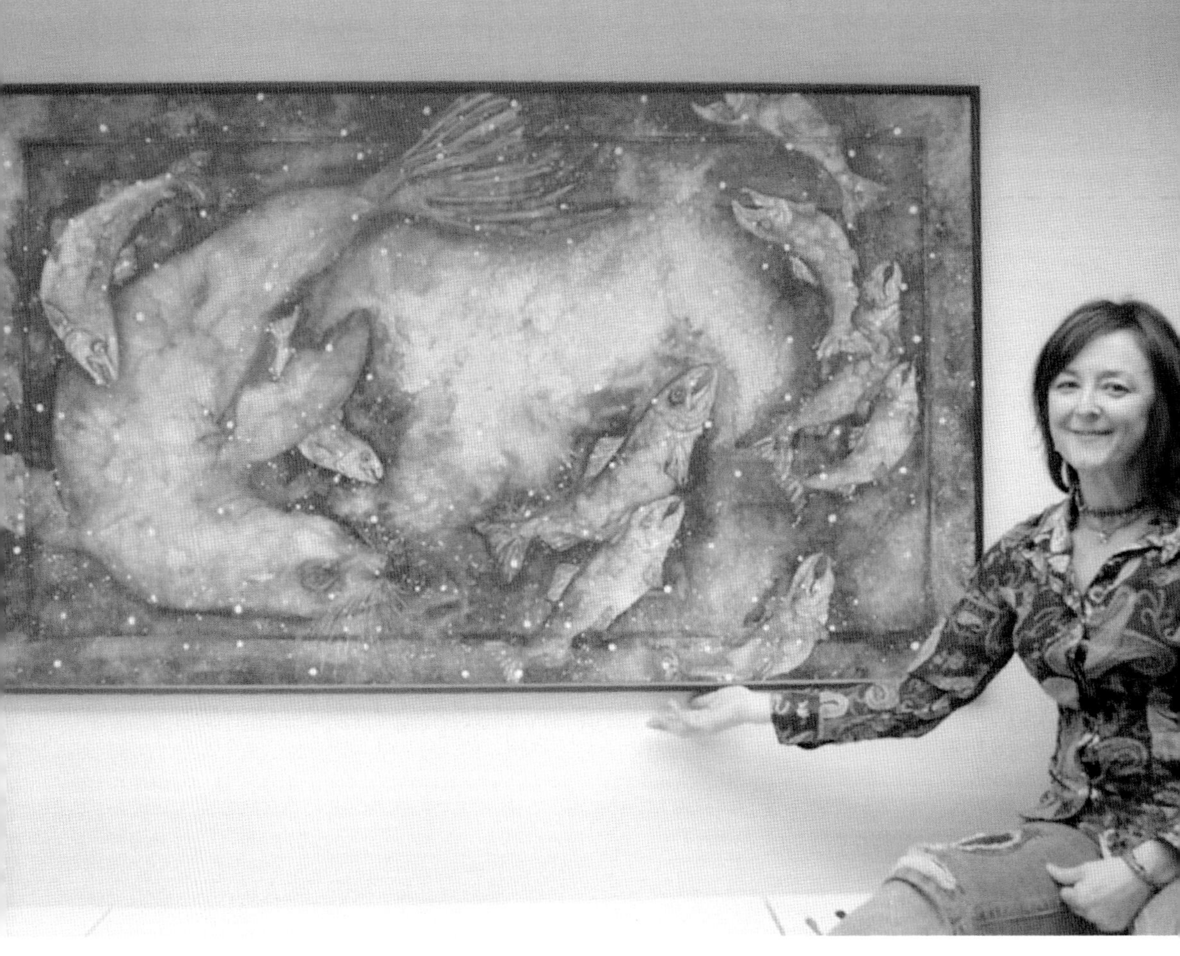

Karla Morreira

Karla Morreira's paintings do not stop at the edges of the paper. Each watercolor piece and each print continues onto the mat board, creating a unique style that is instantly recognizable at the homes, cafés, galleries, and businesses that display her art across the state. An avid diver and a recreational angler, Morreira depicts some of the sea creatures she has encountered and some that populate her dreams. Her land-based subjects include the bears, ravens, and moose near her Whalebone Watercolors Studio in Chugiak. Working with husband Roy, Morreira also produces stained-glass art with a dreamlike quality similar to that in her paintings. (Courtesy of Karla Morreira.)

Jon and Jona Van Zyle

Although artist Jon Van Zyle lives and works locally, his acclaim reaches far beyond the two rivers that border Chugiak-Eagle River. Van Zyle, widely known as "Alaska's artist," has undertaken one-man exhibitions in galleries across North America and Europe for over 30 years. Through such travels, he and wife Jona serve as informal ambassadors for the state, raising Alaska's profile worldwide. Van Zyle is a two-time competitor in the Iditarod Trail Sled Dog Race, official artist for the Iditarod, and a member of the Iditarod Hall of Fame. In addition to an annual race poster, he creates 60 to 80 originals each year and over time has illustrated at least 40 children's books. His most important accomplishment, however, came in 2009 when he designed the state's Decoration of Honor medal for Alaskan soldiers killed in action. Jona Van Zyle is a writer, musher, and multifaceted artist who created an ornament representing Wrangell–St. Elias National Park for the White House Christmas tree in 2007. Both Van Zyles are generous with their time. In between heavy work and exhibition schedules, they open their Birchwood home to the public, hosting dinners for Habitat for Humanity groups from Outside and giving tours of their studio and dog kennels to visitors. (Courtesy Jon and Jona Van Zyle.)

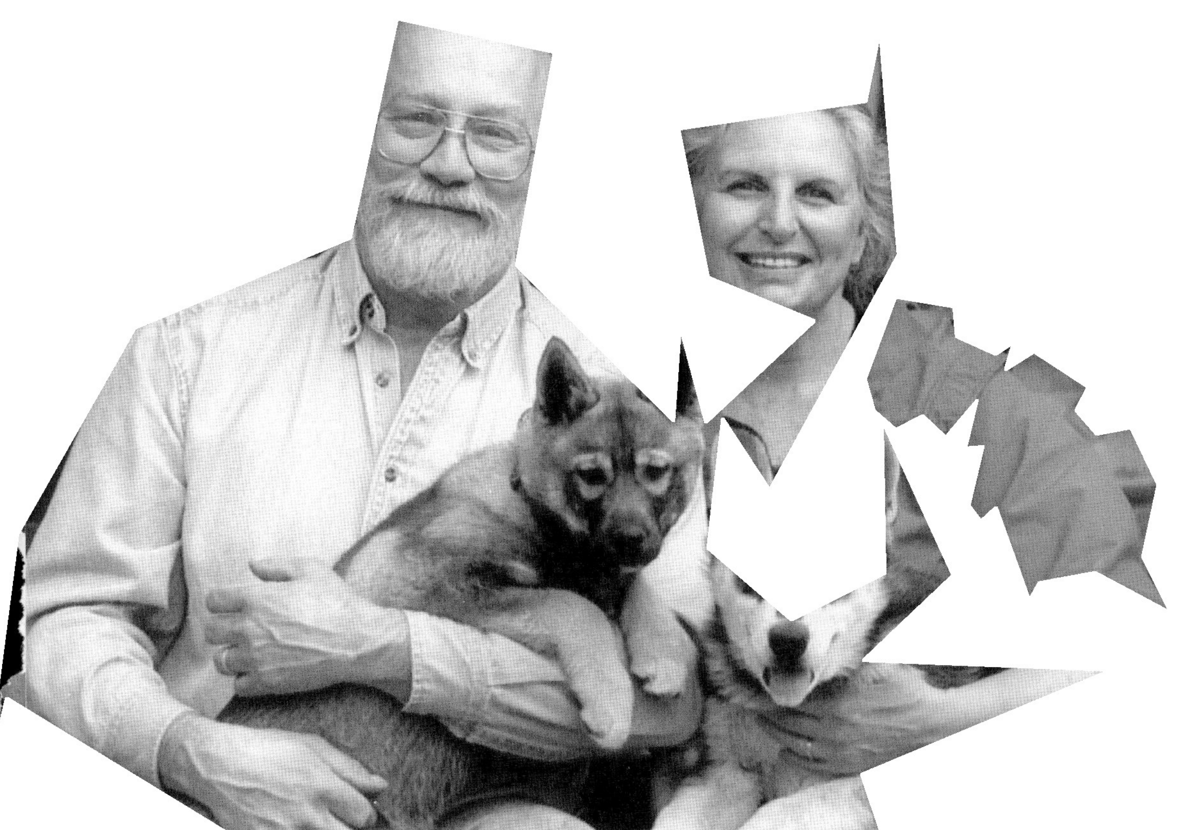

INDEX

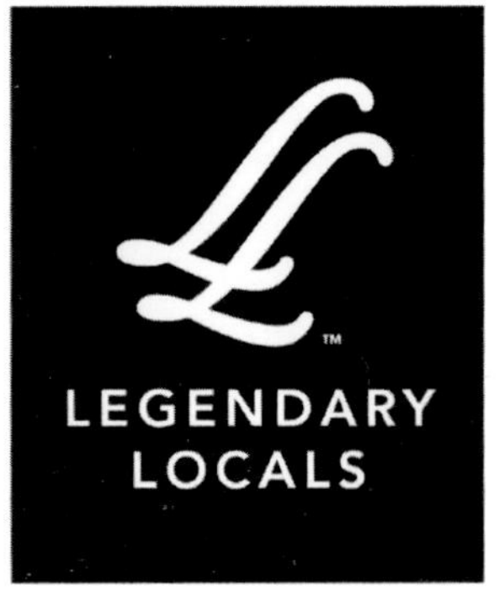

AN IMPRINT OF ARCADIA PUBLISHING